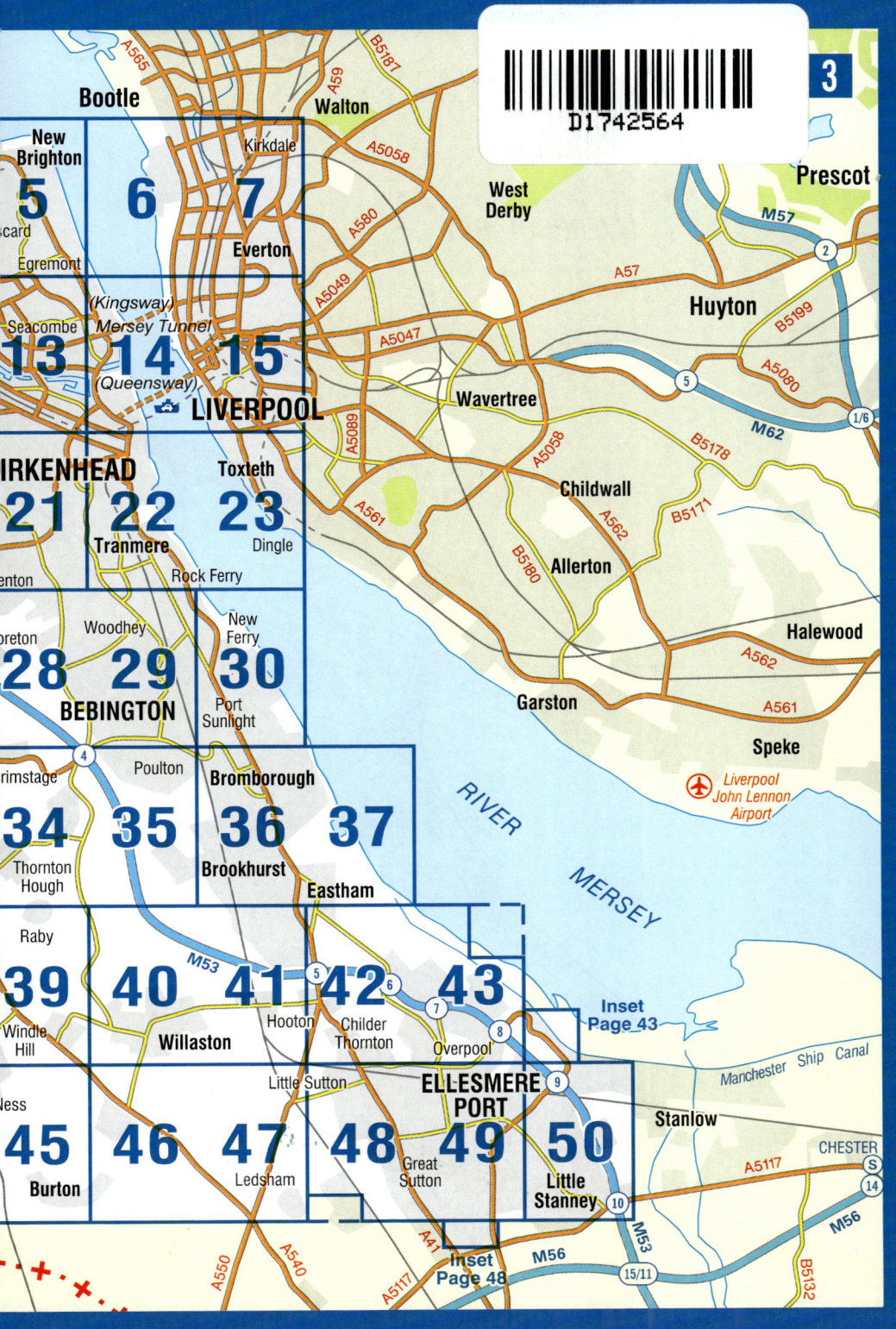

A-Z WIRRAL

CONTENTS

Key to Map Pages   2-3

Map Pages   4-50

Index to Streets, Towns,
Villages, Hospitals etc. and   51-80
selected Places of Interest

REFERENCE

Motorway **M53**

A Road **A551**

Tunnel

B Road **B5138**

Dual Carriageway

One-way Street
Traffic flow on A Roads is also indicated
by a heavy line on the driver's left.

Road Under Construction
Opening dates are correct at the time of publication.

Proposed Road

Restricted Access

Pedestrianized Road

Track & Footpath

Residential Walkway

Railway   Level Crossing   Station   Tunnel

Built-up Area

Local Authority Boundary

Posttown Boundary

Postcode Boundary
(within posttown)

Map Continuation **20**

Car Park (selected) **P**

Church or Chapel †

Cycleway (selected)

Fire Station ■

Hospital **H**

House Numbers (A & B Roads only) 13 8

Information Centre **i**

National Grid Reference ³30

Park & Ride Leasowe **P+**

Police Station ▲

Post Office ★

Safety Camera with Speed Limit
Fixed cameras and long term road works cameras
Symbols do not indicate camera direction **30**

Toilet: without facilities for the Disabled ▽
without facilities for the Disabled   ▽
with facilities for the Disabled ▽
Disabled facilities only ▽

Educational Establishment

Hospital or Healthcare Building

Industrial Building

Leisure or Recreational Facility

Place of Interest

Public Building

Shopping Centre or Market

Other Selected Buildings

SCALE

1:15,840
4 inches to 1 mile

0   ¼   ½   ¾ Mile
6.31 cm to 1 km
10.16 cm to 1 mile

0   250   500   750   1 Kilometre

Copyright of Geographers' A-Z Map Company Limited

Fairfield Road, Borough Green, Sevenoaks, Kent TN15 8PP
Telephone: 01732 781000 (Enquiries & Trade Sales)
01732 783422 (Retail Sales)

www.a-zmaps.co.uk
Copyright © Geographers' A-Z Map Co. Ltd.
Edition 5 2011

KEY TO MAP PAGES

IRISH SEA

Liverpool Bay

4
WALLASEY

8
HOYLAKE

9
Meols

Leasowe
P+

10
Moreton

11

12
Bidston

Upton

Greasby

16
WEST KIRBY

17
Newton
Grange

18
Frankby

19
Woodchurch

20
Noctorum

Caldy

Irby Heath

Thingwall

24

25
Thurstaston

26
Irby
Pensby

Barnston

27

The Dales

HESWALL

31

32
Gayton

33

Mostyn

A548

RIVER DEE
(AFON DYFRDWY)

ENGLAND
WALES

38
NESTON

Little Neston

44

A5026

A55

Holywell
(Treffynnon)

A548

Flint
(Y Fflint)

SCALE

0	1	2 Miles
0	1	2	3 Kilometres

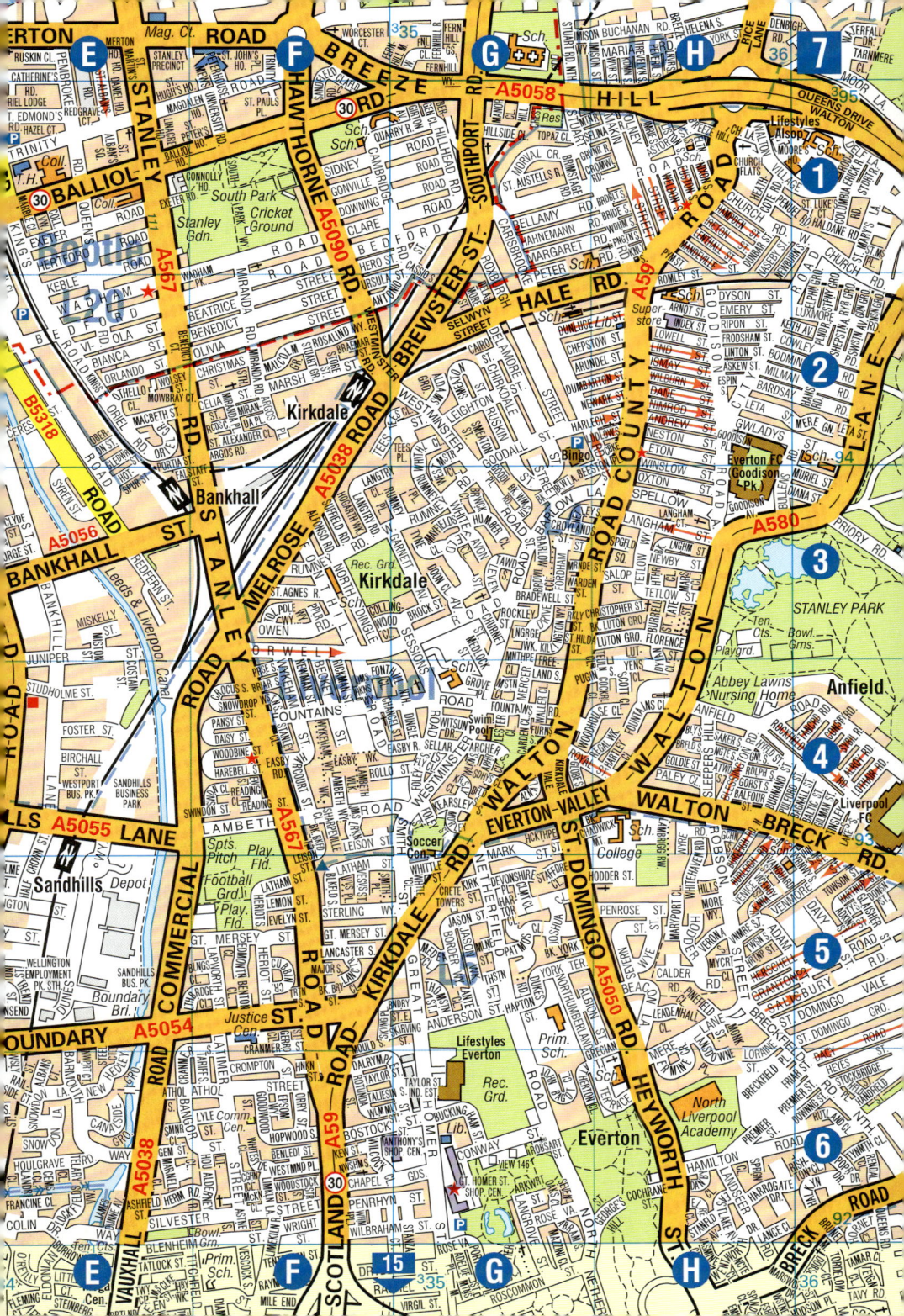

1

I R I S H   S E A

2

91

3

L I V E R P O O L   B A Y

4

³90

HOYLAKE   *Bowling*
Greens

Model
Boating Pond

Comm. Cen.

CLYDESDALE
DOVEDALE
AVONDALE
FERNDALE

TRINITY
HOYLE CT. RD
LAKE RD
MARMION RD
TRINITY RD
SCH

5

Lifeboat Sta.
SAND-
PIPERS
CT.
STRAND RD
GOVERNMENT RD
SEAVIEW RD
GROVE RD
GROVE TER
SHAW ST
Rec.
YEOMAN RD

ADDERLEY
ROAD
GROVE RD
RD

6

NORTH
CABLE
THE MARINE
QUEEN'S
ROAD
WALKER ST.
PLACE
EVANS RD

89
CURZON RD
KINGS
WARREN RD
SANDBANKS
CHERRY
GS.
QUEENS
CT.

MARKET

STABLE
STREET
THE
CROMER
CT.
VALENTIA
RD.
LIGHTHOUSE RD
ROAD
QUADRANT
MONTROSE CT.
ROSECROFT
CT.
BARTON
THE T.H.

HOYLAKE
ROAD

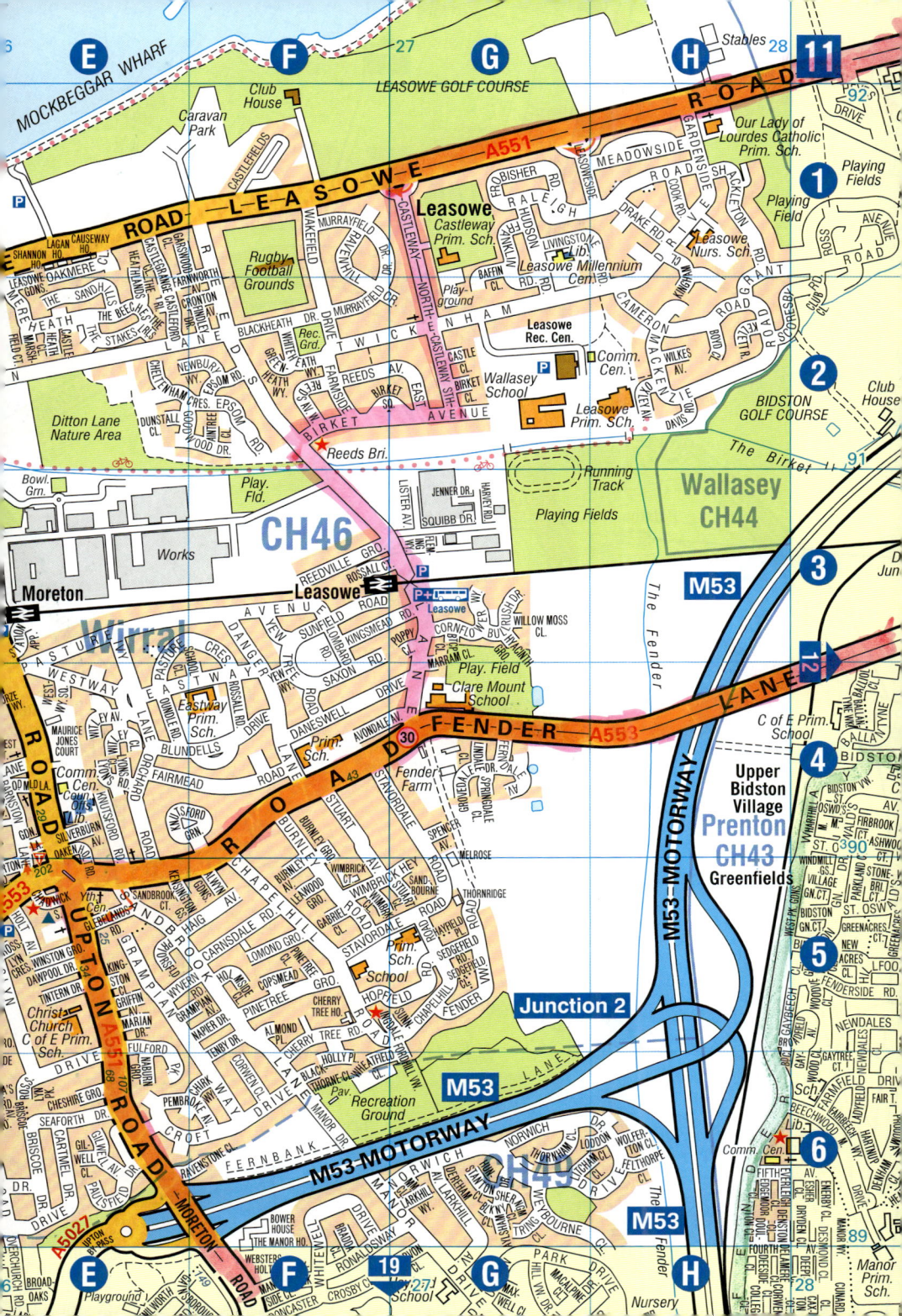

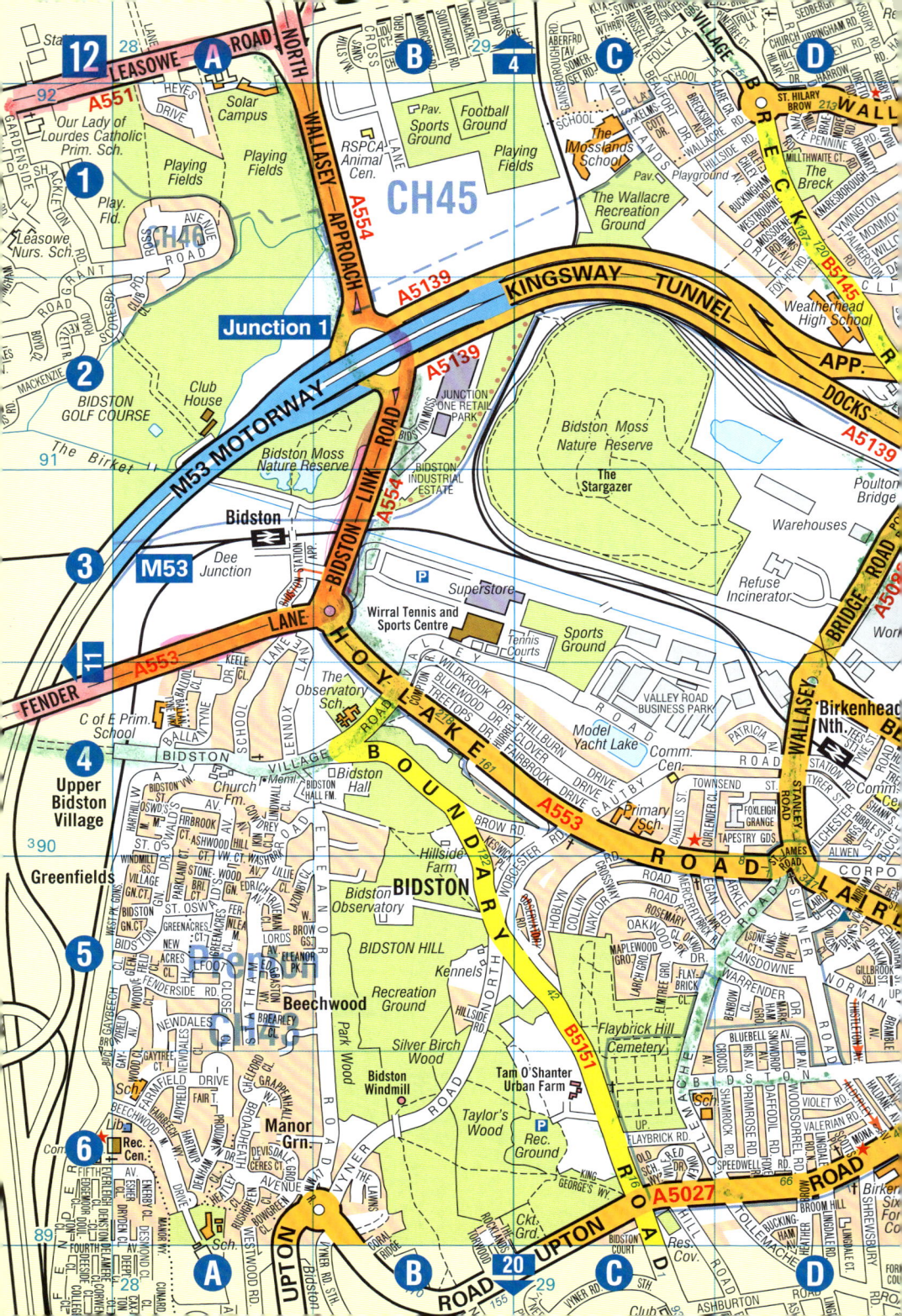

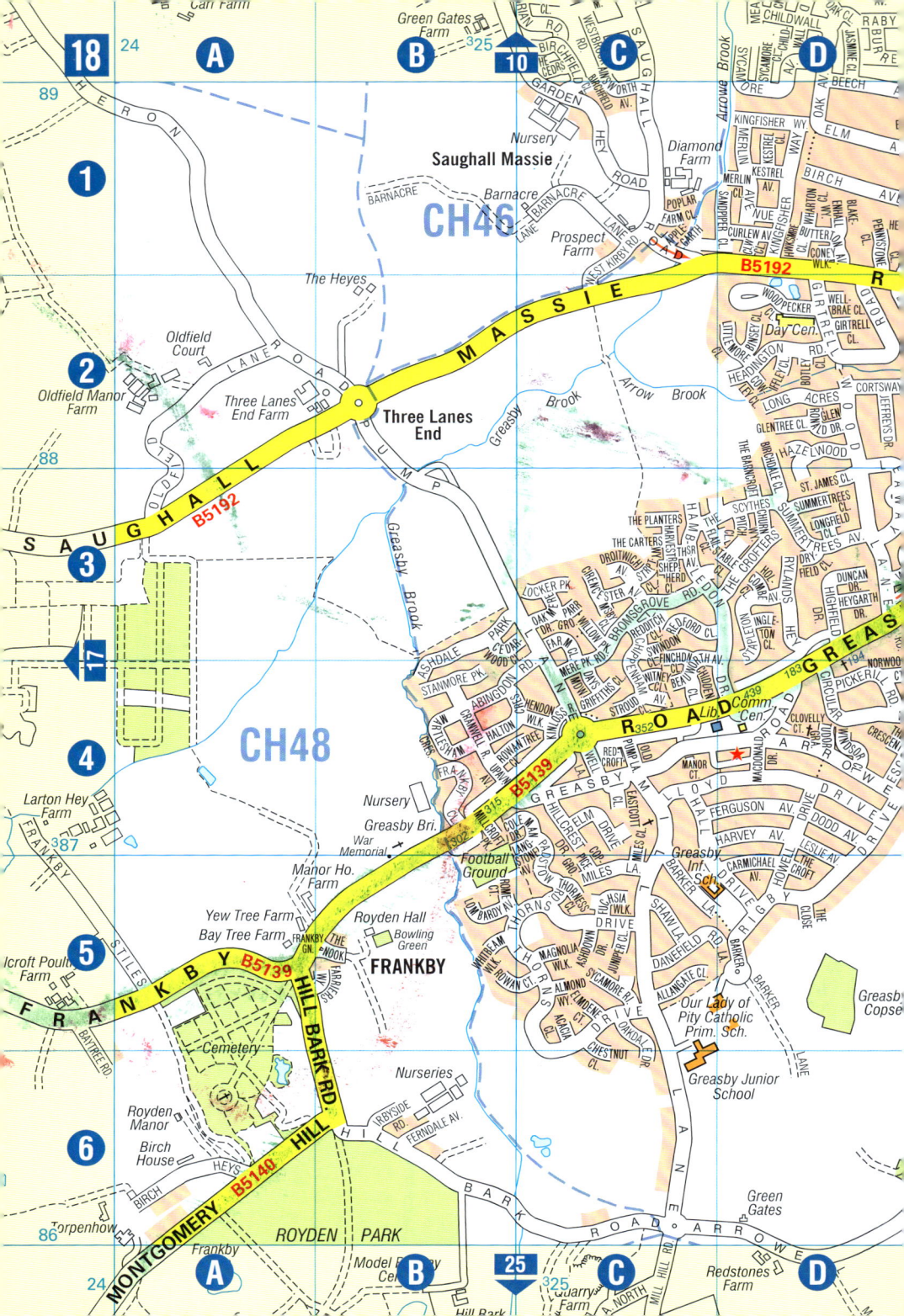

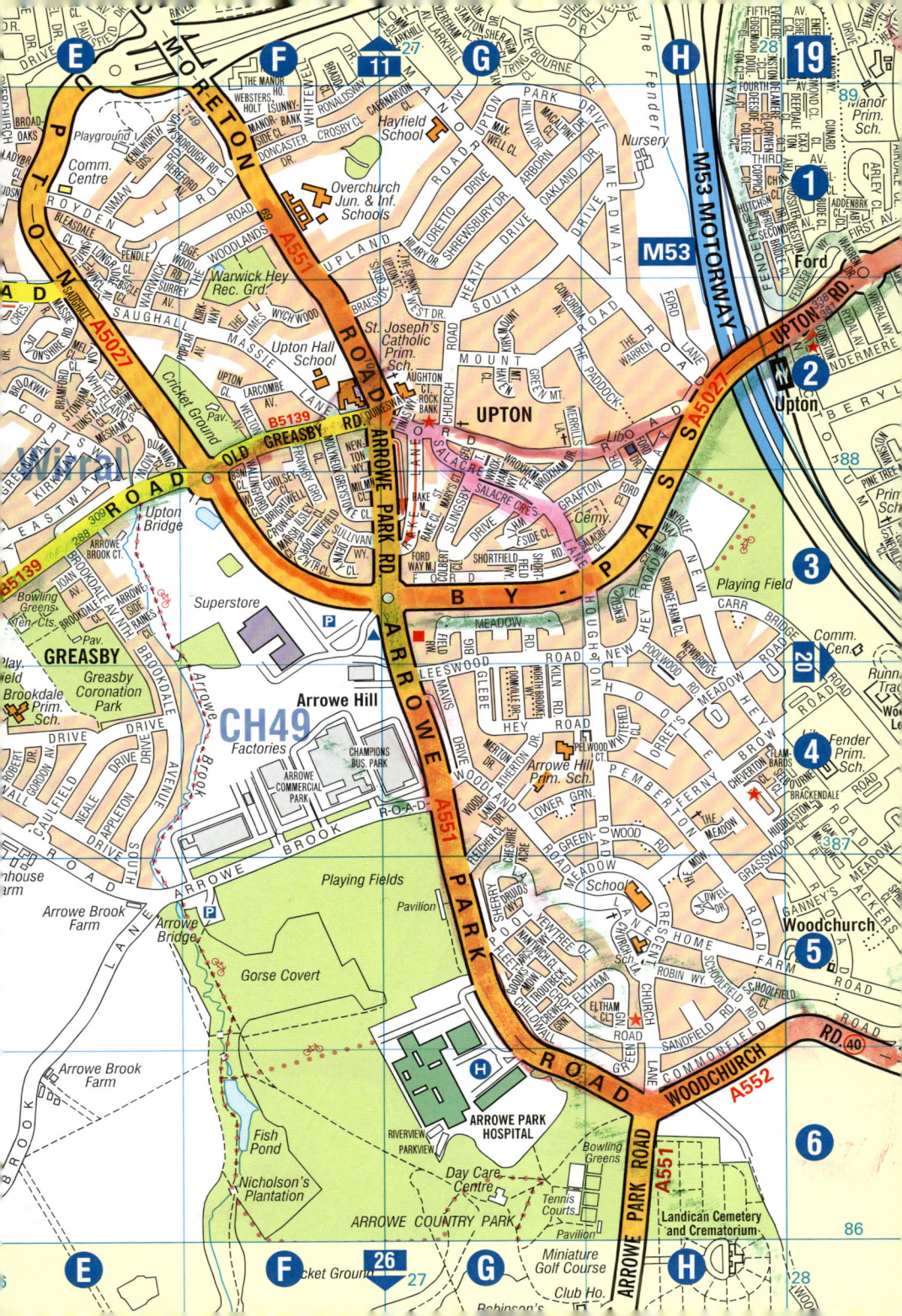

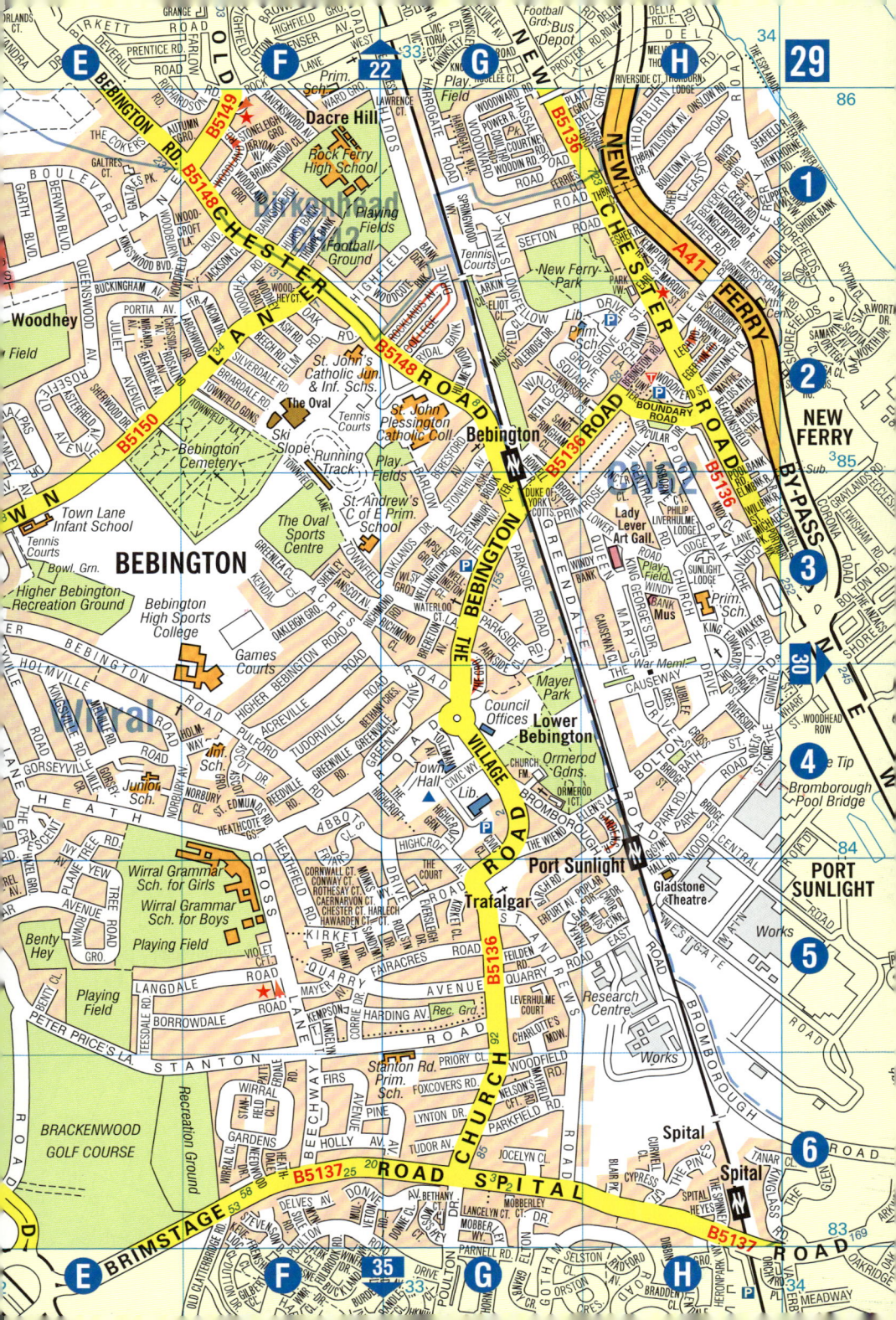

83

1

82

2

R I V E R

3

M E R S E Y

4

81

5

6

3 80

Job's Ferry

Oak Wood

Playing Field

P

P

Eastham Ferry

EASTHAM COUNTRY PARK

Play. Flds.

Eastham Woods

Eastham Woods

Mayfields Remembrance Park

Wood Heath Wy.

Metropolitan College

Playing Field

Custom House

Queen Elizabeth II Dock

Eastham Locks

CHAPEL VW.

PARK

GOLF COURSE

Tank Farm House

Club House

Playing Field

MAYFIELD DR.

SEAVIEW AV.

David ROAD

ST. JOHN'S ROAD

UPPER RD.

LANE

BANKFIELDS

Torr Rec. Grd.

B5132

EASTHAM VILLAGE

Poultry Houses

Oil Storage Depot

Oil Storage Depot

Eastham Hall

RIVACRE ROAD

FINCH ROAD

Eastham House

MANCHESTER SHIP CANAL

Oil Refinery

Tanks

NORTH

DRIVE

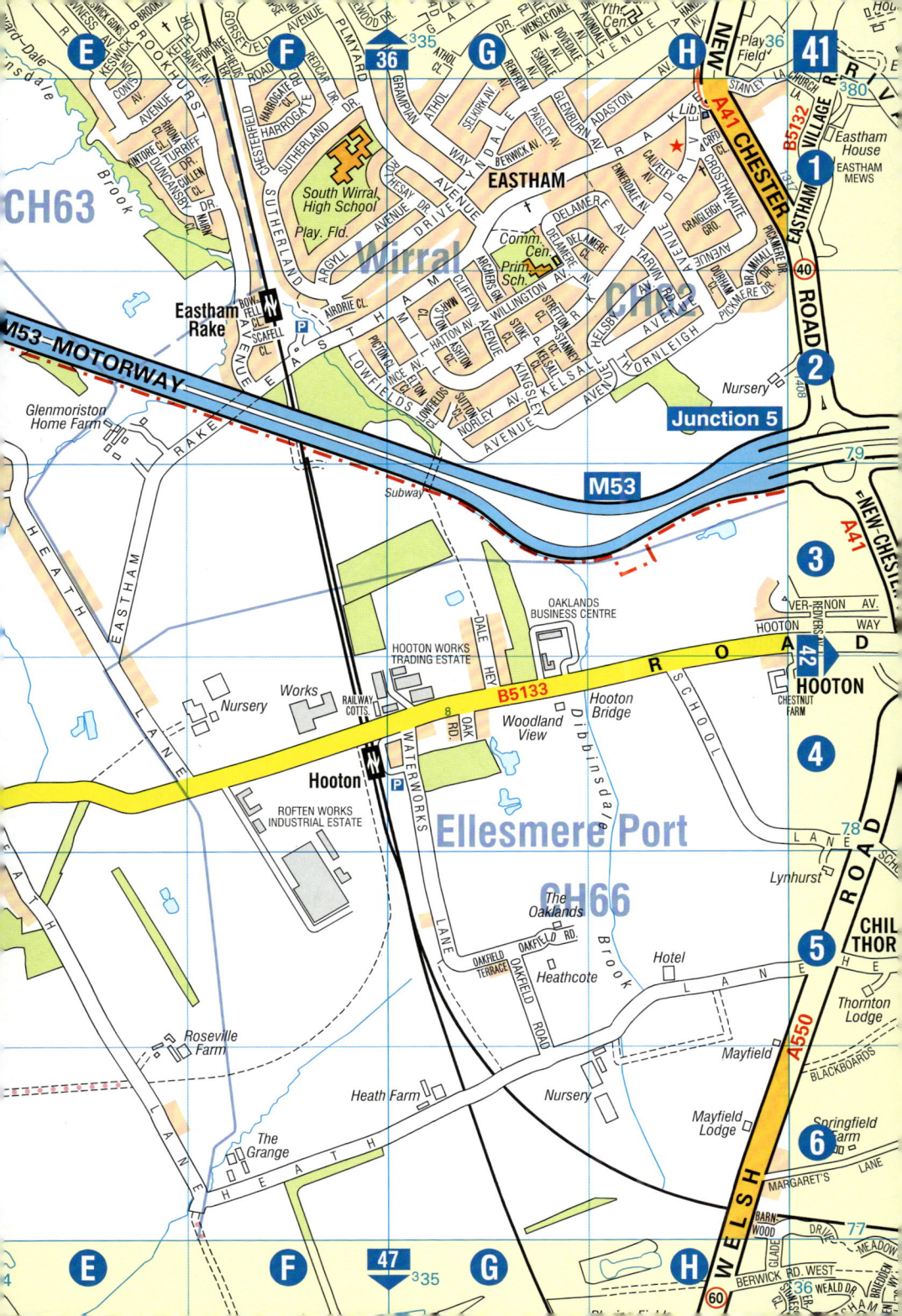

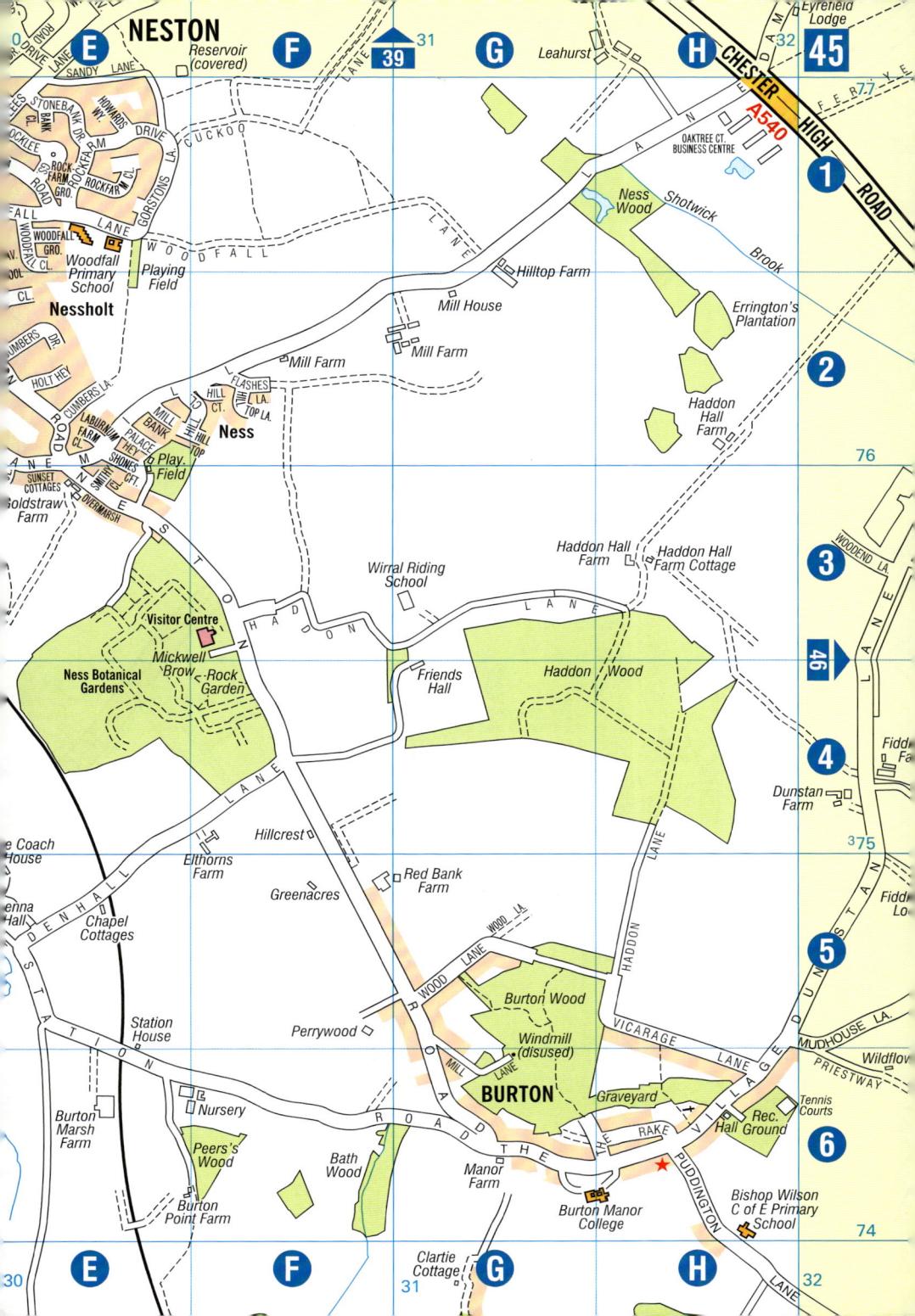

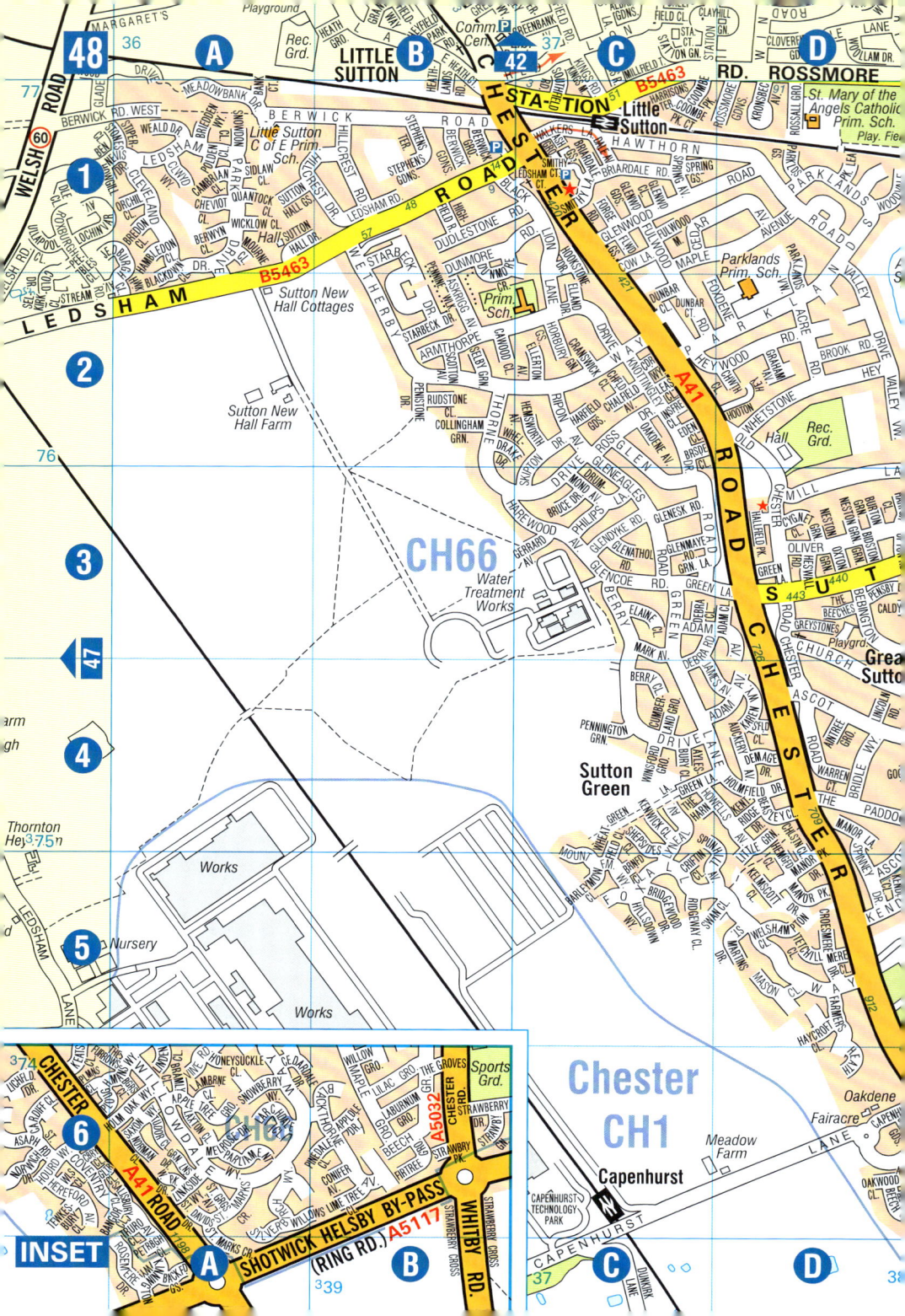

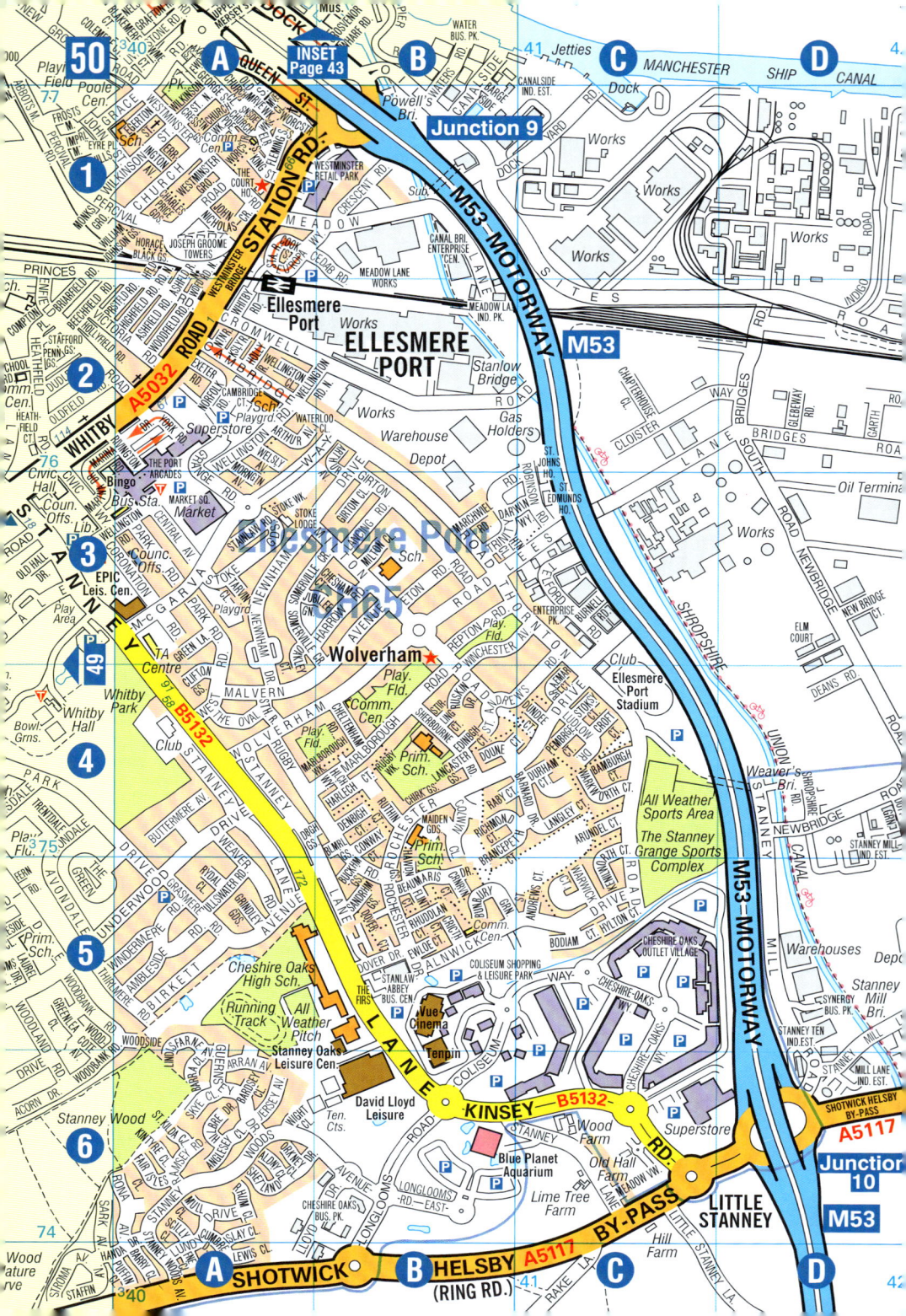

INDEX

Including Streets, Places & Areas, Hospitals etc., Industrial Estates,
Selected Flats & Walkways, Stations and Selected Places of Interest.

HOW TO USE THIS INDEX

1. Each street name is followed by its Postcode District, then by its Locality abbreviation(s) and then by its map reference;
e.g. **Abbey Rd.** CH48: W Kir . . . .5D **16** is in the CH48 Postcode District and the West Kirby Locality and is to be found in square 5D on page **16**.
The page number is shown in bold type.

2. A strict alphabetical order is followed in which Av., Rd., St., etc. (though abbreviated) are read in full and as part of the street name;
e.g. **Ash Tree Apartments** appears after **Ashton St.** but before **Ashtree Cl.**

3. Streets and a selection of flats and walkways that cannot be shown on the mapping, appear in the index with the thoroughfare to which they are
connected shown in brackets; e.g. **Adlington Ho.** L3: Liv . . . .2F **15** (off Henry Edward St.)

4. Addresses that are in more than one part are referred to as not continuous.

5. Places and areas are shown in the index in **BLUE TYPE** and the map reference is to the actual map square in which the town centre or area is located and
not to the place name shown on the map; e.g. **BEBINGTON 3G 29**

6. An example of a selected place of interest is **Hadlow Road Station Mus. . . .6C 40**

7. An example of a station is **Bankhall Station (Rail) . . . .3E 7**, also included is **Park & Ride**.
e.g. **Leasowe (Park & Ride) 3G 11**

8. An example of a Hospital, Walk-in Centre or Hospice is **ARROWE PARK HOSPITAL 6G 19**

GENERAL ABBREVIATIONS

All. : Alley	**Cres.** : Crescent	**La.** : Lane	**Rd.** : Road
App. : Approach	**Cft.** : Croft	**Lit.** : Little	**Shop.** : Shopping
Arc. : Arcade	**Dr.** : Drive	**Lwr.** : Lower	**Sth.** : South
Av. : Avenue	**E.** : East	**Mnr.** : Manor	**Sq.** : Square
Bk. : Back	**Ent.** : Enterprise	**Mans.** : Mansions	**Sta.** : Station
Blvd. : Boulevard	**Est.** : Estate	**Mdw.** : Meadow	**St.** : Street
Bri. : Bridge	**Flds.** : Fields	**M.** : Mews	**Ter.** : Terrace
Bldg. : Building	**Gdn.** : Garden	**Mt.** : Mount	**Twr.** : Tower
Bldgs. : Buildings	**Gdns.** : Gardens	**Mus.** : Museum	**Trad.** : Trading
Bus. : Business	**Ga.** : Gate	**Nth.** : North	**Up.** : Upper
Cvn. : Caravan	**Gt.** : Great	**Pde.** : Parade	**Va.** : Vale
C'way. : Causeway	**Grn.** : Green	**Pk.** : Park	**Vw.** : View
Cen. : Centre	**Gro.** : Grove	**Pas.** : Passage	**Vs.** : Villas
Cl. : Close	**Hgts.** : Heights	**Pav.** : Pavilion	**Vis.** : Visitors
Comn. : Common	**Ho.** : House	**Pl.** : Place	**Wlk.** : Walk
Cnr. : Corner	**Ind.** : Industrial	**Pct.** : Precinct	**W.** : West
Cotts. : Cottages	**Info.** : Information	**Prom.** : Promenade	**Yd.** : Yard
Ct. : Court	**Intl.** : International	**Ri.** : Rise	

LOCALITY ABBREVIATIONS

Aig : **Aigburth**	East : **Eastham**	Liv : **Liverpool**	Rock F : **Rock Ferry**
Back : **Backford**	Ell P : **Ellesmere Port**	Meols : **Meols**	Spit : **Spital**
Barn : **Barnston**	Frank : **Frankby**	More : **Moreton**	Stoak : **Stoak**
Beb : **Bebington**	Grea : **Greasby**	Ness : **Ness**	Store : **Storeton**
Bid : **Bidston**	Gt Sut : **Great Sutton**	Nest : **Neston**	Thing : **Thingwall**
Birke : **Birkenhead**	Hesw : **Heswall**	New B : **New Brighton**	Thorn H : **Thornton Hough**
Boot : **Bootle**	Hghr B : **Higher Bebington**	New F : **New Ferry**	Thurs : **Thurstaston**
Brim : **Brimstage**	Hoot : **Hooton**	Noct : **Noctorum**	Tran : **Tranmere**
Brom : **Bromborough**	Hoy : **Hoylake**	Oxton : **Oxton**	Upton : **Upton**
Burt : **Burton**	Irby : **Irby**	Park : **Parkgate**	Wall : **Wallasey**
Caldy : **Caldy**	Kirkd : **Kirkdale**	Pens : **Pensby**	Walt : **Walton**
Cap : **Capenhurst**	Leas : **Leasowe**	Port S : **Port Sunlight**	W Kir : **West Kirby**
Chil T : **Childer Thornton**	Led : **Ledsham**	Pren : **Prenton**	Whit : **Whitby**
Chor B : **Chorlton-by-Backford**	Lit N : **Little Neston**	Pudd : **Puddington**	Will : **Willaston**
Clau : **Claughton**	Lit Stan : **Little Stanney**	Raby : **Raby**	Woodb : **Woodbank**
Dunk : **Dunkirk**	Lit Sut : **Little Sutton**	Raby M : **Raby Mere**	Woodc : **Woodchurch**

A

Abbey Cl. CH41: Birke 2B 22
Abbeyfield Ho. CH65: Whit . .4G 49
Abbey Rd. CH48: W Kir 5D 16
Abbey St. CH41: Birke 2B 22
Abbot Cl. CH43: Bid 1A 20
Abbots Dr. CH63: Beb 4F 29
Abbotsford St. CH44: Wall . . .3A 14
Abbots M. CH65: Ell P 1H 49
Abbots Quay CH41: Birke . . .1C 22
Abbots Way CH48: W Kir 4E 17
  CH64: Nest 4C 38
Abercromby Sq. L7: Liv 5H 15
Aberdeen St. CH41: Birke 6G 13
Aberford Av. CH45: Wall 6C 4
Aber St. L6: Liv 2H 15
Abingdon Rd. CH49: Grea . . .4B 18
Abram St. L5: Liv 6G 7
Acacia Cl. CH49: Grea 5C 18
Acacia Dr. CH66: Gt Sut 6F 48

Acacia Gro. CH44: Wall 3A 14
  CH48: W Kir 5C 16
Ackers Rd. CH49: Woodc 5A 20
Acland Rd. CH44: Wall 1F 13
Acorn Cl. CH63: Hghr B 3D 28
Acorn Ct. L8: Liv 1H 23
Acorn Dr. CH65: Whit 6H 49
Acrefield Ct. CH42: Tran 6F 21
Acrefield Rd. CH42: Tran 6F 21
Acre La. CH60: Hesw 2E 33
  CH62: Brom 4A 36
  CH63: Brom 4A 36
Acre Rd. CH66: Gt Sut 2D 48
Acres Rd. CH47: Meols 6H 9
  CH63: Beb 3F 29
Acreville Rd. CH63: Beb 4F 29
Acton La. CH44: More 6C 10
Acton Rd. CH42: Rock F 6C 22
Acton St. CH42: Tran 3A 22
Adam Av. CH66: Gt Sut 3C 48
  (not continuous)
Adam Cl. CH66: Gt Sut 3D 48

Adam St. L5: Liv 5H 7
Adaston Av. CH62: East 1H 41
Addenbrook Cl. CH43: Bid . . .1A 20
Addington St. CH44: Wall 2H 13
Addison St. L3: Liv 2F 15
Addison Way L3: Liv 2F 15
Adelaide Pl. L5: Liv 1G 15
Adelaide Rd. CH42: Tran 3G 21
Adelaide St. CH44: Wall 2F 13
Adelphi St. CH41: Birke 1A 22
Adfalent La. CH64: Will 6C 40
Adkins St. L5: Liv 5H 7
Adler Way L3: Liv 4H 23
Adlington Ho. L3: Liv 2F 15
  (off Henry Edward St.)
Adlington St. L3: Liv 2F 15
  (off Fontenoy St.)
Admiral Gro. L8: Liv 2H 23
  (off High Pk. St.)
Admiral St. L8: Liv 2H 23
Agnes Gro. CH44: Wall 6G 5
Agnes Jones Ho. L8: Liv 5H 15

Agnes Rd. CH42: Tran 4A 22
Aigburth Gro. CH46: More 5D 10
Ailsa Rd. CH45: Wall 6E 5
Ainsdale Cl. CH61: Thing 4C 26
  CH63: Brom 6A 36
Ainsworth Av. CH46: More 1C 18
Ainsworth St. L3: Liv 4G 15
Aintree Cl. CH46: Leas 2F 11
Aintree Gro. CH66: Gt Sut 4D 48
Airdale Cl. CH43: Bid 1A 20
Airdrie Cl. CH62: East 2F 41
Aire Cl. CH65: Ell P 6G 43
Airlie Rd. CH47: Hoy 1D 16
Akbar, The CH60: Hesw 1G 31
Alabama Way CH41: Birke 1B 22
Alastair Cres. CH43: Pren 6D 20
Albany, The L3: Liv 3E 15
  (off Old Hall St.)
Albany Gdns. CH66: Lit Sut . . .6C 42
Albany Rd. CH42: Rock F 5A 22
Albemarle Rd. CH44: Wall 2H 13
Albert Dock L3: Liv 5E 15

Albert Dr.—Backford Rd.

Albert Dr. CH64: Nest 5B **38**
Albert Rd. CH42: Tran 3G **21**
CH47: Hoy 1D **16**
CH48: W Kir 6C **16**
Albert St. CH45: New B 2G **5**
Albion Pl. CH45: New B 3F **5**
Albion St. CH41: Birke 1B **22**
(not continuous)
CH45: New B 3E **5**
L5: Liv 5G **7**
Aldams Gro. L4: Kirkd 2G **7**
Alder Dr. CH66: Gt Sut 6F **49**
Alderley Av. CH41: Birke 6D **12**
Alderley Rd. CH44: Wall 2F **13**
CH47: Hoy 6D **8**
Alderney Cl. CH65: Ell P 6A **50**
Alderney Rd. L5: Liv 6F **7**
Alder Rd. CH63: Hghr B 5D **28**
Aldersey St. L3: Liv 2F **15**
Aldersgate CH42: Rock F 5B **22**
Aldford Cl. CH43: Oxton 5C **20**
CH63: Brom 5H **35**
Aldgate CH65: Ell P 2G **49**
Alexander Dr. CH61: Pens 6A **26**
Alexander Wlk. *L4: Walt 3H 7*
(off Florence St.)
Alexander Way *L8: Liv 3H 23*
(off Park Hill Rd.)
Alexandra Ct. *CH45: New B 3E 5*
(off Alexandra Rd.)
Alexandra Dr.
CH42: Rock F 6A **22**
Alexandra Rd. CH43: Oxton . . .2G **21**
CH45: New B 3E **5**
CH48: W Kir 6C **16**
Alexandra St. CH65: Ell P 2G **43**
Alexandra Ter. *L8: Liv 6H 15*
(off Princes Rd.)
Alex Cl. L8: Liv 1H **23**
Alfonso Rd. L4: Kirkd 3F **7**
Alfred M. L1: Liv 6G **15**
Alfred Rd. CH43: Oxton 2G **21**
CH44: Wall 4A **14**
Alison Av. CH42: Rock F 4B **22**
Alistair Dr. CH63: Brom 6A **36**
Allangate Cl. CH49: Grea 5C **18**
Allans Cl. CH64: Nest 1C **44**
Allans Mdw. CH64: Nest 1C **44**
Allcot Av. CH42: Tran 5H **21**
Allerton Gro. CH42: Tran 4A **22**
Allerton Rd. CH42: Tran 4H **21**
CH45: Wall 5E **5**
Allonby Cl. CH43: Noct 3C **20**
Allport La. CH62: Brom 3B **36**
(not continuous)
Allport Rd. CH62: Brom 5A **36**
CH63: Brom 5A **36**
Allports, The CH62: Brom 4B **36**
Alma St. CH41: Birke 1A **22**
CH62: New F 2G **29**
Almond Pl. CH46: More 5F **11**
Almond Way CH49: Grea 5C **18**
Alnwick Dr. CH46: More 5B **10**
CH65: Ell P 5B **50**
Alpha Ct. CH45: Wall 6C **4**
Alpha Dr. CH42: Rock F 6C **22**
Alroy Rd. L4: Walt 4H **7**
Alston Cl. CH62: Brom 2A **36**
Altcar Dr. CH46: More 6D **10**
Althorp St. L8: Liv 4H **23**
Alton Rd. CH43: Oxton 2E **21**
Alvanley Pl. CH43: Oxton 1G **21**
Alvanley Rd. CH66: Gt Sut 3E **49**
Alvanley Way *CH66: Gt Sut . . .3E 49*
(off Gawsworth Rd.)
Alvega Cl. CH62: New F 2A **30**
Alverstone Av. CH41: Birke 6D **12**
Alverstone Rd. CH44: Wall 2H **13**
Alvina La. L4: Walt 4G **7**
Alwen St. CH41: Birke 4D **12**
Alwyn Gdns. CH46: More 5F **11**
Amberley Av. CH46: More 6C **10**
Amberley Cl. CH46: More 6C **10**
Amberley St. L8: Liv 6H **15**
Ambleside Av. CH46: More 5D **10**
Ambleside Cl. CH61: Thing 3C **26**
CH62: Brom 4C **36**
Ambleside Rd. CH65: Ell P 5A **50**
Amelia Cl. L6: Liv 2H **15**
Amery Gro. CH42: Tran 5G **21**
Amidian Ct. *CH44: Wall 2F 13*
(off Poulton Rd.)
Amity St. L8: Liv 2H **23**
Anchorage, The
CH64: Park 6A **38**
L3: Liv 1F **23**
Anchor Courtyard *L3: Liv 5E 15*
(off Gower St.)
Anderson Cl. CH61: Irby 3C **26**
Anderson Ct. CH62: Brom 5B **36**
Anderson St. L5: Liv 5G **7**
(not continuous)
Andrew Ho. *L8: Liv 6H 15*
(off Birley Ct.)
Andrew St. L4: Walt 2H **7**
Andrew's Wlk. CH60: Hesw . . .3D **32**
ANFIELD 4H **7**
Anfield Rd. L4: Walt 4H **7**
Anglesea Way L8: Liv 3H **23**
Anglesey Cl. CH65: Ell P 6A **50**
Anglesey Rd. CH44: Wall 6F **5**
CH48: W Kir 3C **16**
Anglican Ct. *L8: Liv 6G 15*
(off Blair St.)
Angus Rd. CH63: Brom 5A **36**
Ann Cl. CH66: Lit Sut 6D **42**
Annesley Rd. CH44: Wall 2G **13**
Anscot Av. CH63: Beb 3F **29**
Anson St. L3: Liv 3H **15**
Anstey Cl. CH46: More 4B **10**
Anthony's Way CH60: Hesw . . .4C **32**
Anthorn Cl. CH43: Noct 3B **20**
Antonio St. L20: Boot 2F **7**
Antons Rd. CH61: Pens 4C **26**
Antrim Dr. CH66: Gt Sut 5F **49**
Anzacs, The CH62: Port S 3A **30**
Apex Ct. CH62: Brom 2C **36**
Apollo Ct. *CH44: Wall 6H 5*
(off Rudgrave Sq.)
Appin Rd. CH41: Birke 2A **22**
Appleby Gro. CH62: Brom 5B **36**
Appledale Dr. CH66: Whit 6B **48**
Applegarth CH46: More 1C **18**
Appleton Dr. CH49: Grea 4E **19**
CH65: Whit 4F **49**
Apple Tree Gro.
CH66: Gt Sut 6A **48**
Apsley Av. CH45: Wall 5F **5**
Apsley Gro. CH63: Beb 3G **29**
Apsley Rd. CH62: New F 1H **29**
Aqua Complex, The 4G **7**
Arborn Dr. CH49: Upton 1G **19**
Arcade, The CH65: Ell P 2G **49**
Archbishop Warlock Ct.
L3: Liv 1E **15**
Archer Cl. L4: Kirkd 4G **7**
Archers Ct. *CH49: Woodc 5G 19*
(off Childwall Grn.)
Archers Cft. CH62: Brom 2B **36**
Archers Grn. CH62: East 1G **41**
Archer St. L4: Kirkd 4G **7**
Archers Way CH49: Woodc . . .5G **19**
CH66: Gt Sut 6E **49**
Arch Vw. Cres. L1: Liv 5G **15**
Arden Dr. CH64: Nest 1C **44**
Arderne Cl. CH63: Spit 1H **35**
Argos Pl. L20: Kirkd 2F **7**
Argos Rd. L20: Kirkd 2F **7**
Argyle Ct. *L1: Liv 5F 15*
(off Argyle St.)
Argyle St. CH41: Birke 1A **22**
L1: Liv 5F **15**
Argyle St. Sth. CH41: Birke . . .2A **22**
Argyll Av. CH62: East 1F **41**
Arkle Rd. CH43: Bid 5D **12**
Ark Royal Way CH41: Tran 3B **22**
Arkwood Cl. CH62: Spit 6A **30**
Arkwright St. L5: Liv 6G **7**
Arley Cl. CH43: Bid 1A **20**
Arley St. L3: Liv 1E **15**
Arlington Ct. CH43: Oxton 2D **20**
Arlington Rd. CH45: Wall 5C **4**
Armstrong Quay L3: Liv 4H **23**
Armthorpe Dr. CH66: Lit Sut . . .2B **48**
Arno Ct. CH43: Oxton 4F **21**
Arnold Cres. L8: Liv 1H **23**
Arnold St. CH45: Wall 6F **5**
Arno Rd. CH43: Oxton 4F **21**
Arnot St. L4: Walt 2H **7**
Arnot Way CH63: Hghr B 3D **28**
Arnside Rd. CH43: Oxton 3E **21**
CH45: Wall 6F **5**
Arrad St. L7: Liv 5H **15**
Arran Av. CH65: Ell P 6A **50**
Arrowe Av. CH46: More 6D **10**
Arrowe Brook Ct.
CH49: Grea 3E **19**
Arrowe Brook La.
CH49: Grea 6D **18**
Arrowe Brook Rd.
CH49: Woodc 5F **19**
Arrowe Commercial Pk.
CH49: Upton 4F **19**
Arrowe Country Pk. 6F **19**
Arrowe Ct. *CH49: Woodc 5G 19*
(off Childwall Grn.)
ARROWE HILL 4F **19**
ARROWE PARK HOSPITAL . . .6G **19**
Arrowe Pk. Rd.
CH49: Upton, Woodc 2G **19**
Arrowe Rd. CH49: Grea 4D **18**
Arrowe Side CH49: Grea 3E **19**
Art Ho. Sq. *L1: Liv 5G 15*
(off Fleet St.)
Arthur Av. CH65: Ell P 2A **50**
(not continuous)
Arthur St. CH41: Birke 6G **13**
(not continuous)
Arundel Av. CH45: Wall 5D **4**
Arundel Cl. CH61: Pens 4A **26**
Arundel Ct. CH65: Ell P 4C **50**
Arundel St. L4: Walt 2G **7**
Asbury Rd. CH45: Wall 5B **4**
Ascot Dr. CH63: Beb 4F **29**
CH66: Gt Sut 4D **48**
Ascot Gro. CH63: Beb 4F **29**
Ashbourne Cl.
CH66: Gt Sut 6E **49**
Ashbrook Ter. CH63: Beb 3G **29**
Ashburnham Way L3: Liv 2G **15**
Ashburton Av. CH43: Clau 1D **20**
Ashburton Rd. CH43: Clau 1C **20**
CH44: Wall 1F **13**
CH48: W Kir 4D **16**
Ashby Cl. CH46: More 4B **10**
Ash Cl. CH66: Gt Sut 6F **49**
Ashcroft Dr. CH61: Hesw 6B **26**
Ashdale Pk. CH49: Grea 4B **18**
Ashdown Dr. CH49: Grea 5C **18**
Ashfield Cres. CH62: Brom . . .3B **36**
Ashfield Ho. *CH64: Nest 5C 38*
(off Churchill Way)
Ashfield Rd. CH62: Brom 3A **36**
CH65: Ell P 2A **50**
Ashfield Rd. Nth.
CH65: Ell P 2A **50**
Ashfield St. L5: Liv 6E **7**
Ashford Rd. CH41: Birke 3G **21**
CH47: Meols 5E **9**
Ash Gro. CH45: New B 4G **5**
CH66: Lit Sut 1C **48**
Ashlea Rd. CH61: Pens 6B **26**
Ashley Av. CH47: Meols 4H **9**
Ashley St. CH42: Rock F 5B **22**
Ashmore Cl. CH48: Caldy 3A **24**
Ash Rd. CH42: Tran 3H **21**
CH63: Hghr B 2F **29**
Ashton Cl. CH62: East 2G **41**
Ashton Ct. CH48: W Kir 6C **16**
Ashton Dr. CH48: W Kir 6C **16**
ASHTON HOUSE HOSPITAL . . .3F **21**
Ashton St. L3: Liv 3H **15**
Ash Tree Apartments
CH44: Wall 2H **13**
Ashtree Cl. CH64: Lit N 6D **38**
Ashtree Cft. CH64: Will 6C **40**
Ashtree Dr. CH64: Lit N 1E **45**
Ashtree Farm Ct.
CH64: Will 5C **40**
Ash Vs. CH44: Wall 3G **13**
Ashville Rd. CH41: Birke 1E **21**
CH43: Clau 1E **21**
CH44: Wall 3H **13**
Ashway CH60: Hesw 5D **32**
Ashwell St. L8: Liv 6G **15**
Ashwood Cl. CH66: Gt Sut 6D **48**
Ashwood Ct. CH43: Bid 4A **12**
Askew Cl. CH44: Wall 1H **13**
Askew St. L4: Walt 2H **7**
Askrigg Av. CH66: Lit Sut 2B **48**
Aspen Cl. CH60: Hesw 3F **33**
CH66: Gt Sut 6E **49**
Aspendale Rd. CH42: Tran 3H **21**
Aspinall St. CH41: Birke 6G **13**
Asquith Av. CH41: Birke 6F **13**
Asterfield Av. CH63: Hghr B . . .2E **29**
Aston Cl. CH43: Oxton 4D **20**
Astonwood Rd. CH42: Tran . . .4H **21**
Astor St. L4: Walt 1H **7**
Athelstan Cl. CH62: Brom 2B **36**
Atherton Cl. L5: Liv 6G **7**
Atherton Ct. *CH45: New B 3E 5*
(off Alexandra Rd.)
Atherton Dr. CH49: Woodc 4G **19**
Atherton Ho. CH45: New B 3F **5**
Atherton Rd. CH65: Ell P 1F **49**
Atherton St. CH45: New B 2E **5**
Athol Cl. CH62: East 6C **36**
Athol Dr. CH62: East 1G **41**
Athol St. CH41: Birke 6A **14**
L5: Liv 6E **7**
(Bangor St., not continuous)
L5: Liv 6D **6**
(Denbigh St., not continuous)
Atlantic Pav. L3: Liv 5E **15**
Atlantic Point L3: Liv 2F **15**
Atlantic Way L3: Liv 2F **23**
Atlas Way CH66: Ell P 6F **43**
Atterbury St. L8: Liv 2G **23**
Attwood St. L4: Walt 4H **7**
Atworth Ter. *CH64: Will 5B 40*
(off Neston Rd.)
Auburn Rd. CH45: Wall 4E **5**
Aubynes, The CH45: Wall 4C **4**
Auckery Av. CH66: Gt Sut 4D **48**
Audlem Av. CH43: Oxton 4D **20**
Audley St. L3: Liv 3G **15**
Aughton Ct. CH49: Upton 2G **19**
Austin St. CH44: Wall 3E **13**
Autumn Gro. CH42: Rock F 1E **29**
Avelon Cl. CH43: Noct 2B **20**
Avenue, The CH62: Brom 3A **36**
Avon Cl. CH64: Nest 1C **44**
L4: Kirkd 3G **7**
Avondale CH65: Whit 4H **49**
Avondale Av. CH46: More 4F **11**
CH62: East 6D **36**
Avondale Rd. CH47: Hoy 6D **8**
Avon St. CH41: Birke 4D **12**
Awesome Walls Climbing Cen.
. . . . .6D **6**
Axholme Cl. CH61: Thing 4D **26**
Axholme Rd. CH61: Thing 4C **26**
Aylesbury Av. CH43: Oxton 5C **20**
Aylesbury Cl. CH66: Gt Sut . . .4C **48**
Aylesbury Rd. CH45: New B 4G **5**
Aylsham Dr. CH49: Upton 6G **11**
Aysgarth Rd. CH45: Wall 5D **4**

B

Bk. Barlow La. L4: Kirkd 3G **7**
Bk. Beau St. L5: Liv 1G **15**
Bk. Bedford St. *L7: Liv 5H 15*
(off Cambridge St.)
Bk. Berry St. *L1: Liv 5G 15*
(off Seel St.)
Bk. Blackfield Ter. L4: Kirkd 4F **7**
Bk. Bold St. *L1: Liv 4G 15*
(off Newington)
Bk. Boundary Cl. L5: Kirkd 5F **7**
Bk. Bridport St. *L3: Liv 3G 15*
(off Hotham St.)
Bk. Canning St. L8: Liv 5H **15**
Bk. Catharine St. *L8: Liv 5H 15*
(off Little St Bride St.)
Bk. Chadwick Mt. L5: Liv 4G **7**
Bk. Colquitt St. L1: Liv 5G **15**
Bk. Commutation Row
L3: Liv 3G 15
(off London Rd.)
Bk. Egerton St. Nth. *L8: Liv . . .6H 15*
(off Egerton St.)
Bk. Egerton St. Sth. *L8: Liv . . .6H 15*
(off Egerton St.)
Bk. Falkner St. Sth. L8: Liv 5H **15**
Backford Cl. CH43: Oxton 4C **20**
Backford Gdns. CH1: Back 6A **48**
Backford Rd. CH61: Irby 4H **25**

Bk. Guilford St.—Berrylands Cl.

Bk. Guilford St. L6: Liv 2H 15
Bk. Hope Pl. L1: Liv 5G 15
(off Pilgrim St.)
Bk. Huskisson St. L8: Liv 6H 15
Bk. Knight St. L1: Liv 5G 15
(off Berry St.)
Bk. Langham St. L4: Walt 3H 7
Bk. Leeds St. L3: Liv 2D 14
Bk. Lime St. L1: Liv 4F 15
(off Elliot St.)
Bk. Little Canning St.
L8: Liv 6H 15
(off Lit. Canning St.)
Bk. Luton Gro. L4: Walt 3H 7
Bk. Maryland St. L1: Liv 5G 15
(off Baltimore St.)
Bk. Menai St. CH41: Birke 1G 21
Bk. Mulberry St. L7: Liv 5H 15
Bk. Oliver St. CH41: Birke 1A 22
(off Argyle St.)
Bk. Percy St. L8: Liv 6H 15
(off Percy St.)
Bk. Pickop St. L3: Liv 3E 15
(off Vauxhall Rd.)
Bk. Price St. CH41: Birke 6H 13
Bk. Renshaw St. L1: Liv 4G 15
Bk. Rockfield Rd. L4: Walt 4H 7
(off Blessington Rd.)
Back St Bride St. L8: Liv 5H 15
(off Little St Bride St.)
Bk. Sandon St. L8: Liv 6H 15
Back Seaview CH47: Hoy 6D 8
Bk. Seel St. L1: Liv 5F 15
(off Steel St.)
Bk. Sir Howard St. L8: Liv 5H 15
(off Sir Howard St.)
Bk. Westminster Rd.
L4: Kirkd 3G 7
Bk. York Ter. L5: Liv 5G 7
Baden Ct. CH48: W Kir 4C 16
Bader Cl. CH61: Pens 6A 26
Badger Bait CH64: Lit N 1D 44
Badgers Cl. CH66: Gt Sut 6A 48
Badgers Pk. CH64: Lit N 1D 44
Badgers Rake La.
CH66: Led 4E 47
Badger's Set CH48: Caldy 3B 24
Badger Way CH43: Pren 1G 27
Badminton St. L8: Liv 4H 23
Baffin Cl. CH46: Leas 1G 11
Bagnall St. L4: Walt 4H 7
Baildon Grn. CH66: Lit Sut 2B 48
(off Dunmore Rd.)
Bailey Av. CH65: Ell P 1F 49
Bailey St. L1: Liv 5G 15
Baker Dr. CH66: Gt Sut 4E 49
Bakewell Cl. CH66: Gt Sut 6E 49
Bala Gro. CH44: Wall 2E 13
Balfour Rd. CH43: Oxton 2F 21
CH44: Wall 3E 13
Balfour St. L4: Walt 4H 7
Ballantyne Dr. CH43: Bid 4A 12
Ballantyne Wlk. CH43: Bid 4A 12
Ballard Rd. CH48: W Kir 4G 17
Ball Av. CH45: New B 3E 5
Balliol Cl. CH43: Bid 4A 12
Balliol Ho. L20: Boot 1E 7
Balliol Rd. L20: Boot 1E 7
Ball's Rd. CH43: Oxton 3F 21
Balls Rd. E. CH41: Birke 2G 21
Balmoral Gdns. CH43: Pren 6D 20
CH65: Ell P 4B 50
Balmoral Gro. CH43: Noct 4B 20
Balmoral Rd. CH45: New B 2G 5
Baltic St. L4: Walt 4H 7
Baltimore St. L1: Liv 5G 15
Bamburgh Ct. CH65: Ell P 4C 50
Banbury Way CH43: Oxton 5C 20
Banff Av. CH63: East 6B 36
Bangor Cl. CH66: Gt Sut 6A 48
Bangor Rd. CH45: Wall 5B 4
Bangor St. L5: Liv 6E 7
Bank Cl. CH64: Lit N 1E 45
Bank Dene CH42: Rock F 1G 29
Bankfield Ct. CH62: Brom 6D 30
Bankfields Dr. CH62: East 6F 37
Bankfield St. L20: Kirkd 3D 6
Bankhall La. L20: Kirkd 3E 7
Bankhall Station (Rail) 3E 7
Bankhall St. L20: Kirkd 3E 7

Bank Hey CH64: Lit N 2D 44
Banks, The CH45: Wall 4C 4
Bank's Av. CH47: Meols 5F 9
Bankside Rd. CH42: Rock F 1F 29
Banks Rd. CH48: W Kir 5C 16
CH60: Hesw 4G 31
Bank St. CH41: Birke 1A 22
Bankville Rd. CH42: Tran 4A 22
Banning Cl. CH41: Birke 6H 13
Barberry Cl. CH46: More 5B 10
Barclay St. L8: Liv 3H 23
Barcombe Rd. CH60: Hesw 2F 33
Bardsay Rd. L4: Walt 2H 7
Bardsey Cl. CH65: Ell P 6A 50
Barford Cl. CH43: Bid 1H 19
Barford Grange CH64: Will 5D 40
Barker La. CH49: Grea 5C 18
(not continuous)
Barker Rd. CH61: Irby 3B 26
Barkis Cl. L8: Liv 2H 23
Barleyfield CH61: Pens 5A 26
Barleymow Cl.
CH66: Gt Sut 5C 48
Barlow Av. CH63: Beb 3G 29
Barlow La. L4: Kirkd 3G 7
Barlow St. L4: Kirkd 3G 7
Barmouth Rd. CH45: Wall 5B 4
Barmouth Way L5: Liv 6E 7
Barnacre Dr. CH64: Park 3A 38
Barnacre La. CH46: More 1B 18
Barnard Dr. CH65: Ell P 4C 50
Barnard Rd. CH43: Oxton 2F 21
Barncroft CH61: Pens 6B 26
Barncroft, The CH49: Grea 3D 18
Barnes Grn. CH63: Spit 1G 35
Barnfield Cl. CH47: Meols 4G 9
CH66: Gt Sut 5C 48
Barn Hey CH47: Hoy 2C 16
Barn Hey Cres. CH47: Meols 5H 9
Barnsdale Av. CH61: Thing 4D 26
BARNSTON 6E 27
Barnston Av. CH65: Ell P 2F 49
Barnston La. CH46: More 4E 11
Barnston Rd. CH60: Hesw 4D 32
CH61: Barn, Thing 2D 26
Barnston Towers Cl.
CH60: Hesw 3E 33
Barnwell Av. CH44: Wall 6F 5
Barnwood CH66: Lit Sut 6H 41
Barren Gro. CH43: Oxton 3F 21
Barrington Rd. CH44: Wall 2G 13
Barry Cl. CH65: Ell P 6A 50
Barrymore Way
CH63: Brom 5H 35
Barton Cl. CH47: Hoy 1B 16
Barton Hey Dr. CH48: Caldy 3A 24
Barton Rd. CH47: Hoy 1B 16
Barton St. CH41: Birke 1G 21
(not continuous)
Baskervyle Cl. CH60: Hesw 5C 32
Baskervyle Rd. CH60: Hesw 5C 32
Basnett St. L1: Liv 4F 15
Bassendale Rd.
CH62: Brom 1C 36
Bassenthwaite Av.
CH43: Noct 2B 20
Bath St. CH62: Port S 4H 29
L3: Liv 3D 14
Bathwood Dr. CH64: Lit N 2C 44
Baumville Dr. CH63: Spit 1F 35
Bayhorse La. L3: Liv 3H 15
Baysdale Cl. L8: Liv 3H 23
Bayswater Ct. CH45: Wall 5B 4
Bayswater Gdns. CH45: Wall 4B 4
Bayswater Rd. CH45: Wall 5B 4
Baytree Cl. CH66: Gt Sut 6F 49
Baytree Rd. CH42: Tran 4A 22
CH48: Frank 5H 17
Bay Vw. Dr. CH45: Wall 4A 4
Beachcroft Rd. CH47: Meols 4G 9
Beach Gro. CH45: Wall 4G 5
Beach Rd. CH47: Hoy 1B 16
Beach Wlk. CH48: W Kir 1A 24
Beacon Ct. CH60: Hesw 3C 32
Beacon Dr. CH48: W Kir 5E 17
Beacon Ho. L5: Liv 1G 15
(off Portland Pl.)
Beacon La. CH60: Hesw 3C 32
L5: Liv 5H 7
Beacon Pde. CH60: Hesw 3C 32

Beacons, The CH60: Hesw 4C 32
Beaconsfield Cl.
CH42: Tran 4B 22
Beaconsfield Rd.
CH62: New F 2H 29
Beasley Cl. CH66: Gt Sut 4D 48
Beatles Story, The 5E 15
Beatrice Av. CH63: Hghr B 2E 29
Beatrice St. L20: Boot 2F 7
Beatty Cl. CH48: Caldy 3A 24
Beaufort Dr. CH44: Wall 6C 4
Beaufort Rd. CH41: Birke 4D 12
Beaufort St. L8: Liv 1G 23
(Hill St.)
L8: Liv 1G 23
(Mann St.)
L8: Liv 2G 23
(Northumberland St.)
Beaumaris Ct. CH43: Oxton 2F 21
Beaumaris Dr. CH61: Thing 3D 26
CH65: Ell P 5B 50
Beaumaris Rd. CH45: Wall 5B 4
Beaumaris St. L20: Kirkd 3E 7
(not continuous)
Beau St. L3: Liv 1G 15
Beauworth Av. CH49: Grea 4C 18
BEBINGTON 3G 29
Bebington Rd.
CH42: Rock F, Tran 5H 21
CH62: New F 3G 29
CH63: Beb 3G 29
CH66: Gt Sut 3D 48
Bebington Station (Rail) 2G 29
Beckenham Rd.
CH45: New B 2F 5
Becket St. L4: Kirkd 4F 7
(not continuous)
Beckett Gro. CH63: Hghr B 2D 28
Beckwith Ct. CH41: Birke 5G 13
(off Beckwith St.)
Beckwith St. CH41: Birke 5F 13
L1: Liv 5F 15
Beckwith St. E. CH41: Birke 6H 13
Bedford Av. CH42: Rock F 6A 22
CH65: Whit 5G 49
Bedford Av. E. CH65: Whit 5H 49
Bedford Cl. L7: Liv 5H 15
Bedford Ct. CH42: Rock F 5B 22
L7: Liv 6H 15
(off Bedford St. Sth.)
Bedford Dr. CH42: Rock F 6H 21
Bedford Pl. CH42: Rock F 5C 22
L20: Boot 2D 6
Bedford Rd. CH42: Rock F 5B 22
CH45: Wall 5F 5
L4: Walt 2E 7
L20: Boot 2E 7
Bedford Rd. E.
CH42: Rock F 5C 22
Bedford St. Nth. L7: Liv 4H 15
Bedford St. Sth. L7: Liv 5H 15
(not continuous)
Bedford Wlk. L7: Liv 5H 15
(off Bedford Cl.)
Beech Av. CH49: Upton 1D 18
CH61: Pens 5C 26
Beech Ct. CH42: Tran 3H 21
Beechcroft Dr. CH65: Whit 4H 49
Beechcroft Rd. CH44: Wall 3G 13
Beeches, The CH42: Rock F 6C 22
CH46: Leas 2E 11
CH66: Gt Sut 3D 48
Beechfield Cl. CH60: Hesw 4C 32
Beechfield Rd. CH65: Ell P 2H 49
Beech Gro. CH66: Whit 6B 48
Beech Hey La. CH64: Will 4D 40
Beech Rd. CH42: Tran 3G 21
CH60: Hesw 3E 33
CH63: Hghr B 2F 29
Beechway CH63: Beb 6F 29
Beechways Dr. CH64: Nest 6B 38
BEECHWOOD 5A 12
Beechwood Av. CH45: Wall 6C 4
Beechwood Ct.
CH49: Woodc 6H 19
(off Childwall Grn.)
Beechwood Dr. CH43: Bid 6A 12
CH66: Gt Sut 6D 48
Beechwood Recreation Cen.
6A 12

Beechwood Rd.
CH62: Brom 3A 36
Beeston Cl. CH43: Bid 1A 20
Beeston Dr. CH61: Pens 5B 26
Beeston Grn. CH66: Gt Sut 2E 49
Beeston St. L4: Kirkd 3G 7
Beetham Plaza L2: Liv 4E 15
(off The Strand)
Beetham Twr. L3: Liv 3D 14
(off Old Hall St.)
Belfield Dr. CH43: Oxton 4F 21
Belford Dr. CH46: More 5C 10
Belfry Cl. CH46: More 4B 10
Belgrave Av. CH44: Wall 1G 13
Belgrave Dr. CH65: Ell P 2F 49
Belgrave St. CH44: Wall 6F 5
Bellamy Rd. L4: Walt 1G 7
Belldene Gro. CH61: Hesw 1B 32
Belle Vue Rd. CH44: Wall 3A 14
Bellfield Cres. CH45: New B 3E 5
Bell Rd. CH44: Wall 2H 13
Belltower Rd. L20: Kirkd 4D 6
Bellward Cl. CH63: Spit 1F 35
Belmont CH41: Birke 2G 21
Belmont Av. CH62: Brom 2A 36
Belmont Dr. CH61: Pens 5C 26
Belmont Gro. CH43: Oxton 2G 21
Belmont Rd. CH45: New B 2F 5
CH48: W Kir 4D 16
Beloe St. L8: Liv 3H 23
Belvidere Rd. CH45: Wall 5D 4
Benbow Cl. CH43: Bid 5D 12
Benbow St. L20: Boot 1D 6
Bendee Av. CH64: Lit N 6E 39
Bendee Rd. CH64: Lit N 6D 38
Benedict Cl. CH49: Woodc 3H 19
Benedict Ct. L20: Boot 2E 7
Benedict St. L20: Boot 2F 7
Benledi St. L5: Liv 6F 7
Bennet's La. CH47: Meols 3G 9
Bennett Cl. CH64: Will 5C 40
Bennetts Hill CH43: Oxton 3F 21
Bennett Wlk. CH61: Pens 6B 26
Ben Nevis Dr. CH66: Lit Sut 1H 47
Ben Nevis Rd. CH42: Tran 5H 21
Benson Cl. CH49: Upton 3F 19
Benson St. L1: Liv 4G 15
Bentfield Cl. CH63: Hghr B 2D 28
Bentfield Gdns.
CH63: Hghr B 2D 28
Bentham Cl. CH43: Noct 4C 20
Bentinck Cl. CH41: Birke 1G 21
Bentinck Pl. CH41: Birke 1G 21
Bentinck St. CH41: Birke 1G 21
(not continuous)
L5: Liv 6D 6
Bentley Rd. CH43: Oxton 3F 21
CH61: Pens 4B 26
Benton Cl. L5: Liv 5F 7
Bent Way CH60: Hesw 2C 32
Benty Cl. CH63: Hghr B 5E 29
Benty Farm Gro.
CH61: Pens 4C 26
Benty Heath La. CH64: Will 2A 40
CH66: Hoot 2A 40
Beresford Av. CH63: Beb 2G 29
Beresford Cl. CH43: Oxton 2E 21
Beresford Ct. CH43: Oxton 2E 21
CH63: Beb 2G 29
(off Beresford Av.)
Beresford Rd. CH43: Oxton 2D 20
CH45: Wall 4D 4
L8: Liv 3H 23
Beresford St. L5: Liv 1G 15
L20: Boot 2D 6
Berey's Bldgs. L3: Liv 3E 15
(off Bixteth St.)
Bergen Cl. L20: Boot 1G 7
Berkeley Av. CH43: Pren 6D 20
Berkeley Ct. CH49: Woodc 5G 19
(off Childwall Grn.)
Berkeley Dr. CH45: New B 4G 5
Berkley Cl. L8: Liv 1H 23
Berkley St. L8: Liv 6H 15
Bermuda Rd. CH46: More 4C 10
Bernard Av. CH45: New B 4G 5
Berner St. CH41: Birke 5H 13
Berry Cl. CH66: Gt Sut 4C 48
Berry Dr. CH66: Gt Sut 3C 48
Berrylands Cl. CH46: More 4D 10

Berrylands Rd.—Bridge Farm Cl.

Berrylands Rd. CH46: More ... 4D **10**
Berry St. L1: Liv ... 5G **15**
L20: Boot ... 1D **6**
Berry St. Ind. Est. *L20: Boot ... 1D 6*
(off Berry St.)
Bertha Gdns. CH41: Birke ... 5D **12**
Bertha St. CH41: Birke ... 5D **12**
Bertram Cl. CH47: Meols ... 5F **9**
Bertram Dr. CH47: Meols ... 5E **9**
Bertram Dr. Nth. CH47: Meols ... 5F **9**
Berwick Av. CH62: East ... 1G **41**
Berwick Cl. CH46: More ... 5B **10**
Berwick Gdns.
CH66: Lit Sut ... 1B **48**
Berwick Gro. CH66: Lit Sut ... 1B **48**
Berwick Rd. CH66: Lit Sut ... 1A **48**
Berwick Rd. W.
CH66: Lit Sut ... 1H **47**
Berwyn Av. CH47: Hoy ... 6E **9**
CH61: Thing ... 3C **26**
Berwyn Blvd. CH63: Hghr B ... 1E **29**
Berwyn Cl. CH66: Lit Sut ... 1A **48**
Berwyn Dr. CH61: Hesw ... 1B **32**
Berwyn Rd. CH44: Wall ... 6G **5**
Beryl Rd. CH43: Noct ... 2A **20**
Bessborough Rd.
CH43: Oxton ... 3F **21**
Bessemer St. L8: Liv ... 3H **23**
Beta Cl. CH62: New F ... 2G **29**
Bethany Ct. CH63: Spit ... 6G **29**
Bethany Cres. CH63: Beb ... 4F **29**
Bettisfield Av. CH62: Brom ... 6B **36**
Beverley Dr. CH60: Hesw ... 5D **32**
Beverley Gdns.
CH61: Thing ... 3D **26**
Beverley Rd. CH45: Wall ... 5D **4**
CH62: New F ... 1H **29**
Beverley Way CH66: Lit Sut ... 6C **42**
Bevington Bush L3: Liv ... 2F **15**
Bevington Hill L3: Liv ... 1F **15**
Bevington St. L3: Liv ... 1F **15**
Bevyl Rd. CH64: Park ... 3A **38**
Bewey Cl. L8: Liv ... 3G **23**
Bianca St. L20: Boot ... 2E **7**
Bickerstaffe St. L3: Liv ... 2G **15**
Bickerton Av. CH63: Hghr B ... 1D **28**
Bidder St. L3: Liv ... 2G **15**
Bidson Link Rd. CH44: Wall ... 3B **12**
BIDSTON ... 5B **12**
Bidston Av. CH41: Birke ... 6C **12**
CH45: Wall ... 5C **4**
Bidston Ct. CH43: Noct ... 6C **12**
Bidston Grn. CH66: Gt Sut ... 3D **48**
Bidston Grn. Ct. CH43: Bid ... 5A **12**
Bidston Grn. Dr. CH43: Bid ... 5A **12**
Bidston Hall Farm
CH43: Bid ... 4A **12**
Bidston Ind. Est.
CH44: Wall ... 2B **12**
Bidston Link Rd. CH43: Bid ... 3B **12**
Bidston Moss CH44: Wall ... 2B **12**
Bidston Moss Nature Reserve
... 2C **12**
Bidston Rd.
CH43: Clau, Oxton ... 1C **20**
Bidston Station (Rail) ... 3A **12**
Bidston Sta. App.
CH43: Bid ... 3A **12**
Bidston Vw. CH43: Bid ... 4A **12**
Bidston Village Rd.
CH43: Bid ... 4A **12**
Bidston Windmill ... 6B **12**
Big Meadow Rd.
CH49: Woodc ... 3G **19**
Billings Cl. L5: Kirkd ... 5F **7**
Binsey Cl. CH49: Upton ... 2D **18**
Birchall St. L20: Kirkd ... 4E **7**
Birch Av. CH49: Upton ... 1D **18**
Birch Cl. CH43: Oxton ... 4F **21**
Birchdale Cl. CH49: Grea ... 2D **18**
Birches, The CH44: Wall ... 3A **14**
CH64: Nest ... 3D **38**
Birches Cl. CH60: Hesw ... 3C **32**
Birchfield CH46: More ... 6C **10**
Birchfield Cl. CH46: More ... 1C **18**
Birchfield St. L3: Liv ... 2G **15**
Birch Gro. CH45: New B ... 4G **5**
CH66: Whit ... 6G **49**
Birch Heys CH48: Frank ... 6A **18**
Birchmere CH60: Hesw ... 1A **32**
Birchridge Cl. CH62: Spit ... 1A **36**
Birch Rd. CH43: Oxton ... 4F **21**
CH47: Meols ... 5G **9**
CH63: Beb ... 5G **29**
Birch St. L5: Liv ... 6D **6**
Birchview Way CH43: Noct ... 2B **20**
Birchway CH60: Hesw ... 5E **33**
Birchwood Av. CH41: Birke ... 6A **14**
Birchwood Cl. CH41: Birke ... 6H **13**
CH66: Gt Sut ... 6D **48**
Birkdale Av. CH63: Brom ... 5A **36**
BIRKENHEAD ... 1B **22**
Birkenhead Central Station (Rail)
... 2A **22**
Birkenhead North Station (Rail)
... 4D **12**
Birkenhead Park Station (Rail)
... 5F **13**
Birkenhead Priory ... 1B **22**
Birkenhead Rd. CH44: Wall ... 4A **14**
CH47: Hoy, Meols ... 5E **9**
CH64: Will ... 3H **39**
Birket Av. CH46: Leas ... 2F **11**
Birket Cl. CH46: Leas ... 2G **11**
Birket Ho. CH41: Birke ... 6H **13**
Birket Sq. CH46: Leas ... 2F **11**
Birkett Av. CH65: Ell P ... 5A **50**
Birkett Rd. CH42: Rock F ... 6A **22**
CH48: W Kir ... 3D **16**
Birkett St. L3: Liv ... 2G **15**
Birley Ct. L8: Liv ... 6H **15**
Birnam Rd. CH44: Wall ... 2H **13**
Bishop Rd. CH44: Wall ... 3F **13**
Bishops Ct. CH43: Oxton ... 4F **21**
Bishops Gdns. CH65: Ell P ... 2G **49**
Bishop Sheppard Ct. L3: Liv ... 1E **15**
Bisley St. CH45: Wall ... 6F **5**
Bispham Dr. CH47: Meols ... 6G **9**
Bispham Ho. *L3: Liv ... 2F 15*
(off Lace St.)
Bixteth St. L3: Liv ... 3E **15**
Blackboards La.
CH66: Chil T ... 6A **42**
Blackburne Pl. L8: Liv ... 5H **15**
Blackburne Ter. *L8: Liv ... 5H 15*
(off Blackburne Pl.)
Blackdown Cl.
CH66: Lit Sut ... 2A **48**
Blackeys La. CH64: Nest ... 5C **38**
Blackfield St. L5: Kirkd ... 5F **7**
Blackheath Dr. CH46: Leas ... 2F **11**
Black Horse Cl.
CH48: W Kir ... 4E **17**
Black Horse Hill
CH48: W Kir ... 5E **17**
Black Lion La.
CH66: Lit Sut ... 1B **48**
Blackpool St. CH41: Birke ... 2A **22**
Blackstairs Rd. CH66: Ell P ... 6F **43**
Blackstock St. L3: Liv ... 2E **15**
Blackstone St. L5: Liv ... 5D **6**
Blackthorne Av. CH66: Whit ... 6B **48**
Blackthorne Cl. CH46: More ... 6F **11**
Blair Ct. CH43: Clau ... 1F **21**
Blair Pk. CH63: Spit ... 6H **29**
Blair St. L8: Liv ... 6G **15**
Blakeley Brow
CH63: Raby M ... 5G **35**
Blakeley Ct. CH63: Raby M ... 5G **35**
Blakeley Dell
CH63: Raby M ... 5H **35**
Blakeley Dene
CH63: Raby M ... 4H **35**
Blakeley Rd. CH63: Raby M ... 4G **35**
Blakemere Ct. CH65: Ell P ... 2G **43**
Blakeney Cl. CH49: Upton ... 6G **11**
Blakenhall Way
CH49: Upton ... 1D **18**
Blaydon Wlk. CH43: Clau ... 1C **20**
Bleasdale Cl. CH49: Upton ... 1E **19**
Blenheim Rd. CH44: Wall ... 6H **5**
Blenheim St. L5: Liv ... 1E **15**
Blessington Rd. L4: Walt ... 4H **7**
Bletchley Av. CH44: Wall ... 1D **12**
Blithedale Ct. *CH42: Rock F ... 6C 22*
(off The Hawthornes)
Bloomsbury Ct. CH47: Hoy ... 1C **16**
Bluebell Av. CH41: Birke ... 5D **12**
Bluebell La. CH64: Nest ... 4G **39**
Bluecoat, The ... 4F **15**
Bluecoat Chambers *L1: Liv ... 4F 15*
(off School La.)
Bluefields St. L8: Liv ... 6H **15**
Blue Planet Aquarium ... 6B **50**
Bluewood Dr. CH41: Birke ... 4B **12**
Blundells Dr. CH46: More ... 4E **11**
Blundell St. L1: Liv ... 6F **15**
Blyth Rd. CH63: Brom ... 4A **36**
BMB Ind. Pk. CH44: Wall ... 2D **12**
Boathouse La. CH64: Park ... 3A **38**
Bob Paisley Ct. *L5: Liv ... 5H 7*
(off Adkins St.)
Bodiam Ct. CH65: Ell P ... 5C **50**
Bodley St. L4: Walt ... 4H **7**
Bodmin Rd. L4: Walt ... 2H **7**
Bolde Way CH63: Spit ... 2G **35**
Bold Pl. L1: Liv ... 5G **15**
Bold St. L1: Liv ... 4F **15**
Bollington Cl. CH43: Oxton ... 4D **20**
Bolton Rd. CH62: Port S ... 4H **29**
Bolton Rd. E. CH62: Port S ... 3A **30**
Bolton St. L3: Liv ... 4G **15**
Bond St. L3: Liv ... 1F **15**
BOOTLE ... 1D **6**
Bootle Oriel Road Station (Rail)
... 1D **6**
Border Rd. CH60: Hesw ... 3D **32**
Border Way L5: Liv ... 5G **7**
Borough Pavement
CH41: Birke ... 1A **22**
Borough Pl. *CH41: Birke ... 1A 22*
(off Grange Rd. E.)
Borough Rd. CH41: Birke ... 4G **21**
CH42: Rock F, Tran ... 4G **21**
CH44: Wall ... 2H **13**
Borough Rd. E. CH41: Birke ... 1A **22**
CH44: Wall ... 3A **14**
Borough Way CH44: Wall ... 3A **14**
Borrowdale Rd.
CH46: More ... 5D **10**
CH63: Beb ... 5E **29**
Bosnia St. L8: Liv ... 4H **23**
Bostock Grn. CH65: Ell P ... 1F **49**
Bostock St. L5: Liv ... 6F **7**
Boswell Rd. CH43: Pren ... 6D **20**
Bosworth Cl. CH63: Spit ... 1F **35**
Botley Cl. CH49: Upton ... 2D **18**
Boulevard, The
CH65: Gt Sut ... 2F **49**
L8: Liv ... 1H **23**
Boulton Av. CH48: W Kir ... 3D **16**
CH62: New F ... 1H **29**
Boundary La. CH60: Hesw ... 3C **32**
Boundary Pk. CH64: Park ... 6B **38**
Boundary Rd.
CH43: Bid, Noct ... 4B **12**
CH48: W Kir ... 1B **24**
CH62: Port S ... 2H **29**
Boundary St. L5: Liv ... 5D **6**
Boundary St. E. L5: Liv ... 5G **7**
Bousfield St. L4: Walt ... 4G **7**
Bowdon Rd. CH45: Wall ... 5E **5**
Bower Ho. CH49: Upton ... 6F **11**
Bower Rd. CH60: Hesw ... 3E **33**
Bowfell Cl. CH62: East ... 2F **41**
Bowgreen Cl. CH43: Bid ... 6A **12**
Bowland Cl. CH62: Brom ... 2B **36**
Bowness Av. CH43: Pren ... 5E **21**
CH63: Brom ... 6A **36**
Bowood St. L8: Liv ... 4H **23**
Bowring Dr. CH64: Park ... 4A **38**
Bowring St. L8: Liv ... 3H **23**
Bowscale Cl. CH49: Upton ... 2E **19**
Boyd Cl. CH46: Leas ... 2H **11**
Brackendale CH49: Woodc ... 4A **20**
Bracken Dr. CH48: W Kir ... 5G **17**
Brackenhurst Dr.
CH45: New B ... 4G **5**
Bracken La. CH63: Hghr B ... 4D **28**
Bracken Rd. CH66: Gt Sut ... 3E **49**
Brackenside CH60: Hesw ... 1B **32**
Brackenwood Rd.
CH63: Hghr B ... 4D **28**
Brackley Cl. CH44: Wall ... 2E **13**
Bradda Cl. CH49: Upton ... 6F **11**
Bradden Cl. CH63: Spit ... 1H **35**
Bradewell Cl. L4: Kirkd ... 3G **7**
Bradewell St. L4: Kirkd ... 3G **7**
Bradgate Cl. CH46: More ... 4B **10**
Bradman Cl. CH45: Wall ... 6F **5**
Bradman Rd. CH46: More ... 4C **10**
Bradmoor Rd. CH62: Brom ... 3B **36**
Bradwall Cl. CH65: Whit ... 3G **49**
Bradwell Cl. CH48: W Kir ... 5F **17**
Braehaven Rd. CH45: New B ... 4G **5**
Braemar Ct. CH65: Ell P ... 4C **50**
Braemar Ho. CH43: Oxton ... 2D **20**
Braemar St. L20: Kirkd ... 2F **7**
Braemore Rd. CH44: Wall ... 1D **12**
Braeside Cl. CH66: Gt Sut ... 2C **48**
Braeside Gdns.
CH49: Upton ... 2F **19**
Braid St. CH41: Birke ... 5H **13**
Braidwood Ct. *CH41: Birke ... 2G 21*
(off Mount Gro.)
Bramble Av. CH41: Birke ... 5D **12**
Bramble Way CH46: More ... 3D **10**
Bramblewood Cl.
CH43: Noct ... 3B **20**
Bramerton Ct. CH48: W Kir ... 4C **16**
Bramford Cl. CH49: Upton ... 2E **19**
Bramhall Cl. CH48: W Kir ... 5F **17**
Bramhall Dr. CH62: East ... 2H **41**
Bramley Av. CH63: Hghr B ... 2E **29**
Bramley Cl. CH66: Gt Sut ... 6A **48**
Brampton Dr. L8: Liv ... 5H **15**
Bramwell Av. CH43: Pren ... 6E **21**
Brancepeth Ct. CH65: Ell P ... 4B **50**
Brancote Ct. CH43: Clau ... 1D **20**
Brancote Gdns. CH43: Clau ... 1D **20**
CH62: Brom ... 4B **36**
Brancote Mt. CH43: Clau ... 1D **20**
Brancote Rd. CH43: Clau ... 1D **20**
Brandon St. CH41: Birke ... 1B **22**
Brasenose Rd. L20: Boot ... 1D **6**
Brassey St. CH41: Birke ... 5F **13**
L8: Liv ... 1G **23**
Brattan Rd. CH41: Birke ... 3G **21**
Braunton Rd. CH45: Wall ... 5E **5**
Bray St. CH41: Birke ... 5F **13**
Brearley Cl. CH43: Bid ... 5A **12**
Breck, The CH66: Ell P ... 6E **43**
Breckfield Pl. L5: Liv ... 6H **7**
Breckfield Rd. Nth. L5: Liv ... 5H **7**
Breck Pl. CH44: Wall ... 2E **13**
Breck Rd. CH44: Wall ... 1D **12**
L5: Liv ... 1H **15**
Breckside Av. CH44: Wall ... 1C **12**
Brecon Dr. CH66: Gt Sut ... 6E **49**
Brecon Rd. CH42: Tran ... 6G **21**
Bredon Cl. CH66: Lit Sut ... 1A **48**
Breeze Cl. *L9: Walt ... 1H 7*
(off Breeze La.)
Breeze Hill L9: Walt ... 1F **7**
L20: Boot ... 1F **7**
Breezehill Cl. CH64: Nest ... 5D **38**
Breezehill Pk. CH64: Nest ... 5D **38**
Breezehill Rd. CH64: Nest ... 5D **38**
Breeze La. L9: Walt ... 1H **7**
Brenig St. CH41: Birke ... 4D **12**
Brentwood Ct.
CH49: Woodc ... 5G 19
(off Childwall Grn.)
Brentwood St. CH44: Wall ... 2G **13**
Brereton Av. CH63: Beb ... 3G **29**
Brett St. CH41: Birke ... 5F **13**
Brewster St. L4: Kirkd ... 2G **7**
L20: Boot ... 2G **7**
Brian Av. CH61: Irby ... 3B **26**
Briardale Gdns.
CH66: Lit Sut ... 1C **48**
Briardale Rd. CH42: Tran ... 3G **21**
CH44: Wall ... 3A **14**
CH63: Hghr B ... 2F **29**
CH64: Will ... 5C **40**
CH66: Lit Sut ... 1C **48**
Briar Dr. CH60: Hesw ... 3C **32**
Briarfield Rd. CH60: Hesw ... 3C **32**
CH65: Ell P ... 2H **49**
Briar St. L4: Kirkd ... 4F **7**
Briarswood Cl.
CH42: Rock F ... 1F **29**
Briary Cl. CH60: Hesw ... 2D **32**
Brick St. L1: Liv ... 6F **15**
Bride St. L4: Walt ... 1H **7**
Bridge Ct. CH48: W Kir ... 4C **16**
CH64: Nest ... 6C **38**
Bridgecroft Rd. CH45: Wall ... 5F **5**
Bridge Farm Cl.
CH49: Woodc ... 3H **19**

Bridge Mdw. CH66: Gt Sut 5F 49
Bridgenorth Rd.
　CH61: Pens 5A 26
Bridge Rd. CH48: W Kir 4C 16
Bridges Rd. CH65: Ell P 2D 50
Bridge St. CH41: Birke 6A 14
　　　　　　　　　　(not continuous)
　CH62: Port S 4H 29
　　　　　　　　　　(not continuous)
　CH64: Nest 6C 38
　L20: Boot 1D 6
Bridgewater St. L1: Liv 6F 15
Bridgewood Dr.
　CH66: Gt Sut 5C 48
Bridle Av. CH44: Wall 3A 14
Bridle Cl. CH43: Bid 1H 19
　CH62: Brom 4C 36
Bridle Pk. CH62: Brom 4C 36
Bridle Rd. CH44: Wall 3A 14
　CH62: Brom, East 4A 36
Bridle Way CH66: Gt Sut 4D 48
Bridport St. L3: Liv 3G 15
Briedden Way
　CH66: Lit Sut 1A 48
Brighton St. CH44: Wall 1H 13
Bright St. CH41: Birke 1G 21
　　　　　　　　　　(not continuous)
　L6: Liv 2H 15
Brightwell Cl. CH49: Upton . .3F 19
Brill St. CH41: Birke 5F 13
BRIMSTAGE 1B 34
Brimstage Av.
　CH63: Hghr B 1D 28
Brimstage Cl. CH60: Hesw . .4E 33
Brimstage Grn. CH60: Hesw . .3F 33
Brimstage Hall 1A 34
Brimstage La.
　CH63: Brim, Store 1B 34
Brimstage Rd. CH60: Hesw . .4E 33
　CH63: Beb, Brim, Hghr B
　　　　　　　　　　　　　　. . .4E 33
　L4: Walt 1G 7
Brindley St. CH41: Birke 2G 21
Brinley Cl. CH62: Brom 6B 36
Brisbane Av. CH45: New B . . .3E 5
Briscoe Av. CH46: More 6E 11
Briscoe Dr. CH46: More 6E 11
Bristol Av. CH44: Wall 1G 13
Bristol Dr. CH66: Gt Sut 6E 49
Britannia Cres. L8: Liv 4H 23
Britannia Ho. CH41: Birke . . .1B 22
Britannia Rd. CH45: Wall 1E 13
Broadbelt St. L4: Walt 1H 7
Broad Birches CH65: Ell P . . .1G 49
Broadfield Av. CH43: Bid 5H 11
Broadfield Cl. CH43: Bid 6H 11
Broadheath Av. CH43: Bid . . .6A 12
Broadlake CH64: Will 5B 40
Broadland Gdns.
　CH66: Gt Sut 5F 49
Broadland Rd. CH66: Gt Sut . .5F 49
Broad La. CH60: Hesw 2F 31
Broadmead CH60: Hesw 4E 33
Broadoaks CH49: Upton 1E 19
Broadstone Dr. CH63: Spit . . .1F 35
Broadway CH45: Wall 6D 4
　CH49: Grea 2E 19
　CH63: Hghr B 2D 28
Broadway Av. CH45: Wall 6D 4
Brockley Av. CH45: New B . . .2F 5
Brock St. L4: Kirkd 3G 7
BROMBOROUGH 3A 36
BROMBOROUGH POOL 4B 30
BROMBOROUGH PORT 6C 30
Bromborough Rake Station (Rail)
　. . . . . .3A 36
Bromborough Rd.
　CH63: Beb 4G 29
Bromborough Station (Rail)
　. . . . . .4A 36
Bromborough Village Rd.
　CH62: Brom 2C 36
Brome Way CH63: Spit 1H 35
Bromley Cl. CH60: Hesw 4A 32
Bromley Rd. CH45: New B . . .4E 5
Brompton Av. CH44: Wall 1G 13
Brompton Way
　CH66: Gt Sut 6E 49

Bromsgrove Rd. CH49: Grea . .3C 18
Bronington Av. CH62: Brom . .5B 36
Bronte St. L3: Liv 4G 15
Brook Cl. CH44: Wall 6G 5
Brookdale Av. Nth.
　CH49: Grea 3E 19
Brookdale Av. Sth.
　CH49: Grea 3E 19
Brookdale Cl. CH49: Grea . . .3E 19
Brookfield Dr.
　CH48: W Kir 5D 16
Brookfield Rd. CH48: W Kir . .5D 16
Brook Hey CH64: Park 3A 38
Brook Hey Dr. CH64: Park . . .3A 38
BROOKHURST 6A 36
Brookhurst Av. CH62: East . . .5A 36
　CH63: Brom, East 5A 36
Brookhurst Cl. CH63: Brom . .6A 36
Brookhurst Rd. CH63: Brom . .5A 36
Brookland Rd. CH41: Birke . . .2H 21
Brooklands CH41: Birke 6H 13
Brooklands Gdns.
　CH64: Park 4A 38
Brooklands Rd. CH64: Park . . .4A 38
Brook La. CH64: Park 3A 38
Brooklet Rd. CH60: Hesw 3E 33
Brooklyn Dr. CH65: Gt Sut . . .2F 49
Brook Mdw. CH61: Irby 2A 26
Brook Rd. CH66: Gt Sut 2D 48
Brooks All. L1: Liv 4F 15
Brookside Cres.
　CH49: Upton 2D 18
Brookside Dr. CH49: Upton . .2E 19
Brook St. CH41: Birke 5G 13
　CH62: Port S 3G 29
　CH64: Nest 5C 38
　L3: Liv 3D 14
Brook St. E. CH41: Birke 6A 14
Brook Ter. CH48: W Kir 5C 16
Brookthorpe Cl. CH45: Wall . .5G 5
Brook Wlk. CH61: Irby 2H 25
Brookway CH43: Pren 6C 20
　CH45: Wall 6E 5
　CH49: Grea 2E 19
Brook Well CH46: Lit N 2C 44
Broomfield Cl. CH60: Hesw . .2G 31
Broom Hill CH43: Clau 6D 12
Broomlands CH60: Hesw 3B 32
Broomleigh Cl.
　CH43: Hghr B 4D 28
Broseley Av. CH62: Brom 2A 36
Broster Av. CH46: More 5C 10
Broster Cl. CH46: More 5C 10
Brosters La. CH47: Meols 5F 9
Brotherton Cl. CH62: Brom . . .2A 36
Brotherton Park &
　Dibbinsdale Local Nature Reserve
　. . . . . .1A 36
Brougham Av. CH42: Tran . . .3B 22
Brougham Rd. CH44: Wall . . .2H 13
Broughton Av. CH48: W Kir . .4C 16
Broughton Rd. CH44: Wall . . .2F 13
Brow La. CH60: Hesw 4B 32
Browning Av. CH42: Rock F . .6B 22
Browning Dr. CH65: Gt Sut . . .3F 49
Browning Grn. CH65: Gt Sut . .3F 49
　　　　　　　　　　(off Browning Dr.)
Browning Rd. CH45: Wall 6B 4
Brownlow Hill L3: Liv 4G 15
Brownlow Rd. CH62: New F . .2H 29
Brownlow St. L3: Liv 4H 15
Brow Rd. CH43: Bid 4B 12
Brow Side L5: Liv 1H 15
Broxton Av. CH43: Pren 5D 20
　CH48: W Kir 4D 16
Broxton Rd. CH45: Wall 5D 4
　CH65: Ell P 2E 49
Bruce Cres. CH63: Brom 5A 36
Bruce Dr. CH66: Gt Sut 3C 48
Bruera Rd. CH65: Gt Sut 3F 49
Brunel M. L6: Liv 6H 7
Brunel Rd. CH62: Brom 2D 36
Brunsborough Cl.
　CH62: Brom 5A 36
Brunsfield Cl. CH46: More . . .6C 10
Brunstath Cl. CH60: Hesw . . .2E 33
Brunswick Bus. Pk. L3: Liv . . .2F 23
　　　　　　　　　　(not continuous)
Brunswick Cl. L4: Kirkd 3G 7
Brunswick Ct. CH41: Birke . . .6A 14
　　　　　　　　　　(off Brunswick M.)

Brunswick Cres.
　CH66: Gt Sut 4E 49
Brunswick Ent. Cen. L3: Liv . .2F 23
Brunswick M. CH41: Birke . . .6A 14
Brunswick Pl. L20: Kirkd 3D 6
Brunswick Rd. L6: Liv 2H 15
Brunswick Station (Rail) 3G 23
Brunswick St. L2: Liv 4E 15
　L3: Liv 4D 14
Brunswick Way L3: Liv 2F 23
Bryanston Rd. CH42: Tran . . .5E 21
Bryce Cl. CH62: Brom 6A 30
Bryce Dr. CH62: Brom 6A 30
Bryce Wlk. CH62: Brom 5A 30
Bryn Bank CH44: Wall 1G 13
Brynmoss Av. CH44: Wall . . .1D 12
Bryony Way CH42: Rock F . . .1F 29
Brythen St. L1: Liv 4F 15
BT Convention Cen. 6E 15
Buccleuch St. CH41: Birke . . .4D 12
Buchanan Rd. CH44: Wall . . .2H 13
　L9: Walt 1H 7
Buckingham Av. CH43: Clau . .6D 12
　CH63: Hghr B 2E 29
Buckingham Gdns.
　CH65: Ell P 5B 50
Buckingham Rd.
　CH44: Wall 1D 12
Buckingham St. L5: Liv 6G 7
Buckland Dr. CH63: Spit 1F 35
Buckley Ct. CH64: Will 5B 40
Buckley La. CH64: Will 5B 40
Bude Cl. CH43: Bid 1A 20
Bude Ho. CH43: Bid 1A 20
　　　　　　　　　　　　(off Bude Cl.)
Budworth Cl. CH43: Oxton . . .3C 20
Budworth Ct. CH43: Oxton . . .2D 20
Budworth Rd.
　CH43: Noct, Oxton 3C 20
　CH66: Gt Sut 5E 49
Buerton Cl. CH43: Noct 3C 20
Buffs La. CH60: Hesw 2D 32
Buggen La. CH64: Nest 5B 38
Buildwas Rd. CH44: Nest 3C 38
Bulkeley Rd. CH44: Wall 2H 13
Bullens Rd. L4: Walt 3H 7
Bull Hill CH64: Lit N 1D 44
Bullrush Dr. CH46: More 3G 11
Bulrushes, The L17: Aig 4H 23
Bulwer St. CH42: Rock F 5B 22
Bunbury Grn. CH65: Ell P 5B 50
Burbo Way CH45: Wall 3C 4
Burden Rd. CH46: More 5C 10
Burdett Av. CH63: Spit 1F 35
Burdett Cl. CH63: Spit 1G 35
Burdett Rd. CH45: Wall 6B 4
　CH66: Gt Sut 5E 49
Burford Av. CH44: Wall 2D 12
Burgess St. L3: Liv 3G 15
Burleigh M. L5: Liv 5H 7
　　　　　　　　　　(off Burleigh M. Sth.)
Burleigh Rd. Nth. L5: Liv 5H 7
Burleigh Rd. Sth. L5: Liv 5H 7
Burlingham Av. CH48: W Kir . .6F 17
Burlington Rd. CH45: New B . .2F 5
Burlington St. CH41: Birke . . .1A 22
　L3: Liv 1E 15
Burnand St. L4: Walt 4H 7
Burnell Rd. CH65: Ell P 3C 50
Burnley Av. CH46: More 5F 11
Burnley Gro. CH46: More 4F 11
Burnley Rd. CH46: More 4F 11
Burns Av. CH45: Wall 6E 5
Burns Cl. CH66: Gt Sut 3E 49
Burnside Av. CH44: Wall 4F 13
Burnside Rd. CH44: Wall 4F 13
Burrell Cl. CH42: Tran 6G 21
Burrell Ct. CH42: Tran 6G 21
Burrell Dr. CH46: More 6D 10
Burrell Rd. CH42: Tran 6G 21
Burrell St. L4: Walt 3H 7
Burroughs Gdns. L3: Liv 1F 15
Burrows Ct. L3: Liv 1E 15
BURTON 6H 45
Burton Av. CH45: Wall 6C 4
Burton Cl. L1: Liv 5F 15
Burton Grn. CH66: Gt Sut 3D 48
Burton Rd.
　CH64: Lit N, Ness 6C 38
Burton St. L5: Kirkd 5E 7

Busby's Cotts. CH45: New B . . .3F 5
Bushell Cl. CH64: Nest 6D 38
Bushell Ct. CH43: Oxton 3E 21
Bushell Rd. CH64: Nest 6D 38
Bush Way CH60: Hesw 3H 31
Bute St. L5: Liv 2G 15
　　　　　　　　　　(not continuous)
Buttercup Cl. CH46: More 3G 11
Butterfield St. L4: Walt 4H 7
Buttermere Av. CH43: Noct . . .1A 20
　CH65: Ell P 4A 50
Buttermere Cl. CH41: Birke . . .2G 21
　　　　　　　　　　(off Penrith St.)
Butterton Av. CH49: Upton . . .1D 18
Button St. L2: Liv 4F 15
Buxton La. CH44: Wall 6C 4
Buxton Rd. CH42: Rock F 5C 22
Byerley St. CH44: Wall 2H 13
Byles St. L8: Liv 3H 23
Byng St. L20: Boot 1D 6
Byrne Av. CH42: Rock F 6B 22
Byrne Avenue Recreation Cen.
　. .6B 22
Byrom St. L3: Liv 3F 15
Byron Cl. CH43: Pren 1H 21

C

Cablehouse L2: Liv 3E 15
　　　　　　　　　　(off Cheapside)
Cable Rd. CH47: Hoy 6C 8
Cable Yd., The L2: Liv 3E 15
　　　　　　　　　　(off Cheapside)
Caernarvon Cl.
　CH49: Upton 1G 19
Caernarvon Ct. CH63: Beb . . .5F 29
　CH65: Ell P 5B 50
Caerwys Gro. CH42: Tran 3A 22
Cains Brewery 1G 23
Cairo St. L4: Kirkd 6G 7
Caithness Dr. CH45: Wall 5G 5
Caithness Gdns.
　CH43: Pren 6D 20
Calday Grange Cl.
　CH48: W Kir 6F 17
Calday Grange Swimming Pool
　. .5F 17
Caldbeck Rd. CH62: Brom . . .1B 36
Calder Av. CH43: Pren 5E 21
Calder Rd. CH63: Hghr B 4D 28
　L5: Liv 5H 7
Calder Way CH66: Gt Sut 2C 48
Caldicott Av. CH62: Brom 4B 36
Caldwell Dr. CH49: Woodc . . .5H 19
CALDY 2B 24
Caldy Chase Dr.
　CH48: Caldy 2B 24
Caldy Ct. CH48: W Kir 6D 16
Caldy Dr. CH66: Gt Sut 3D 48
Caldy Pk. CH48: W Kir 1A 24
Caldy Rd. CH45: Wall 6F 5
　CH48: Caldy, W Kir 6D 16
Caldy Wood CH48: Caldy 2B 24
Caledonia St. L7: Liv 5H 15
Callaghan Cl. L5: Liv 6F 7
Calmet Cl. L5: Liv 5G 7
Calne Cl. CH61: Irby 2H 25
Calthorpe Way CH43: Noct . . .1B 20
Calveley Av. CH62: East 1H 41
Calveley Cl. CH43: Noct 4C 20
Cambrian Cl. CH46: More 6B 10
　　　　　　　　　　(off Cambrian Rd.)
　CH66: Lit Sut 1A 48
Cambrian Rd. CH46: More . . .6C 10
Cambridge Ct. CH65: Ell P . . .3A 50
　L7: Liv 5H 15
Cambridge Rd. CH42: Tran . . .5F 21
　CH45: New B 4F 5
　CH62: Brom 3C 36
　CH65: Ell P 2A 50
　L20: Boot 1F 7
Cambridge St. L7: Liv 5H 15
　　　　　　　　　　(not continuous)
Camden Cl. CH49: Woodc . . .3H 19
Camden Pl. CH41: Birke 1A 22
Camden Rd. CH65: Ell P 2G 49
Camden St. L3: Liv 3G 15
Cameron Rd. CH46: Leas 2H 11
Cammell Ct. CH43: Clau 1F 21

Campbell Sq. *L1: Liv* 5F 15
(off Campbell St.)
Campbell St. L1: Liv 5F 15
Campbeltown Rd.
　CH41: Tran 3B 22
Camperdown St.
　CH41: Birke 1B 22
Canada Blvd. L3: Liv 4D 14
Canal Bri. Ent. Cen.
　CH65: Ell P 1B 50
Canalside CH65: Ell P 1B 50
Canalside Gro. L5: Liv 6E 7
Canalside Ind. Est.
　CH65: Ell P 1C 50
Canal St. L20: Boot 1D 6
Candia Towers L5: Liv 5G 7
(off Jason St.)
Cannell Ct. CH64: Will 5C 40
Canning Pl. L1: Liv 5E 15
Canning St. CH41: Birke 6A 14
　L8: Liv 5H 15
Cannock Cl. CH66: Gt Sut 6E 49
Cannon Hill CH43: Clau 1F 21
Cannon Mt. CH43: Clau 1F 21
Cannon St. CH65: Ell P 2G 49
Canterbury Cl.
　CH66: Gt Sut 6A 48
Canterbury Rd.
　CH42: Rock F 6C 22
　CH44: Wall 2G 13
Canterbury St. L3: Liv 2G 15
Canterbury Way L3: Liv 2H 15
Capenhurst Gdns.
　CH66: Gt Sut 6D 48
Capenhurst La. CH1: Cap 6C 48
　CH65: Whit 4F 49
　CH66: Gt Sut 6D 48
Capenhurst Station (Rail) 6C 48
Capenhurst Technology Pk.
　CH1: Cap 6C 48
Capital Gate L3: Liv 3H 15
Captain Charles Jones Wlk.
　CH44: Wall 6H 5
(off Webster Av.)
Carden Cl. L4: Kirkd 4G 7
Cardiff Cl. CH66: Gt Sut 6A 48
Cardigan Av. CH41: Birke 1H 21
Cardigan Rd. CH45: New B . . .4F 5
Cardus Cl. CH46: More 5B 10
Carey Av. CH63: Hghr B 3D 28
Cargill Gro. CH42: Rock F . . .1H 29
Carham Rd. CH47: Hoy 1E 17
Carisbrooke Cl.
　CH48: Caldy 1A 24
Carisbrooke Pl. L4: Kirkd 2H 7
Carisbrooke Rd.
　L4: Kirkd, Walt 1G 7
　L20: Boot 1G 7
Carlaw Rd. CH42: Tran 5E 21
Carlett Blvd. CH62: East 6D 36
Carlett Pk. CH62: East 5D 36
Carlisle M. CH43: Oxton 2G 21
Carlton Cl. CH64: Park 3A 38
Carlton Cres. CH66: Ell P 5F 43
Carlton La. CH47: Meols 5E 9
Carlton Mt. CH42: Tran 4A 22
Carlton Rd. CH42: Tran 3G 21
　CH45: New B 3F 5
　CH63: Beb 5H 29
Carlton St. L3: Liv 1D 14
Carlton Ter. CH47: Meols 5E 9
Carlyle Cres. CH66: Gt Sut . . .3E 49
Carmarthen Cres. L8: Liv 1F 23
Carmel Cl. CH45: New B 2F 5
Carmichael Av. CH49: Grea . . .5D 18
Carnforth Cl. CH41: Birke 2G 21
Carnoustie Cl. CH46: More . . .4B 10
Carnsdale Rd. CH46: More . . .5F 11
Carol Dr. CH60: Hesw 3E 33
Caroline Cl. CH43: Oxton 2F 21
Carpenter's La.
　CH48: W Kir 5D 16
Carpenters Row L1: Liv 5F 15
Carr Bri. Rd. CH49: Woodc . . .3H 19
Carr Gate CH46: More 6B 10
Carr Hey CH46: More 6B 10
Carr Hey Cl. CH49: Woodc . . .5A 20
Carr Ho. La. CH46: More 5B 10
Carrick Dr. CH65: Whit 5H 49
Carrington Rd. CH45: Wall . . .5G 5

Carrington St. CH41: Birke . . .5E 13
Carr La. CH46: More 4A 10
　CH47: Hoy 1D 16
　CH47: Meols 4H 9
　CH48: W Kir 2F 17
Carr La. Ind. Est.
　CH47: Hoy 1E 17
Carrock Rd. CH62: Brom 1C 36
Carrow Cl. CH46: More 6B 10
Carruthers St. L3: Liv 2E 15
Carsgoe Rd. CH47: Hoy 1E 17
Carsthorne Rd. CH47: Hoy . . .1E 17
Carters, The CH49: Grea 3C 18
Carter St. L8: Liv 6H 15
Carterton Rd. CH47: Hoy 1E 17
Cartmel Cl. CH41: Birke 2G 21
Cartmel Dr. CH46: More 6E 11
　CH66: Gt Sut 5F 49
Carver St. L3: Liv 2H 15
Caryl Gro. L8: Liv 3G 23
Caryl St. L8: Liv 2G 23
(Atterbury St.)
　L8: Liv 2G 23
(Park St.)
　L8: Liv 1F 23
(Stanhope St.)
Cases St. L1: Liv 4F 15
Cashel Rd. CH41: Birke 3F 13
Cassio St. L20: Boot 1G 7
Castlebridge Ct.
　CH42: Rock F 6B 22
(off Old Chester Rd.)
Castle Cl. CH46: Leas 2G 11
Castle Ct. CH48: W Kir 6D 16
Castle Dr. CH60: Hesw 3B 32
　CH65: Whit 4G 49
Castlefields CH46: Leas 1F 11
Castleford Ri. CH46: Leas 2E 11
Castlegrange Cl.
　CH46: Leas 1E 11
Castleheath Cl. CH46: Leas . . .2E 11
Castle Hill *L2: Liv* 4F 15
(off Lwr. Castle St.)
Castle Mt. CH60: Hesw 3B 32
(off The Mount)
Castle Rd. CH45: Wall 5E 5
Castle St. CH41: Birke 1B 22
　L2: Liv 4E 15
Castleway Nth. CH46: Leas . . .1G 11
Castleway Sth.
　CH46: Leas 2G 11
Catharine St. L8: Liv 5H 15
Cathcart St. CH41: Birke 6H 5
Cathedral Cl. L1: Liv 6G 15
Cathedral Ct. *L1: Liv* 6H 15
(off Gambier Ter.)
Cathedral Ga. L1: Liv 5G 15
Cathedral Wlk. L3: Liv 4H 15
Catherine St. CH41: Birke 1H 21
Caulfield Dr. CH49: Grea 4E 19
Causeway, The
　CH62: Port S 4H 29
Causeway Ct. CH62: Port S . . .3H 29
Causeway Ho. CH46: Leas 1E 11
Cavell Dr. CH65: Whit 3G 49
Cavendish Dr.
　CH42: Rock F 6H 21
Cavendish Gdns.
　CH65: Whit 3G 49
Cavendish Rd. CH41: Birke . . .6F 13
　CH45: New B 2F 5
Cavendish St. CH41: Birke . . .5F 13
Cavern Club, The 4E 15
(off Mathew St.)
Cavern Quarter 4E 15
(off Mathew St.)
Cavern Walks *L2: Liv* 4E 15
(off Mathew St.)
Cawood Cl. CH66: Lit Sut 2B 48
Caxton Cl. CH43: Bid 1A 20
　CH66: Gt Sut 3E 49
Cazneau St. L3: Liv 2F 15
Cearns Rd. CH43: Oxton 2E 21
Cecil Rd. CH42: Tran 5F 21
　CH45: Wall 4G 5
　CH62: New F 1H 29
Cedab Rd. CH65: Ell P 1B 50
Cedar Av. CH63: Hghr B 5E 29
　CH66: Lit Sut 1C 48
Cedardale Rd. CH66: Whit 6A 48

Cedar Gro. CH64: Nest 5D 38
Cedars, The CH46: More 6C 10
Cedar St. CH41: Birke 2H 21
Cedarway CH60: Hesw 6D 32
Cedarwood Cl. CH49: Grea . . .3B 18
Celia St. L20: Kirkd 2F 7
Celtic Rd. CH47: Meols 4G 9
Celtic St. L8: Liv 1H 23
Cemeas Cl. L5: Liv 6E 7
Central Av. CH62: Brom 2A 36
　CH65: Ell P 3A 50
Central Gdns. *L1: Liv* 4G 15
(off Benson St.)
Central Pk. Av. CH44: Wall 1G 13
Central Rd. CH62: Port S 3H 29
(Osborne Ct.)
　CH62: Port S 4H 29
(Wood St.)
Central Shop. Cen. L1: Liv 4F 15
Central Station (Rail) 4F 15
Centurion Cl. CH47: Meols 4G 9
Centurion Dr. CH47: Meols 4G 9
Century Bldgs. L3: Liv 3F 23
Ceres Cl. CH43: Bid 6A 12
Ceres St. L20: Kirkd 2E 7
Cestrian Dr. CH61: Thing 4C 26
Chadwick Ct. Ind. Cen.
　L3: Liv 2D 14
Chadwick St. CH46: More 5E 11
　L3: Liv 1D 14
Chalfield Av. CH66: Gt Sut 2C 48
Chalfield Cl. CH66: Gt Sut 2C 48
Chalkwell Dr. CH60: Hesw 4E 33
Challis St. CH41: Birke 4C 12
Chaloner St. L3: Liv 6F 15
Chamberlain St.
　CH41: Tran 3A 22
　CH44: Wall 3E 13
Champions Bus. Pk.
　CH49: Upton 4F 19
Chancel St. L4: Kirkd 4F 7
Chandlers Edge *CH65: Ell P* . .2H 43
(off Grosvenor Wharf Rd.)
Change La. CH64: Will 5D 40
Channel, The CH45: Wall 3C 4
Chantrell Rd. CH48: W Kir 5G 17
Chantry Cl. CH43: Bid 1H 19
Chantry Wlk. CH60: Hesw 5C 32
Chapel Cl. *CH65: Ell P* 2G 43
(off Grace Rd.)
Chapel Gdns. L5: Liv 6F 7
Chapelhill Rd. CH46: More 5F 11
Chapel La.
　CH1: Cap, Woodb 6G 47
　CH66: Led 6G 47
Chapel M. CH65: Whit 3H 49
Chapel Rd. CH47: Hoy 5E 9
Chapel St. L3: Liv 3D 14
Chapel Ter. L20: Boot 1D 6
Chapel Vw. CH62: East 5E 37
Chapman Cl. L8: Liv 2G 23
Chapterhouse Cl.
　CH65: Ell P 2C 50
Charing Cross CH41: Birke 2H 21
Charlcombe St. CH42: Tran . . .3H 21
Charlecote St. L8: Liv 4H 23
Charles Price Gdns.
　CH65: Ell P 1A 50
Charles Rd. CH47: Hoy 1D 16
Charles St. CH41: Birke 6H 13
Charleston Cl.
　CH66: Gt Sut 4D 48
Charleston Rd. L8: Liv 3H 23
Charlesville CH43: Oxton 2F 21
Charlesville Ct. CH43: Oxton . . .2F 21
Charlotte Rd. CH44: Wall 6H 5
Charlotte's Mdw.
　CH63: Beb 5G 29
Charlotte Way *L1: Liv* 4F 15
(off St John's Cen.)
Charlton Ct. CH43: Clau 1D 20
Charlwood Cl. CH43: Bid 1A 20
Charter Cres. CH66: Gt Sut . . .4E 49
Charter Ho. *CH44: Wall* 1H 13
(off Church St.)
Chase, The CH60: Hesw 3C 32
　CH63: Brom 6A 36
Chase Dr. CH66: Gt Sut 5E 49
Chase Way CH66: Gt Sut 5E 49
　L5: Liv 1G 15

Chatham Rd. CH42: Rock F . . .5C 22
Chatham St. L7: Liv 5H 15
　L8: Liv 5H 15
Chatsworth Av. CH44: Wall . . .1G 13
Chatsworth Cl.
　CH66: Gt Sut 2D 48
Chatsworth Rd.
　CH42: Rock F 5C 22
　CH61: Pens 4B 26
Chaucer St. L3: Liv 2F 15
Cheapside L2: Liv 3E 15
Cheapside All. *L2: Liv* 3E 15
(off Cheapside)
Cheddon Way CH61: Pens 5A 26
Chelford Cl. CH43: Bid 6A 12
Chelmsford Cl. L4: Kirkd 4F 7
(off Harcourt St.)
Chelsea, The *CH45: New B* . . .2G 5
(off Tower Prom.)
Cheltenham Cres.
　CH46: Leas 2E 11
Cheltenham Rd. CH45: Wall . . .5C 4
　CH65: Ell P 4B 50
Chenotrie Gdns.
　CH43: Noct 2B 20
Chepstow Av. CH44: Wall 1G 13
Chepstow St. L4: Walt 2G 7
Cheriton Av. CH48: W Kir 5F 17
Cherrybank CH44: Wall 3F 13
Cherry Brow Ter. *CH64: Will* . .5B 40
(off Hadlow Rd.)
Cherry Cl. CH64: Nest 5G 39
Cherry Gdns. CH47: Hoy 6D 8
Cherry Gro. CH66: Whit 6G 49
Cherry Sq. CH44: Wall 1F 13
Cherry Tree Ho.
　CH46: More 5F 11
Cherry Tree M. CH60: Hesw . . .3C 32
Cherry Tree Rd.
　CH46: More 5F 11
Chesham Ct. CH65: Ell P 3B 50
Cheshire Acre
　CH49: Woodc 4G 19
Cheshire Gro. CH46: More 6E 11
Cheshire Oaks Bus. Pk.
　CH65: Ell P 6B 50
Cheshire Oaks Outlet Village
　CH65: Ell P 5C 50
Cheshire Oaks Way
　CH65: Ell P 5C 50
Cheshire Way CH61: Pens 6B 26
Chesney Cl. L8: Liv 1G 23
Chesnut Gro. CH42: Tran 3H 21
Chester Ct. CH63: Beb 5F 29
Chesterfield Rd. CH62: East . . .1F 41
Chesterfield St. L8: Liv 6G 15
Chester High Rd.
　CH64: Burt, Nest 6F 33
　CH66: Led 4E 39
Chester Rd. CH60: Hesw 4D 32
　CH64: Nest 6C 38
　CH65: Whit 6B 48
　CH66: Chil T, Gt Sut, Hoot, Lit Sut
　 . . . . .4A 42
　CH66: Whit 6B 48
Chester St. CH41: Birke 1B 22
　CH44: Wall 2E 13
　L8: Liv 6G 15
Chestnut Av. CH66: Gt Sut 6F 49
Chestnut Cl. CH49: Grea 6C 18
Chestnut Farm CH66: Hoot . . .4A 42
Chestnut Gro. CH62: Brom 3A 36
Chestnuts, The CH64: Will 5B 40
Cheswood Ct.
　CH49: Woodc 5G 19
(off Childwall Grn.)
Chetwynd Cl. CH43: Oxton . . .3D 20
Chetwynd Rd. CH43: Oxton . . .2E 21
Cheverton Cl. CH49: Woodc . . .4H 19
Cheviot Cl. CH42: Tran 6H 21
　CH66: Lit Sut 1A 48
Cheviot Rd. CH42: Tran 6G 21
Chidden Cl. CH49: Grea 4C 18
Childer Cres. CH66: Lit Sut . . .6B 42
Childer Ct. CH66: Lit Sut 6B 42
CHILDER THORNTON 5A 42
Childwall Av. CH46: More 6D 10
Childwall Cl. CH46: More 6D 10
Childwall Ct. CH66: Ell P 5F 43
Childwall Gdns. CH66: Ell P . . .5F 43

Childwall Grn.—Cornwall Ct.

Childwall Grn.
CH49: Woodc 5G **19**
Childwall Rd. CH66: Ell P 5F **43**
Chilhem Cl. L8: Liv 3H **23**
Chiltern Rd. CH42: Tran 6G **21**
Chilton Dr. CH66: Gt Sut 5E **49**
China Farm La.
CH48: W Kir 3G **17**
Chippenham Av.
CH49: Grea 3C **18**
Chirkdale St. L4: Kirkd 2G **7**
(not continuous)
Chirk Gdns. CH65: Ell P 4B **50**
Chirk Way CH46: More 6F **11**
Chisenhale St. L3: Liv 1E **15**
Cholmondeley Rd.
CH48: W Kir 5D **16**
CH65: Gt Sut 3F **49**
Cholsey Cl. CH49: Upton 3F **19**
Chorley Way CH63: Spit 2G **35**
Chorlton Gro. CH45: Wall 6B **4**
Christchurch Rd.
CH43: Oxton 3F **21**
Christian St. L3: Liv 2G **15**
Christie Cl. CH66: Hoot 3A **42**
Christleton Cl. CH43: Oxton 5B **20**
Christleton Dr. CH66: Ell P 1E **49**
Christmas St. L20: Kirkd 2F **7**
Christopher Dr. CH62: East 6E **37**
Christophers Cl.
CH61: Pens 5C **26**
Christopher St. L4: Walt 3H **7**
Chung Hok Ho. *L1: Liv 6G* ***15***
(off Pine M.)
Church All. L1: Liv 4F **15**
Church Cl. CH44: Wall 1H **13**
Church Cres. CH44: Wall 3A **14**
Church Dr. CH62: Port S 3H **29**
Church Farm CH63: Beb 4G **29**
Church Farm Ct.
CH60: Hesw 4B **32**
CH64: Will 5B **40**
Church Farm Organics 4F 25
Church Flats L4: Walt 1H **7**
Church Gdns. CH44: Wall 1H **13**
Church Hill CH45: Wall 6D **4**
Churchill Av. CH41: Birke 6F **13**
Churchill Ct. CH64: Nest 5C **38**
Churchill Gro. CH44: Wall 6G **5**
Churchill Way CH64: Nest 5C **38**
Churchill Way Nth. L3: Liv 3F **15**
Churchill Way Sth. L3: Liv 3F **15**
Churchlands *CH44: Wall 3A* ***14***
(off Bridle Rd.)
Church La. CH44: Wall 1H **13**
(not continuous)
CH49: Woodc 5H **19**
CH61: Thurs 4F **25**
CH62: Brom 2B **36**
CH62: East 1A **42**
CH64: Nest 6C **38**
CH66: Gt Sut 3D **48**
L4: Walt 1H **7**
Churchmeadow Cl.
CH44: Wall 1H **13**
Church Mdw. La.
CH60: Hesw 4A **32**
Church M. CH42: Rock F 6C **22**
Church Pde. CH65: Ell P 1A **50**
Church Rd. CH42: Tran 4H **21**
CH44: Wall 3A **14**
CH48: W Kir 6C **16**
CH49: Upton 2G **19**
CH63: Beb 6G **29**
CH63: Thorn H 5B **34**
L4: Walt 1H **7**
Church Rd. W. L4: Walt 1H **7**
Church Sq. CH62: Brom 2B **36**
Church St. CH41: Birke 1B **22**
(not continuous)
CH44: Wall 1H **13**
CH65: Ell P 1A **50**
L1: Liv 4F **15**
L20: Boot 1C **6**
Church Ter. CH42: Tran 4H **21**
Church Vw. L20: Boot 1D **6**
Churchview Rd. CH41: Birke 5F **13**
Church Wlk. CH48: W Kir 6D **16**
CH65: Ell P 1A **50**
L20: Boot 1D **6**
Churchwood Cl.
CH62: Brom 2B **36**
Churchwood Ct.
CH49: Woodc 6H ***19***
(off Childwall Grn.)
Churnet St. L4: Kirkd 3G **7**
Churn Way CH49: Grea 3D **18**
Churton Av. CH43: Oxton 4D **20**
Cinnamon Bldg., The
L1: Liv 5F ***15***
(off Henry St.)
Circle 109 *L1: Liv 5F* ***15***
(off Henry St.)
Circular Dr. CH49: Grea 4D **18**
CH60: Hesw 2B **32**
CH62: Port S 2H **29**
Circular Rd. CH41: Birke 2H **21**
Cirencester Av. CH49: Grea 3C **18**
Citrine Rd. CH44: Wall 3H **13**
City Lofts *L3: Liv 2D* ***14***
(off Waterloo Rd.)
L3: Liv 3D ***14***
(off William Jessop Way)
City Rd. L4: Walt 2H **7**
City Sq. *L2: Liv 3E* ***15***
(off Tithebarn St.)
Civic Cl. CH63: Beb 4G **29**
Civic Way CH63: Beb 4G **29**
CH65: Ell P 3H **49**
CLAIRE HOUSE CHILDREN'S HOSPICE 2D 34
Clare Cres. CH44: Wall 1D **12**
Clare Dr. CH65: Whit 5H **49**
Claremont Ct. CH45: Wall 5D **4**
Claremont Rd. CH48: W Kir 4D **16**
Claremont Way
CH63: Hghr B 1D **28**
Claremount Dr. CH63: Beb 5F **29**
Claremount Rd.
CH45: Wall 4D **4**
Clarence Rd. CH42: Tran 4G **21**
CH44: Wall 3H **13**
Clarence St. L3: Liv 4G **15**
Clarendon Cl. CH43: Oxton 2G **21**
Clarendon Rd. CH44: Wall 2H **13**
Clare Rd. L20: Boot 1F **7**
Clare Way CH45: Wall 6D **4**
Claribel St. L8: Liv 1H **23**
Clarke Av. CH42: Rock F 5A **22**
CLATTERBRIDGE CENTRE FOR ONCOLOGY 2D 34
CLATTERBRIDGE HOSPITAL 2D 34
Clatterbridge Rd.
CH63: Spit 4D **34**
CLAUGHTON 6D 12
Claughton Dr. CH44: Wall 2F **13**
Claughton Firs CH43: Oxton 3F **21**
Claughton Grn. CH43: Oxton 2E **21**
Claughton Pl. CH41: Birke 1G **21**
Claughton Rd. CH41: Birke 1G **21**
Clayfield Cl. L20: Boot 1F **7**
Clayhill Grn. CH66: Lit Sut 6C **42**
Clayhill Ind. Est.
CH64: Nest 3C **38**
Clayhill Light Ind. Pk.
CH64: Nest 3C **38**
Clay St. L3: Liv 1D **14**
Clayton La. CH44: Wall 3E **13**
Clayton Pl. CH41: Birke 2G **21**
Clayton Sq. *L1: Liv 4F* ***15***
(off Church St.)
Clayton Sq. Shop. Cen.
L1: Liv 4F **15**
Clayton St. CH41: Birke 2G **21**
Cleaver Heath Nature Reserve 1H 31
Clee Hill Rd. CH42: Tran 6G **21**
Clegg St. L5: Liv 1G **15**
Clement Gdns. L3: Liv 1E **15**
Cleopas St. L8: Liv 3H **23**
Cleveland Dr. CH66: Lit Sut 1A **48**
Cleveland Sq. L1: Liv 5F **15**
Cleveland St. CH41: Birke 5F **13**
Cleveley Rd. CH47: Meols 5G **9**
Cliff, The CH45: New B 3D **4**
Cliff Dr. CH44: Wall 6H **5**
Cliffe Rd. CH64: Lit N 2D **44**
Clifford Rd. CH44: Wall 2G **13**
Clifford St. CH41: Birke 5E **13**
L3: Liv 3G **15**
Cliff Rd. CH44: Wall 2D **12**
Clifton Av. CH62: East 2G **41**
Clifton Ct. CH41: Birke 2H **21**
Clifton Cres. CH41: Birke 1A **22**
Clifton Gdns. CH65: Ell P 4A **50**
Clifton Ga. *CH41: Birke 2A* ***22***
(off Clifton Rd.)
Clifton Gro. CH44: Wall 1H **13**
L5: Liv 1G **15**
CLIFTON PARK 2H 21
Clifton Rd. CH41: Birke 2H **21**
Clipper Vw. CH62: New F 1A **30**
Clive Rd. CH43: Oxton 3G **21**
Cloister Way CH65: Ell P 2C **50**
Close, The CH49: Grea 5D **18**
CH61: Irby 3H **25**
CH63: Hghr B 6H **21**
Closeburn Av. CH60: Hesw 5A **32**
Clovelly Ct. CH49: Grea 4D **18**
Clover Birches CH65: Ell P 1G **49**
Clover Dr. CH41: Birke 4C **12**
Cloverfield Gdns.
CH66: Lit Sut 6D **42**
Clwyd St. CH41: Birke 1H **21**
CH45: New B 4E **5**
Clwyd Way CH66: Lit Sut 1A **48**
Clydesdale CH65: Whit 4H **49**
Clydesdale Rd. CH44: Wall 6H **5**
CH47: Hoy 5D **8**
Clyde St. CH42: Rock F 5B **22**
L20: Kirkd 3E **7**
Coalbrookdale Rd.
CH64: Nest 3D **38**
Coal St. L3: Liv 3G **15**
Coastal Dr. CH45: Wall 4B **4**
Coastal Point *CH46: Leas 1E* ***11***
(off Leasowe Rd.)
Coastguard La. CH64: Park 4A **38**
Cobden Av. CH42: Tran 4B **22**
Cobden Ct. CH42: Tran 4B **22**
Cobden Pl. CH42: Tran 4B **22**
Cobden St. L6: Liv 2H **15**
Cobham Rd. CH46: More 5D **10**
Coburg St. CH41: Birke 1H **21**
Coburg Wharf L3: Liv 1E **23**
Cochrane St. L5: Liv 6H **7**
Cockburn St. L8: Liv 3H **23**
Cockerell Cl. L4: Walt 4H **7**
Cockspur St. L3: Liv 3E **15**
Cockspur St. W. L3: Liv 3E **15**
Cokers, The CH42: Rock F 1E **29**
Colbert Ct. CH49: Upton 3G **19**
Coldstream Dr.
CH66: Lit Sut 2H **47**
Coleman Dr. CH49: Grea 4B **18**
Colemere Ct. CH65: Ell P 6H **43**
Colemere Dr. CH61: Thing 3D **26**
Coleridge Dr. CH62: New F 2G **29**
Cole St. CH43: Oxton 1G **21**
Colin Dr. L3: Liv 6E **7**
Coliseum Shop. & Leisure Pk.
CH65: Ell P 5B **50**
Coliseum Way CH65: Ell P 6B **50**
College Cl. CH43: Bid 1H **19**
CH45: Wall 5C **4**
College Dr. CH63: Beb 2G **29**
College La. L1: Liv 4F **15**
College St. Nth. L6: Liv 2H **15**
College St. Sth. L6: Liv 2H **15**
College Vw. L20: Boot 1E **7**
Colliery Grn. Cl.
CH64: Lit N 2C **44**
Colliery Grn. Ct.
CH64: Lit N 2C **44**
Colliery Grn. Dr.
CH64: Lit N 2C **44**
Collingham Grn.
CH66: Lit Sut 2B **48**
Collingwood Cl. L4: Kirkd 3F **7**
Collingwood Rd. CH63: Beb 5H **29**
Collin Rd. CH43: Bid 5C **12**
Colmore Av. CH63: Spit 2F **35**
Colonnades, The L3: Liv 5D **14**
Colquitt St. L1: Liv 5G **15**
Columbia La. CH43: Oxton 3F **21**
Columbia Rd. CH43: Oxton 3F **21**
L4: Walt 1H **7**
Columbus Dr. CH61: Pens 6A **26**
Columbus Quay L3: Liv 4G **23**
Column Rd.
CH48: Caldy, W Kir 5E **17**
Colville Rd. CH44: Wall 1E **13**
Colwyn Cl. CH65: Ell P 4B **50**
Colwyn St. CH41: Birke 5E **13**
Combermere St. L8: Liv 1H **23**
Comely Av. CH44: Wall 1G **13**
Comely Bank Rd.
CH44: Wall 1H **13**
Commercial Rd.
CH62: Brom 6C **30**
L5: Kirkd 5E **7**
Commonfield Rd.
CH49: Woodc 6H **19**
Commutation Row L3: Liv 3G **15**
Compass Ct. CH45: Wall 3D **4**
Compton Pl. CH65: Ell P 2H **49**
Compton Rd. CH41: Birke 4B **12**
Comus St. L3: Liv 2F **15**
Concert Sq. *L1: Liv 4F* ***15***
(off Concert St.)
Concert St. L1: Liv 4F **15**
Concordia Av. CH49: Upton 2G **19**
Coney Wlk. CH49: Upton 1D **18**
Conifer Cl. CH66: Whit 6B **48**
Coningsby Dr. CH45: Wall 1E **13**
Coningsby Rd. L4: Walt 4H **7**
Coniston Av. CH43: Noct 2A **20**
CH45: Wall 4C **4**
CH63: East 1E **41**
Coniston Cl. CH66: Hoot 4B **42**
Coniston Rd. CH61: Irby 3H **25**
CH64: Nest 1C **44**
Connaught Cl. CH41: Birke 5E **13**
Connaught Ho. CH41: Birke 1C **22**
Connaught Way CH41: Birke 5E **13**
Connolly Ho. L20: Boot 1F **7**
Constance St. L3: Liv 3H **15**
Constantine Av.
CH60: Hesw 2C **32**
Convent Cl. CH42: Tran 3H **21**
Conville Blvd.
CH63: Hghr B 1E **29**
Conway Cl. CH63: Hghr B 4D **28**
Conway Ct. CH63: Beb 5F **29**
CH65: Ell P 4B **50**
Conway Dr. CH41: Birke 1H **21**
Conway Park Station (Rail) 6A 14
Conway St. CH41: Birke 6H **13**
(not continuous)
L5: Liv 6G **7**
Cookes Cl. CH64: Nest 4C **38**
Cook Rd. CH46: Leas 1H **11**
Cookson St. L1: Liv 6G **15**
Cook St. CH41: Birke 2H **21**
CH65: Ell P 1A **50**
L2: Liv 4E **15**
Coombe Pk. CH66: Lit Sut 1C **48**
Coombe Pk. Ct.
CH66: Lit Sut 1C **48**
Coombe Rd. CH61: Irby 2A **26**
Cooperage Cl. L8: Liv 3G **23**
Copeland Cl. CH61: Pens 5A **26**
Copperas Hill L3: Liv 4G **15**
Copperfield Cl. L8: Liv 2H **23**
Coppice, The CH45: Wall 4E **5**
Coppice Cl. CH43: Bid 1H **19**
Coppice Grange
CH46: More 6C **10**
Coppice Gro. CH49: Grea 5C **18**
Copse Gro. CH61: Irby 2A **26**
Copsmead CH46: More 5F **11**
Coral Ridge CH43: Bid 6B **12**
Corbyn St. CH44: Wall 4A **14**
Corfu St. CH41: Birke 1G **21**
Corinthian St.
CH42: Rock F 5B **22**
Corinth Twr. *L5: Liv 5G* ***7***
(off Anderson St.)
Corinto St. L8: Liv 6H **15**
Cormorant Ct. CH45: Wall 3C **4**
Cornelius Dr. CH61: Pens 4B **26**
Cornfield Cl. CH66: Gt Sut 6F **49**
Cornflower Way
CH46: More 3G **11**
Cornhill L1: Liv 5F **15**
Corniche Rd. CH62: Port S 3H **29**
Corn St. L8: Liv 2G **23**
Cornwall Ct. CH63: Beb 5F **29**

Cornwall Dr. CH43: Pren 6E 21
Cornwallis St. L1: Liv 5F 15
(not continuous)
Cornwell Cl. CH62: New F 1H 29
Corona Rd. CH62: Port S 3A 30
Coronation Av.
CH45: New B 4F 5
Coronation Bldgs.
CH45: Wall 6F 6
(off Wallasey Rd.)
CH48: W Kir 3E 17
Coronation Dr. CH62: Brom . . .6B 30
Coronation Rd. CH47: Hoy . . .1B 16
CH65: Ell P 3H 49
(not continuous)
Corporation Rd.
CH41: Birke 5D 12
Corrie Dr. CH63: Beb 5F 29
Cortsway CH49: Grea 2E 19
Cortsway W. CH49: Grea 2D 18
Corwen Cl. CH43: Bid 1H 19
CH46: More 6F 11
Corwen Rd. CH47: Hoy 6E 9
Costain St. L20: Kirkd 4E 7
Cotswold Rd. CH42: Tran . . .6G 21
Cottage Cl. CH63: Brom 6A 36
CH64: Lit N 6C 38
Cottage Dr. E. CH60: Hesw . . .6B 32
Cottage Dr. W. CH60: Hesw . . .6B 32
Cottage St. CH41: Birke 6H 13
Cottesmore Dr. CH60: Hesw . . .3F 33
Cotton Exchange Bldg.
L3: Liv 3E 15
(off Old Hall St.)
Cotton St. L3: Liv 1D 14
Cottonwood L17: Aig 5H 23
Coulsdon Pl. L8: Liv 3H 23
Coulthard Rd.
CH42: Rock F 1G 29
County Rd. L4: Walt 2H 7
Court, The CH63: Beb 5G 29
CH64: Lit N 1D 44
Courtenay Rd. CH47: Hoy . . .1C 16
Court Ho., The CH65: Ell P . . .1A 50
Courtier Cl. L5: Liv 1G 15
Courtney Av. CH44: Wall 2E 13
Courtney Rd. CH42: Rock F . . .1G 29
Courtyard, The CH64: Will 5B 40
Covent Gdn. L2: Liv 4E 15
Coventry Av. CH66: Gt Sut 6A 48
Coventry St. CH41: Birke . . .1H 21
Covertside CH48: W Kir 5F 17
Cowan Dr. L6: Liv 1H 15
Cowdrey Av. CH43: Bid 4A 12
Cow La. CH66: Lit Sut 1C 48
Cowley Cl. CH49: Upton 2D 18
Cowley Rd. L4: Walt 2H 7
Coxheath CH42: Rock F 6C 22
Craig Gdns. CH66: Ell P 6E 43
Craigleigh Gro. CH62: East . . .1H 41
Cranbourne Av. CH41: Birke . . .6E 13
CH46: More 6D 10
CH47: Meols 4G 9
Cranford Cl. CH62: East 1H 41
Cranford St. CH44: Wall 3G 13
Cranmer St. L5: Liv 6E 7
(not continuous)
Cranswick Grn.
CH66: Lit Sut 2C 48
Cranwell Rd. CH49: Grea 4B 18
Craven Cl. CH41: Birke 1H 21
Craven St. CH41: Birke 1G 21
L3: Liv 3G 15
Creek, The CH45: Wall 3C 4
Crescent, The CH48: W Kir . . .5C 16
CH49: Grea 4D 18
CH60: Hesw 5D 32
CH61: Pens 3B 26
CH63: Hghr B 4E 29
CH65: Gt Sut 2F 49
Crescent Rd. CH44: Wall 1G 13
CH65: Ell P 1B 50
Cressida Av. CH63: Hghr B . . .2E 29
Cressingham Rd.
CH45: New B 3F 5
Cressington Av. CH42: Tran . . .6H 21
Cressington Gdns.
CH65: Ell P 1A 50
Cresson Ct. CH43: Oxton 2D 20

Cresswell St. L6: Liv 1H 15
(not continuous)
Crete Towers L5: Kirkd 5G 7
Crewe Grn. CH49: Woodc 5G 19
Criccieth Ct. CH65: Ell P 5B 50
Criftin Cl. CH66: Gt Sut 5C 48
Crocus Av. CH41: Birke 6D 12
Crocus St. L5: Kirkd 4F 7
Croesmere Dr.
CH66: Gt Sut 5D 48
Croft, The CH49: Grea 5D 18
Croft Av. CH62: Brom 2A 36
Croft Av. E. CH62: Brom 1B 36
Croft Bus. Cen.
CH62: Brom 1C 36
Croft Bus. Pk. CH62: Brom . . .1C 36
Croft Cl. CH43: Noct 3C 20
CH62: Brom 2B 36
Croft Cotts. CH66: Chil T 5A 42
(off School La.)
Croft Ct. CH65: Ell P 4C 50
Croft Dr. CH46: More 6E 11
CH48: Caldy 3A 24
Croft Dr. E. CH48: Caldy 2B 24
Croft Dr. W. CH48: Caldy 2A 24
Croft Edge CH43: Oxton 4F 21
Croften Dr. CH64: Lit N 2C 44
Crofters, The CH49: Grea 3D 18
Crofters Cl. CH66: Gt Sut 6E 49
Crofters Heath CH66: Gt Sut . . .6E 49
Croft Grn. CH62: Brom 6B 30
Croft La. CH62: Brom 2B 36
Crofton Rd. CH42: Tran 4A 22
Croftsway CH60: Hesw 3H 31
Croft Technology Pk.
CH62: Brom 2D 36
Croft Trade Pk. CH62: Brom . .1C 36
Cromarty Rd. CH44: Wall 1D 12
Cromer Dr. CH45: Wall 6E 5
Cromer Rd. CH47: Hoy 6C 8
Crompton St. L5: Liv 6F 7
Cromwell Rd. CH65: Ell P 2A 50
L4: Walt 1H 7
Cronton Av. CH46: Leas 2F 11
Croome Dr. CH48: W Kir 5E 17
Cropper St. L1: Liv 4G 15
Crosby Cl. CH49: Upton 1F 19
Crosby Gro. CH64: Will 4D 40
Crosfield Rd. CH44: Wall 2G 13
Cross, The CH62: Brom 2C 36
CH64: Nest 5C 38
Crossdale Rd. CH62: Brom . . .5B 36
Crosshall St. L1: Liv 3F 15
Cross Hey Av. CH43: Noct 2B 20
Cross La. CH45: Wall 6B 4
CH63: Beb 5F 29
CH64: Lit N 2C 44
Crossley Av. CH66: Lit P 1E 49
Crossley Dr. CH60: Hesw 3H 31
Cross St. CH41: Birke 1B 22
CH62: Port S 4H 29
CH64: Nest 5C 38
Crossway CH43: Bid 5C 12
Crossway, The CH63: Raby . . .1G 39
Crossways CH62: Brom 6B 30
Crosthwaite Av. CH62: East . . .1H 41
Croughton Ct. CH66: Ell P 5F 43
Croughton Rd. CH66: Ell P . . .5F 43
Crowmarsh Cl. CH49: Upton . . .3F 19
Crown St. L7: Liv 3H 15
Crow St. L8: Liv 1F 23
Croxteth Av. CH44: Wall 1F 13
Croylands St. L4: Kirkd 3G 7
Crump St. L1: Liv 6G 15
Crutchley Av. CH41: Birke 5F 13
Cubbin Cres. L5: Kirkd 5F 7
Cuckoo La.
CH64: Lit N, Nest 1F 45
Cuerden St. L3: Liv 3F 15
Cullen Cl. CH63: East 1F 41
Cumberland Av. CH43: Pren . . .5E 21
Cumberland Gro.
CH66: Gt Sut 4C 48
Cumberland Rd.
CH45: New B 4G 5
Cumberland St. L1: Liv 3E 15
Cumbers Dr. CH64: Ness 2E 45
Cumbers La. CH64: Ness 2E 45
Cumbrae Dr. CH65: Ell P 6A 50
Cumbria Cl. CH66: Gt Sut 6E 49

Cummings St. L1: Liv 5G 15
Cunard Av. CH44: Wall 6H 5
Cunard Cl. CH43: Bid 1A 20
Cunliffe St. L2: Liv 3E 15
Cunningham Cl.
CH48: Caldy 3A 24
Cunningham Dr.
CH63: Brom 4A 36
Curlender Cl. CH41: Birke . . .4C 12
Curlew Av. CH49: Upton 1D 18
Curlew Cl. CH49: Upton 1D 18
Curlew Ct. CH46: More 4C 10
Curlew Way CH46: More 4C 10
Curwell Cl. CH63: Spit 6H 29
Curzon Av. CH41: Birke 6F 13
CH45: New B 3F 5
Curzon Rd. CH42: Tran 5F 21
CH47: Hoy 6C 8
Custom Ho. Pl. L1: Liv 5E 15
Cygnet Cl. CH65: Gt Sut 3D 48
Cypress Av. CH66: Gt Sut 6F 49
Cypress Cft. CH63: Spit 6H 29
Cyprus Ter. CH45: New B 4F 5

D

DACRE HILL 1F 29
Dacre St. CH41: Birke 1A 22
L20: Boot 2D 6
Dacy Rd. L5: Liv 6H 7
Daffodil Rd. CH41: Birke 6D 12
Daisy La. CH44: Wall 2F 13
Daisy St. L5: Kirkd 4F 7
Dale, The CH64: Nest 1B 44
Dale Av. CH60: Hesw 2B 32
CH62: Brom 3B 36
CH66: Lit Sut 1C 48
Dale Ct. CH60: Hesw 3B 32
Dale Dr. CH65: Gt Sut 2F 49
Dale End Rd. CH61: Barn 5E 27
Dale Gdns. CH60: Hesw 2H 31
CH65: Whit 4H 49
Dale Hey CH44: Wall 2F 13
CH66: Hoot 3G 41
Dalehurst Cl. CH44: Wall 1H 13
Dale Rd. CH62: Brom 5B 36
Dale Vw. CH61: Pens 4C 26
Daleside Cl. CH61: Irby 3B 26
Dale St. L2: Liv 3E 15
Dalesway CH60: Hesw 3A 32
Dale Vw. Cl. CH61: Pens 4C 26
Dalmorton Rd. CH45: New B . . .3F 5
Dalrymple St. L5: Liv 6F 7
Dalton Rd. CH45: New B 4G 5
Damhead La. CH64: Will 6H 39
Danby Cl. L5: Liv 6H 7
Dane Cl. CH61: Irby 3B 26
Danefield Rd. CH49: Grea 5C 18
Danehurst Rd. CH45: Wall 4D 4
Danescourt Rd. CH41: Birke . . .5E 13
Dane St. L4: Walt 2H 7
Daneswell Dr. CH46: More 4F 11
Danger La. CH46: More 3F 11
Daniel Ho. L20: Boot 1E 7
Dansie St. L3: Liv 4H 15
Darby Cl. CH64: Lit N 3C 44
Daresbury Rd. CH44: Wall 1E 13
Darleydale Dr. CH62: East 6D 36
Darlington Cl. CH44: Wall 1H 13
Darlington St. CH44: Wall 1H 13
Darmond's Grn.
CH48: W Kir 4D 16
Darnley St. L8: Liv 2G 23
Darwen St. L5: Liv 6E 7
Darwin Way CH65: Ell P 3B 50
Daryl Rd. CH60: Hesw 2C 32
Daulby St. L3: Liv 4H 15
Davenham Av. CH43: Oxton . . .4D 20
Davenham Rd. CH43: Oxton . . .5D 20
Davenport Cl. CH48: Caldy . . .3A 24
Davenport Rd. CH60: Hesw . . .4A 32
Daventree Rd. CH45: Wall 6F 5
David Lewis St. L1: Liv 4F 15
David Lloyd Leisure
Ellesmere Port 6B 50
David St. L8: Liv 3H 23
Davies St. L1: Liv 3E 15
Davis Rd. CH46: Leas 2H 11
Davy St. L5: Liv 5H 7

Dawlish Rd. CH44: Wall 1D 12
CH61: Irby 4G 25
Dawn Cl. CH64: Ness 2E 45
Dawn Gdns. CH65: Whit 3H 49
Dawpool Cotts. CH48: Caldy . .3E 25
Dawpool Dr. CH46: More 5E 11
CH62: Brom 4A 36
Dawpool Farm CH61: Thurs . . .4F 25
Dawson Av. CH41: Birke 5F 13
Dawson St. L1: Liv 4F 15
Dawson Way L1: Liv 4F 15
(off St John's Cen.)
Dawstone Ri. CH60: Hesw 4B 32
Dawstone Rd. CH60: Hesw 4B 32
Days Mdw. CH49: Grea 4C 18
Deakin St. CH41: Birke 5D 12
Dean Av. CH45: Wall 4D 4
Dean Dillistone Ct. L1: Liv 6G 15
(off Cathedral Ga.)
Dean Patey Ct. L1: Liv 5G 15
Deansgate CH65: Ell P 2G 49
Deans Rd. CH65: Ell P 4D 50
Deans Way CH41: Birke 5D 12
Dearnford Av. CH62: Brom 5B 36
Dearnford Cl. CH62: Brom 5B 36
Debra Cl. CH66: Gt Sut 3C 48
Debra Rd. CH66: Gt Sut 4C 48
Dee La. CH48: W Kir 5C 16
Dee Pk. Cl. CH60: Hesw 5D 32
Dee Pk. Rd. CH60: Hesw 5D 32
Deepdale Cl. CH43: Bid 1A 20
Deerwood Cl. CH66: Lit Sut . . .6D 42
Deerwood Cres.
CH66: Lit Sut 6D 42
Dee Sailing Club 4B 24
Deeside CH60: Hesw 3B 31
CH65: Whit 4H 49
Deeside Cl. CH43: Bid 1H 19
CH65: Whit 5H 49
Deeside Ct. CH64: Park 4A 38
Dee Vw. Cl. CH64: Nest 1C 44
Dee Vw. Rd. CH60: Hesw 3B 32
De Grouchy St.
CH48: W Kir 4D 16
Delamere Av. CH62: East 1G 41
CH66: Gt Sut 2E 49
Delamere Cl. CH43: Bid 1H 19
CH62: East 1G 41
Delamere Dr. CH66: Gt Sut . . .3B 48
Delamere Grn.
CH65: Gt Sut 3E 49
(off Delamere Dr.)
Delamere Gro. CH44: Wall 3A 14
(off Tudor Av.)
Delamore Pl. L4: Kirkd 2G 7
Delamore's Acre CH64: Will . . .5C 40
Delamore St. L4: Kirkd 2G 7
Delavor Cl. CH60: Hesw 3A 32
Delavor Rd. CH60: Hesw 3H 31
Delf La. L4: Walt 1H 7
Dell, The CH42: Rock F 6D 22
Della Robbia Ho.
CH41: Birke 2H 21
(off Clifton Rd.)
Dell Cl. CH63: Brom 5H 35
Dell Ct. CH43: Pren 6D 20
Dell Gro. CH42: Rock F 1H 29
Dell La. CH60: Hesw 4D 32
Delta Rd. E. CH42: Rock F 6D 22
Delta Rd. W. CH42: Rock F . . .6D 22
Delves Av. CH63: Spit 6F 29
Delyn Cl. CH42: Rock F 6A 22
Demage Dr. CH66: Gt Sut 4D 48
Demesne St. CH44: Wall 2A 14
Denbigh Ct. CH65: Ell P 4B 50
Denbigh Gdns. CH65: Ell P . . .4A 50
Denbigh Rd. CH44: Wall 2H 13
L9: Walt 1H 7
Denbigh St. L5: Liv 6D 6
Deneshey Rd. CH47: Meols 5E 9
Denhall La. CH64: Burt 4D 44
Denham Cl. CH43: Bid 6A 12
Denison St. L3: Liv 2D 14
Denman Gro. CH44: Wall 3A 14
(off Tudor Av.)
Denning Dr. CH61: Irby 2H 25
Denny Cl. CH49: Upton 3F 19
Denston Cl. CH43: Bid 6H 11
Dentdale Dr. L5: Liv 1G 15
Denton Dr. CH45: Wall 5G 5

Denton St.—Ellens Cl.

Denton St. L8: Liv 3H 23
Dentwood St. L8: Liv 3H 23
Denwall Ho. *CH64: Nest 5C 38*
(off Churchill Way)
Derby Rd. CH42: Tran 4H 21
CH45: Wall 5E 5
L5: Kirkd 5D 6
L20: Boot 1D 6
L20: Kirkd 5D 6
Derby Sq. L2: Liv 4E 15
Dereham Av. CH49: Upton 6G 11
Derwent Cl. CH63: Hghr B 4D 28
Derwent Dr. CH45: Wall 5E 5
CH61: Pens 5B 26
CH66: Hoot 3B 42
Derwent Rd. CH43: Oxton 3F 21
CH47: Meols 5G 9
CH63: Hghr B 4D 28
Derwent Way CH64: Lit N 6D 38
Desford Cl. CH46: More 4B 10
Desmond Cl. CH43: Bid 6A 12
Deva Rd. CH48: W Kir 5C 16
Deveraux Dr. CH44: Wall 2F 13
Deverill Rd. CH42: Rock F 6A 22
Devisdale Gro. CH43: Bid 6A 12
Devizes Dr. CH61: Irby 2H 25
Devon Av. CH45: Wall 6G 5
Devon Ct. *L5: Liv 6H 7*
(off Tynemouth Cl.)
Devon Dr. CH61: Pens 5A 26
Devon Gdns. CH42: Rock F 6B 22
Devonport St. L8: Liv 2H 23
Devonshire Cl. CH43: Oxton 2F 21
DEVONSHIRE PARK 4G 21
Devonshire Pl. CH43: Oxton 2E 21
L5: Liv 5G 7
(not continuous)
Devonshire Rd. CH43: Oxton 2F 21
CH44: Wall 1F 13
(not continuous)
CH48: W Kir 6E 17
CH49: Upton 2E 19
CH61: Pens 5A 26
Devon St. L3: Liv 3G 15
Dewberry Cl. CH42: Tran 3H 21
Dexter St. L8: Liv 1G 23
Dial Rd. CH42: Tran 4H 21
Diamond St. L5: Liv 1F 15
Diana St. L4: Walt 3H 7
Diane Ho. *L8: Liv 6H 15*
(off Birley Ct.)
Dibbinsdale Rd.
CH63: Brom 3H 35
Dibbins Grn. CH63: Brom 5H 35
Dibbins Hey CH63: Spit 1G 35
Dibbinview Gro. CH63: Spit 1H 35
Dickens Av. CH43: Pren 6D 20
Dickens Cl. CH43: Pren 6D 20
Dickenson St. L1: Liv 5F 15
Dickens St. L8: Liv 1H 23
Dickson St. L3: Liv 1D 14
Digg La. CH46: More 4D 10
DINGLE 4H 23
Dingle Brow L8: Liv 4H 23
Dingle Grange *L8: Liv 4H 23*
(off Dingle Brow)
Dingle Gro. L8: Liv 3H 23
Dingle La. L8: Liv 4H 23
Dingle Mt. L8: Liv 4H 23
Dingle Rd. CH42: Tran 3G 21
L8: Liv 4H 23
Dingwall Dr. CH49: Grea 4E 19
Dinmore Rd. CH44: Wall 1F 13
Dinsdale Rd. CH62: Brom 1C 36
Ditton La. CH46: Leas 2D 10
Dobson St. L6: Liv 1H 15
Dock Rd. CH41: Birke 3E 13
Dock Rd. Nth. CH62: Port S 3A 30
Dock Rd. Sth. CH62: Brom 5B 30
Docks Link CH44: Wall 2D 12
Dock St. CH65: Ell P 2G 43
Dock Yd. Rd. CH65: Ell P 1B 50
Dodd Av. CH49: Grea 4D 18
Doddridge Rd. L8: Liv 2G 23
Dodleston Cl. CH43: Noct 3B 20
Doe's Mdw. Rd.
CH63: Brom 4H 35
Dolphin Cres. CH66: Gt Sut 5E 49
Dombey Pl. *L8: Liv 1H 23*
(off Dombey St.)
Dombey St. L8: Liv 1H 23
Domville Dr. CH49: Woodc 4G 19
Donaldson St. L5: Liv 5H 7
Doncaster Dr. CH49: Upton 1F 19
Donne Av. CH63: Spit 6F 29
Donne Cl. CH63: Spit 6G 29
Don Wlk. CH65: Ell P 6G 43
Doon Cl. L4: Kirkd 3G 7
Dorans La. L2: Liv 4E 15
Dorchester Cl. CH49: Upton 3F 19
Dorchester Pk. CH43: Noct 4B 20
Dorchester Way CH43: Noct 4B 20
Doreen Av. CH46: More 5D 10
Doric St. CH42: Rock F 5B 22
Dorincourt CH43: Oxton 3E 21
Dorrington Wlk. *L5: Liv 1G 15*
(off Roscommon St.)
Dorrit St. L8: Liv 1H 23
Dorset Dr. CH61: Pens 5A 26
Dorset Gdns. CH42: Rock F 6B 22
Dorset Rd. CH45: New B 4E 5
CH48: W Kir 4E 17
Douglas Dr. CH46: More 5D 10
Douglas Pl. L20: Boot 1D 6
Douglas Rd. CH48: W Kir 4F 17
Douglas St. CH41: Birke 1A 22
Doulton Cl. CH43: Bid 6H 11
Doune Ct. CH65: Ell P 4B 50
Douro St. L5: Liv 1G 15
Dove Cl. CH66: Ell P 6G 43
Dovedale Av. CH62: East 6C 36
Dovedale Cl. CH43: Pren 5D 20
Dovedale Rd. CH45: Wall 4E 5
CH47: Hoy 5D 8
Dovepoint Rd. CH47: Meols 4G 9
Dover Cl. CH41: Birke 6H 13
Dover Ct. CH65: Ell P 5B 50
Dover Dr. CH65: Ell P 5B 50
Dover St. L3: Liv 4H 15
Dovesmead Rd.
CH60: Hesw 4E 33
Dovey St. L8: Liv 2H 23
Downes Grn. CH63: Spit 2G 35
Downham Dr. CH60: Hesw 3C 32
Downham Rd. CH42: Tran 4H 21
Downham Rd. Nth.
CH61: Hesw 1C 32
Downham Rd. Sth.
CH60: Hesw 3C 32
Downing Cl. CH43: Oxton 4F 21
Downing Rd. L20: Boot 1F 7
Downing St. L5: Liv 6H 7
Drake Rd. CH46: Leas 1H 11
CH64: Nest 4C 38
Drake St. L20: Boot 2D 6
Draycott St. L8: Liv 4H 23
Drayton Cl. CH61: Irby 4H 25
Drayton Rd. CH44: Wall 2H 13
Drinkwater Gdns. L3: Liv 2G 15
Droitwich Av. CH49: Grea 3C 18
Druids Way CH49: Woodc 5G 19
Drummond Av.
CH66: Gt Sut 3C 48
Drummond Rd. CH47: Hoy 2C 16
Drury La. L2: Liv 4E 15
Dryburgh Way *L4: Kirkd 3G 7*
(off Bradwell St.)
Dryden Cl. CH43: Bid 6A 12
Dryden St. L5: Liv 1F 15
Dryfield Cl. CH49: Grea 3D 18
Dublin Cft. CH66: Gt Sut 6E 49
Dublin St. L3: Liv 1D 14
Duckinfield St. L3: Liv 4H 15
Duck Pond La. CH42: Tran 5E 21
Duddon Cl. CH43: Oxton 4D 20
Dudleston Rd.
CH66: Lit Sut 1B 48
Dudley Cl. CH43: Oxton 3F 21
Dudley Cres. CH65: Hoot 2B 42
Dudley Rd. CH45: New B 3E 5
CH65: Ell P 2H 49
Duke of York Cotts.
CH62: Port S 3G 29
Dukes Rd. L5: Liv 5G 7
Dukes Ter. L1: Liv 5G 15
Duke St. CH41: Birke 4G 13
CH45: New B 3F 5
L1: Liv 5F 15
Duke St. Bri. CH41: Birke 4G 13
Duke St. La. L1: Liv 5F 15
Dumbarton St. L4: Walt 2G 7
Dunbar Cl. CH66: Lit Sut 2C 48
Dunbar Ct. CH66: Lit Sut 2C 48
Dunbar St. L4: Walt 1H 7
Duncan Dr. CH49: Grea 3D 18
Duncansby Dr. CH63: East 1E 41
Duncan St. CH41: Birke 1B 22
L1: Liv 6G 15
Duncote Cl. CH43: Oxton 3E 21
Dundas St. L20: Boot 2D 6
Dundee Ct. CH65: Ell P 4C 50
Dundee Gro. CH44: Wall 2E 13
Dundonald St. CH41: Birke 5E 13
Dunes Way L5: Kirkd 5E 7
Dunham Cl. CH62: East 2H 41
Dunkirk Cres. CH65: Whit 6G 49
Dunkirk Dr. CH65: Whit 6H 49
Dunkirk La. CH1: Dunk 6C 48
CH65: Whit 6G 49
Dunlins Ct. CH45: Wall 3C 4
Dunluce St. L4: Walt 2G 7
Dunmore Cres.
CH66: Lit Sut 1B 48
Dunmore Rd. CH66: Lit Sut 1B 48
Dunnett St. L20: Kirkd 2D 6
Dunning Cl. CH49: Upton 2E 19
Dunraven Rd. CH48: W Kir 5C 16
CH64: Lit N 6E 39
Dunstall Cl. CH46: Leas 2E 11
Dunstan La. CH64: Burt 5A 46
Dunster Gro. CH60: Hesw 4D 32
Durban Rd. CH45: Wall 5F 5
Dures Ct. CH43: Clau 1E 21
Durham Ct. CH65: Ell P 4C 50
Durley Dr. CH43: Pren 6C 20
Durley Pk. Cl. CH43: Pren 1G 27
Dutton Dr. CH63: Spit 1F 35
Dutton Grn. CH2: Lit Stan 4D 50
Dylan Cl. L4: Walt 4H 7
Dyson St. L4: Walt 2H 7

E

Eagle La. CH66: Lit Sut 6D 42
Earle Cres. CH64: Nest 4B 38
Earle Dr. CH64: Park 5B 38
Earle St. L3: Liv 3E 15
Earls Gdns. CH65: Ell P 2H 49
Earlston Rd. CH45: Wall 5E 5
Earl St. CH62: New F 1H 29
Earlswood Cl. CH46: More 5B 10
Easby Rd. L4: Kirkd 4G 7
L5: Kirkd 4F 7
Easby Wlk. L4: Kirkd 4F 7
East Bank CH42: Tran 4G 21
Eastbourne Rd. CH41: Birke 1G 21
Eastbourne Wlk. L6: Liv 1H 15
Eastcott Cl. CH49: Grea 4C 18
Eastcroft Rd. CH44: Wall 2G 13
Eastern Av. CH62: Brom 5B 30
E. Farm M. CH48: Caldy 1D 24
E. Float Quay CH41: Birke 4H 13
EASTHAM 6C 36
Eastham Country Pk. 3E 37
EASTHAM FERRY 3E 37
Eastham M. CH62: East 1A 42
Eastham Rake CH62: East 3E 41
Eastham Rake Station (Rail) 2F 41
Eastham Village Rd.
CH62: East 6E 37
Eastlake Av. L5: Liv 6H 7
Eastleigh Dr. CH61: Irby 2H 25
East O'Hills Cl.
CH60: Hesw 2C 32
Easton Rd. CH62: New F 1H 29
East St. CH41: Birke 3A 14
L3: Liv 3E 15
Eastview Cl. CH43: Noct 3B 20
East Village *L1: Liv 5G 15*
(off Madison Sq.)
Eastway CH46: More 4E 11
CH49: Grea 3E 19
CH66: Lit Sut 6D 42
Eaton Av. CH44: Wall 1G 13
Eaton Rd. CH43: Oxton 2F 21
CH48: W Kir 6C 16
Eaton St. CH44: Wall 6F 5
L3: Liv 2E 15
Ebenezer St. CH42: Rock F 5C 22
Eberle St. L2: Liv 3E 15
Ebony Cl. CH46: More 5B 10
Ebor La. L5: Liv 1G 15
Eccleshall Rd.
CH62: Port S 3A 30
Eccleston Av. CH62: Brom 2A 36
CH66: Ell P 2E 49
Eccleston Cl. CH43: Oxton 4D 20
Echo Arena 6E 15
Echo La. CH48: W Kir 6E 17
Edale Cl. CH62: East 6C 36
Eddisbury Rd. CH44: Wall 6G 5
CH47: Hoy 3C 16
CH48: W Kir 3C 16
CH66: Whit 5F 49
Eden Cl. CH66: Gt Sut 2C 48
Edenhurst Av. CH44: Wall 6G 5
Edenpark Rd. CH42: Tran 4G 21
Eden Sq. *L2: Liv 3E 15*
(off Hatton Gdn.)
Edgar Ct. CH41: Birke 6H 13
Edgar St. L3: Liv 2F 15
Edgbaston Way CH43: Bid 5A 12
Edgefield Cl. CH43: Noct 3B 20
Edgehill Rd. CH46: More 5C 10
Edgemoor Cl. CH43: Bid 6H 11
Edgemoor Dr. CH61: Irby 2G 25
Edgewood Dr. CH62: Brom 6B 36
Edgewood Rd. CH47: Meols 4F 9
CH49: Upton 1F 19
Edinburgh Ct. CH65: Ell P 4B 50
Edinburgh Dr. CH43: Pren 6E 21
Edinburgh Rd. CH45: Wall 6F 5
Edith Rd. CH44: Wall 2A 14
Edmonton Cl. L5: Kirkd 5F 7
Edmund St. L3: Liv 3E 15
Edrich Av. CH43: Bid 5A 12
Edward Pav. L3: Liv 5E 15
Edward Rd. CH47: Hoy 1E 17
Edward St. CH65: Ell P 2G 43
Effingham St. L20: Boot 2D 6
Egan Ct. *CH41: Birke 6A 14*
(off Lord St.)
Egan Rd. CH43: Bid 5C 12
Egbert Rd. CH47: Meols 5E 9
Egerton Ct. CH41: Birke 6A 14
Egerton Dr. CH48: W Kir 5D 16
Egerton Gdns.
CH42: Rock F 6A 22
Egerton Gro. CH45: Wall 6F 5
Egerton Pk. CH42: Rock F 6A 22
Egerton Pk. Cl.
CH42: Rock F 6A 22
Egerton Rd. CH43: Clau 1E 21
CH62: New F 2H 29
Egerton St. CH45: New B 3F 5
CH65: Ell P 1A 50
L8: Liv 6H 15
Egerton Wharf CH41: Birke 5A 14
EGREMONT 6H 5
Egremont Prom. CH44: Wall 5H 5
CH45: Wall 5H 5
Elaine Cl. CH66: Gt Sut 3C 48
Elaine St. L8: Liv 1H 23
Elbrus Dr. CH66: Ell P 6F 43
Elder Gro. CH48: W Kir 5D 16
Elderwood Rd. CH42: Tran 4A 22
Eldon Gro. *L3: Liv 1F 15*
(off Limekiln La.)
Eldonian Way L3: Liv 1E 15
Eldon Pl. L3: Liv 1E 15
Eldon Rd. CH42: Rock F 5B 22
CH44: Wall 1F 13
Eldon St. L3: Liv 1E 15
Eldon Ter. CH64: Nest 6C 38
Eleanor Pk. CH43: Bid 5A 12
Eleanor Rd. CH43: Bid 4B 12
CH46: More 4C 10
Eleanor St. CH65: Ell P 1A 50
L20: Kirkd 2D 6
Elfet St. CH41: Birke 5D 12
Elgar Av. CH62: East 6C 36
Elgar Cl. CH65: Gt Sut 4F 49
Elgin Dr. CH45: Wall 5G 5
Elgin Way CH41: Birke 6A 14
Eliot Cl. CH62: New F 2G 29
Elizabeth St. L3: Liv 3H 15
Elland Dr. CH66: Lit Sut 2C 48
Ellens Cl. L6: Liv 3H 15

Ellen's La. CH63: Beb 4H 29
Elleray Dr. L8: Liv 3H 23
Elleray Pk. Rd. CH45: Wall 4E 5
Ellerman Rd. L3: Liv 4G 23
(not continuous)
Ellerton Av. CH66: Lit Sut 2C 48
Ellesmere Gro. CH45: Wall 5F 5
ELLESMERE PORT 2A 50
Ellesmere Port Golf Cen. 6B 42
ELLESMERE PORT HOSPITAL
. . . . .5G 49
Ellesmere Port Stadium 4C 50
Ellesmere Port Station (Rail)
. . . . .2A 50
Elliot St. L1: Liv 4F 15
Ellis Pl. L8: Liv 2H 23
Elm Av. CH49: Upton 1D 18
Elm Bank L4: Walt 4H 7
(off Walton Breck Rd.)
Elmbank Rd. CH62: New F 3H 29
Elmbank St. CH44: Wall 2G 13
Elm Cl. CH61: Pens 5C 26
Elm Ct. CH63: Hghr B 3D 28
CH65: Ell P 3D 50
Elmdene Ct. CH49: Grea 5C 18
Elm Dr. CH49: Grea 4C 18
Elm Grn. CH64: Will 5B 40
Elm Gro. CH42: Tran 3H 21
CH47: Hoy 6E 9
CH66: Whit 6G 49
Elmore Cl. L5: Liv 6H 7
Elm Pk. Rd. CH45: Wall 4E 5
Elm Rd. CH42: Tran 5F 21
(Elm Rd. Nth.)
CH42: Tran 4H 21
(Walker M.)
CH61: Irby 3B 26
CH63: Hghr B 2F 29
CH64: Will 5B 40
Elm Rd. Nth. CH42: Tran 5F 21
Elms Pk. CH61: Thing 4C 26
Elm St. CH41: Birke 1H 21
CH65: Ell P 2G 43
Elmswood Rd. CH42: Tran 3G 21
CH45: Wall 1H 13
Elm Ter. CH47: Hoy 6E 9
Elm Tree Ct. CH47: Hoy 5E 9
Elmtree Gro. CH43: Bid 5C 12
Elmure Av. CH63: Hghr B 4D 28
Elmwood Dr. CH61: Hesw 1B 32
Elphin Gro. L4: Walt 2H 7
Elstow St. L5: Kirkd 4F 7
Elswick St. L8: Liv 4H 23
Eltham Cl. CH49: Woodc 5H 19
Eltham Grn. CH49: Woodc 5H 19
Elton Cl. CH62: East 2G 41
Elton Dr. CH63: Spit 1G 35
Elton St. L4: Walt 1H 7
Elwyn Rd. CH47: Meols 4G 9
Elwy St. L8: Liv 2H 23
Ely Av. CH46: More 5C 10
Ember Cres. L6: Liv 1H 15
Emerald St. L8: Liv 4H 23
Emerson St. L8: Liv 6H 15
Emery St. L4: Walt 2H 7
Empress Rd. CH44: Wall 1G 13
Emslie Ct. CH64: Park 6A 38
Enerby Cl. CH43: Bid 6A 12
Enfield Rd. CH65: Ell P 2H 49
Enfield Ter. CH43: Oxton 2F 21
Enid St. L8: Liv 1H 23
Ennerdale Av. CH62: East 1H 41
Ennerdale Rd. CH43: Pren 6C 20
CH45: Wall 3D 4
Ennerdale St. L3: Liv 1F 15
Ennisdale Dr. CH48: W Kir 4E 17
Ensor St. L20: Boot 2D 6
Enterprise Pk. CH65: Ell P 3C 50
EPIC Leisure Cen. 3H 49
Epping Ct. CH60: Hesw 2C 32
Epsom Rd. CH46: Leas 2F 11
Epsom Way L5: Liv 6F 7
Epworth Cl. CH43: Clau 1E 21
Epworth Grange CH43: Clau 1E 21
(off Park Rd. W.)
Epworth St. L6: Liv 3H 15
Erfurt Av. CH63: Beb 5G 29
Erica Ct. CH60: Hesw 1A 32
Eric Fountain Rd.
CH65: Ell P 2D 42

Eric Gro. CH44: Wall 1E 13
Eric Rd. CH44: Wall 1E 13
Erin Cl. L8: Liv 1G 23
Ermine Cres. L5: Liv 6H 7
Errington Av. CH65: Ell P 1A 50
Errington St. L5: Kirkd 5E 7
Erskine Ind. Est. L6: Liv 2H 15
Erskine Rd. CH44: Wall 2G 13
Erskine St. L6: Liv 3H 15
Erskine St. Ind. Est. L6: Liv . . .3H 15
(off Prospect St.)
Escolme Dr. CH49: Grea 4D 18
Esher Cl. CH43: Bid 6A 12
CH62: New F 1H 29
Esher Rd. CH62: New F 1H 29
Eskdale Cl. CH65: Whit 4H 49
Eskdale Av. CH46: More 4C 10
CH62: East 6C 36
Esk St. L20: Kirkd 3D 6
Espin St. L4: Walt 2H 7
Esplanade CH42: Rock F 5D 22
Esplanade, The
CH62: New F 6D 22
Essex Rd. CH48: W Kir 4E 17
Ethelbert La. CH47: Meols 5E 9
Ethelbert Rd. CH47: Meols 5E 9
Ethel Rd. CH44: Wall 2H 13
Eton Dr. CH63: Thorn H 5H 33
Eton Rd. CH65: Ell P 3B 50
Eton St. L4: Walt 2H 7
Europa Blvd. CH41: Birke 1A 22
Europa Cen., The
CH41: Birke 1A 22
Europa Pools 1H 21
Europa Sq. CH41: Birke 1A 22
Europa Way CH65: Ell P 1A 50
Euston Gro. CH43: Oxton 2F 21
Euston St. L4: Walt 1H 7
Evans Bus. Pk. CH65: Ell P . . .4F 43
Evans Rd. CH47: Hoy 6D 8
Evelyn Rd. CH44: Wall 2G 13
Evelyn St. L5: Kirkd 5F 7
Everest Cl. CH66: Gt Sut 4F 49
Everest Rd. CH42: Tran 5H 21
Evergreen Cl. CH49: Upton 1E 19
Everleigh Cl. CH43: Bid 6H 11
Eversleigh Dr. CH63: Beb 5G 29
Eversley Pk. CH43: Oxton 4F 21
Eversley St. L8: Liv 1H 23
(not continuous)
EVERTON 6G 7
Everton Brow L3: Liv 2G 15
Everton FC 2H 7
Everton Rd. L6: Liv 1H 15
Everton Valley L4: Walt 4G 7
Everton Vw. L20: Boot 1D 6
Everyman Theatre 4H 15
Evesham Rd. CH45: Wall 5D 4
Ewloe Ct. CH65: Ell P 5B 50
Exchange Flags L2: Liv 3E 15
(off Exchange Pas. E.)
Exchange Pas. E. L2: Liv 3E 15
Exchange Pas. W. L2: Liv 3E 15
Exchange St. E. L2: Liv 3E 15
Exchange St. W. L2: Liv 4E 15
Exeter Rd. CH44: Wall 6G 5
CH65: Ell P 2A 50
L20: Boot 1E 7
Exmoor Cl. CH61: Pens 4B 26
Exmouth Cl. CH41: Birke 1H 21
Exmouth Gdns. CH41: Birke . . .1H 21
Exmouth St. CH41: Birke 1H 21
Exmouth Way CH41: Birke 1H 21
Expressway Bus. Pk.
CH42: Tran 4B 22
Eyre Pl. CH65: Ell P 1H 49

F

Fab4D 4D 14
FACT 5G 15
Fairacres Rd. CH63: Beb 5G 29
Fairbeech M. CH43: Bid 6A 12
Fairbrook Dr. CH41: Birke 4C 12
Fairclough La. CH43: Oxton 3F 21
Fairclough St. L1: Liv 4F 15
Fairfax Rd. CH41: Tran 3A 22
Fairfield Av. CH65: Whit 5G 49
Fairfield Cres. CH46: More 5D 10

Fairfield Dr. CH48: W Kir 4G 17
Fairfield Rd. CH42: Tran 5A 22
Fairhaven Cl. CH42: Rock F 5B 22
Fairhaven Dr. CH63: Brom 4A 36
Fair Isles Cl. CH65: Ell P 4A 50
Fairlawn Cl. CH53: Raby M 5G 35
Fairlawn Cl. CH43: Oxton 2D 20
Fairmead Rd. CH46: More 4E 11
Fairview CH41: Tran 3A 22
Fairview Av. CH45: Wall 6E 5
Fairview Cl. CH43: Oxton 5F 21
CH65: Whit 5G 49
Fairview Way CH61: Pens 6B 26
Fairway Cres. CH62: Brom 5B 30
Fairway Nth. CH62: Brom 5B 30
Fairways CH42: Tran 1B 28
Fairways, The CH48: Caldy 3B 24
Fairways Dr. CH66: Lit Sut 5D 42
Fairway Sth. CH62: Brom 6B 30
Falcongate Ind. Est.
CH41: Birke 4F 13
Falcon Rd. CH41: Birke 3G 21
Falcon St. CH41: Birke 3G 21
CH66: Gt Sut 4F 49
Falkland Rd. CH44: Wall 1H 13
Falkland St. CH41: Birke 5E 13
L3: Liv 3H 15
(not continuous)
Falkner Sq. L7: Liv 5H 15
L8: Liv 6H 15
(not continuous)
Falkner St. L8: Liv 5H 15
(not continuous)
Falkner Ter. L8: Liv 6H 15
(off Up. Parliament St.)
Falstaff St. L20: Kirkd 3E 7
Faraday Rd. CH65: Whit 3G 49
Fareham Cl. CH49: Upton 1E 19
Farley Av. CH62: Brom 2A 36
Farlow Rd. CH42: Rock F 6B 22
Farm Cl. CH49: Grea 3C 18
Far Mdw. La. CH61: Irby 3G 25
Farmers Heath
CH66: Gt Sut 5D 48
Farmfield Dr. CH43: Bid 6A 12
Farmside CH46: Leas 2F 11
Farmstead Way
CH66: Gt Sut 6E 49
Farndon Av. CH45: Wall 5C 4
Farndon Dr. CH48: W Kir 4G 17
Farndon Rd. CH66: Ell P 1E 49
Farndon Way CH43: Oxton 3D 20
Farne Cl. CH65: Ell P 6A 50
Farnworth Av. CH46: Leas 2E 11
Farr Hall Dr. CH60: Hesw 4A 32
Farr Hall Rd. CH60: Hesw 3A 32
Farriers Way CH48: Frank 5B 18
Faversham Way
CH42: Rock F 5B 22
Fazakerley St. L3: Liv 3D 14
Fearnley Rd. CH41: Birke 2H 21
Fearnley Rd. CH41: Birke 2H 21
Feather La. CH60: Hesw 3B 32
Feilden Rd. CH63: Beb 5G 29
Felicity Gro. CH46: More 4D 10
Fell St. CH44: Wall 3A 14
Felthorpe Cl. CH49: Upton 6H 11
Felton Cl. CH46: More 5C 10
Fendale Av. CH46: More 4G 11
Fender Cl. CH49: Woodc 6B 20
Fender La. CH43: Bid 4G 11
CH46: More 4G 11
Fenderside Rd. CH43: Bid 5A 12
Fender Vw. Rd.
CH46: More 5G 11
Fender Way CH43: Bid 1H 19
CH61: Pens 5C 26
Fenwick Rd. CH66: Gt Sut 5E 49
Fenwick St. L2: Liv 4E 15
Ferguson Av. CH49: Grea 4D 18
Fern Cl. CH65: Ell P 1E 49
Fernbank La. CH49: Upton 6F 11
Ferndale Av. CH44: Wall 1G 13
CH48: Frank 6B 18
Ferndale Rd. CH47: Hoy 6D 8
Fern Gro. CH43: Noct 3B 20
Fernhill CH45: New B 3F 5
Fernhill Cl. L20: Boot 1G 7

Fernhill Gdns. L20: Boot 1G 7
Fernhill Mews E. L20: Boot . . .1G 7
(off Fernhill Rd.)
Fernhill Mews W. L20: Boot . . .1G 7
Fernhill Rd. L20: Boot 1G 7
Fernhill Way L20: Boot 1G 7
Fernie Cres. L8: Liv 2H 23
Fernlea M. CH43: Bid 5A 12
Fernlea Rd. CH60: Hesw 3C 32
Fern Rd. CH65: Whit 5G 49
Ferns Cl. CH60: Hesw 2G 31
Ferns Rd. CH63: Hghr B 4D 28
Ferny Brow Rd.
CH49: Woodc 4H 19
Fernyess La. CH64: Will 1A 46
Ferries Cl. CH42: Rock F 1G 29
Ferry Rd. CH62: East 6E 37
Ferryside CH44: Wall 3A 14
Ferry Vw. Rd. CH44: Wall 3A 14
Festival Rd. CH65: Ell P 2F 49
Ffrancon Dr. CH63: Hghr B 2F 29
Field Cl. CH62: New F 1H 29
Field Hey La. CH64: Will 4D 40
(not continuous)
Field Rd. CH45: New B 4F 5
Fieldside Rd.
CH42: Rock F 5A 22
Field St. L3: Liv 2G 15
(not continuous)
Fieldway CH45: Wall 6E 5
CH47: Meols 6H 9
CH60: Hesw 2E 33
CH63: Hghr B 1D 28
CH66: Lit Sut 6B 42
Fieldway Cl. CH41: Birke 5G 13
Fifth Av. CH43: Bid 6H 11
Finch Ct. CH41: Birke 6H 13
Finchdean Cl. CH49: Grea 3C 18
Finch Pl. L3: Liv 3H 15
Findley Dr. CH46: Leas 2F 11
Finney, The CH48: Caldy 3B 24
Finstall Rd. CH63: Spit 1F 35
Firbrook Cl. CH43: Bid 4A 12
Firdene Cres. CH43: Noct 3C 20
Firs, The CH43: Bid 5C 12
CH65: Ell P 5B 50
Firs Av. CH63: Beb 6F 29
Firshaw Rd. CH47: Meols 4E 9
First Av. CH43: Bid 1A 20
Firtree Gro. CH66: Whit 6B 48
Firway CH60: Hesw 6D 32
Fishers La. CH61: Pens 5A 26
Fisher St. L8: Liv 1F 23
Fishguard Cl. L6: Liv 1H 15
Fitness First
Bromborough 6C 30
Fitzclarence Wlk. L6: Liv 1H 15
(off Plumpton St.)
Fitzclarence Way L6: Liv 1H 15
Fitzpatrick Ct. L3: Liv 1E 15
Fitzroy Way L6: Liv 2H 15
Fiveways Pk. CH64: Nest 2D 38
Flag La. CH64: Lit N 6D 38
Flail Cl. CH49: Grea 3C 18
Flambards CH49: Woodc 4H 19
Flashes La. CH64: Ness 2F 45
Flatt La. CH43: Oxton 4D 20
CH65: Ell P 2H 49
Flaxhill CH46: More 4D 10
Flaybrick Cl. CH43: Bid 5C 12
Fleck La.
CH48: Caldy, W Kir 6F 17
Fleetcroft Rd.
CH49: Woodc 5G 19
Fleet St. CH65: Ell P 2G 49
L1: Liv 4F 15
Fleming Ct. L3: Liv 1E 15
Fleming St. CH65: Ell P 1A 50
Fleming Way CH46: Leas 3G 11
Fletcher Av. CH42: Rock F 5A 22
Fletcher Cl. CH49: Woodc 4G 19
Flint Cl. CH64: Nest 1C 44
Flint Ct. CH65: Ell P 5B 50
Flint Dr. CH64: Nest 6C 38
Flint Mdw. CH64: Nest 6C 38
Flint St. L1: Liv 6F 15
Floral Pavilion Theatre 2G 5
Floral Wood L1: Aig 5H 23
Florence Av. CH60: Hesw 2B 32
Florence Rd. CH44: Wall 2A 14

Florence St. CH41: Birke 1H 21
   L4: Walt 3H 7
Flowermead Cl.
   CH47: Meols 4H 9
Focus Bldg., The L3: Liv 3F 15
   (off Crosshall St.)
Folds, The CH63: Thorn H 5A 34
Foley Cl. L4: Kirkd 4G 7
Foley St. L4: Kirkd 4G 7
Folly La. CH44: Wall 6C 4
   (not continuous)
Fontenoy St. L3: Liv 3F 15
Fonthill Cl. L4: Kirkd 4F 7
Fonthill Rd. L4: Kirkd 3F 7
FORD 1A 20
Ford Cl. CH49: Upton 3H 19
Ford Dr. CH49: Upton 2H 19
Fordham St. L4: Kirkd 3G 7
Fordhill Vw. CH46: More 5G 11
Ford La. CH49: Upton 2H 19
Ford Rd. CH49: Upton 2G 19
Ford St. L3: Liv 2E 15
Ford Way M. CH49: Upton 3G 19
Ford Way CH49: Upton 3G 19
Forest Cl. CH47: Meols 4F 9
Forest Ct. CH43: Clau 1D 20
Forest Rd. CH43: Clau 6E 13
   CH47: Meols 4F 9
   CH60: Hesw 2C 32
   CH65: Ell P 6E 43
Forge Rd. CH66: Lit Sut 1C 48
Forge St. L20: Kirkd 3E 7
Fornalls Grn. La.
   CH47: Meols 6G 9
Forrest St. L1: Liv 5F 15
Forth St. L20: Kirkd 2E 7
Fort Perch Rock 2F 5
Fort St. CH45: New B 4G 5
Forwood Rd. CH62: Brom . . .3B 36
Foster St. L20: Kirkd 4E 7
Fotheringay Ct. CH65: Ell P . .5B 50
   (off Rochester Dr.)
Foundation, The L3: Liv 4H 15
Foundry, The L1: Liv 5F 15
   (off Henry St.)
Fountain Rd. CH45: New B 4E 7
Fountains Cl. L4: Walt 4H 7
Fountains Ct. L4: Kirkd 4F 7
   (off Stanley Cl.)
Fountains Rd. L4: Kirkd 4F 7
   (not continuous)
Fountain St. CH42: Tran 4G 21
Four Bridges CH41: Birke 4A 14
Fourth Av. CH43: Bid 1H 19
Fowell Rd. CH45: New B 3F 5
Foxall Way CH66: Gt Sut 5C 48
Foxcover Rd. CH60: Hesw 4E 33
Foxcovers Rd. CH63: Beb 6G 29
Foxdale Cl. CH43: Oxton 2E 21
Foxdene CH66: Lit Sut 2C 48
Foxes Cl. CH43: Oxton 2F 21
Foxfield Rd. CH47: Meols 5F 9
Foxglove Rd. CH41: Birke 6D 12
Foxglove Way CH64: Lit N 2C 44
Fox Hey Rd. CH44: Wall 2D 12
Foxhill Cl. L8: Liv 1H 5
Foxleigh Grange
   CH41: Birke 4D 12
   L3: Liv 1G 15
Fox St. CH41: Birke 1G 21
Foxton Cl. CH46: More 4B 10
Foxwood Cl. CH48: W Kir 4G 17
Francine Cl. L3: Liv 6E 7
Francis Av. CH43: Clau 1F 21
   CH46: More 5D 10
FRANKBY 5B 18
Frankby Av. CH44: Wall 1E 13
Frankby Cl. CH49: Grea 4B 18
Frankby Grn. CH48: Frank . .5A 18
Frankby Gro. CH49: Upton . . .2F 19
Frankby Rd. CH47: Meols 5F 9
   CH48: Frank, W Kir 4F 17
   CH49: Grea 4F 17
Frankby Stiles CH48: Frank . .4H 17
Franklin Rd. CH46: Leas 1G 11
Fraser St. L3: Liv 3G 15
Freeland St. L4: Kirkd 4G 7
Freeman St. CH41: Birke 6A 14
Freemason's Row L3: Liv 2E 15

Frensham Cl. CH63: Spit 1F 35
Friars Cl. CH63: Beb 4F 29
Friar St. L5: Liv 6H 7
Frobisher Rd. CH46: Leas 1G 11
   CH64: Nest 5C 38
Frodsham St. CH41: Tran 3A 22
   (not continuous)
   L4: Walt 2H 7
Frome Cl. CH61: Irby 2H 25
Frome Ct. CH65: Ell P 6H 43
Frost Dr. CH61: Irby 3G 25
Frosts M. CH65: Ell P 1H 49
Fuchsia Cl. CH66: Gt Sut 6F 49
Fuchsia Wlk. CH49: Grea 5C 18
Fulbrook Cl. CH63: Spit 1F 35
Fulbrook Rd. CH63: Spit 1F 35
Fulford Pk. CH46: More 5E 11
Fulton Av. CH48: W Kir 4F 17
Fulton St. L5: Liv 6D 6
Fulwood Gdns.
   CH66: Lit Sut 1C 48
Fulwood M. CH66: Lit Sut 1C 48
Fulwood Rd. CH66: Lit Sut . . .1C 48
Furness Cl. CH49: Upton 1E 19
Furness St. L4: Walt 4G 7
Furrocks Cl. CH64: Ness 2D 44
Furrocks La. CH64: Ness 2D 44
Furrocks Way CH64: Ness 2D 44
Furrows, The CH66: Gt Sut . . .6A 48
Furze Way CH46: More 4E 11

G

Gabriel Cl. CH46: More 5F 11
Gainsborough Rd.
   CH45: Wall 1C 12
   CH49: Upton 1E 19
Gala Bingo
   Bromborough 6C 30
Gala Leo Casino 6F 15
Gallagher Ind. Est.
   CH44: Wall 3F 13
Gallopers La. CH61: Thing . . .3D 26
Galton St. L3: Liv 2D 14
Galtres Ct. CH63: Hghr B 1E 29
Galtres Pk. CH63: Hghr B 1E 29
Gambier Ter. L1: Liv 6H 15
Gamlin St. CH41: Birke 5D 12
Ganneys Mdw. Cl.
   CH49: Woodc 4A 20
Ganney's Mdw. Rd.
   CH49: Woodc 5A 20
Garden Ct. CH42: Tran 6G 21
Garden Hey Rd.
   CH46: More 6B 10
   CH47: Meols 5E 9
Garden La. CH46: More 4E 11
   L5: Liv 1H 15
Gardenside CH46: Leas 1H 11
Gardenside St. L6: Liv 2H 15
Gardens Rd. CH63: Beb 4H 29
Gardner's Row L3: Liv 2F 15
Garfield Ter. CH49: Upton 2G 19
Garnett Av. L4: Kirkd 3G 7
Garrick Av. CH46: More 5C 10
Garrick Rd. CH43: Pren 1H 27
Garswood Cl. CH46: Leas 1E 11
Garswood St. L8: Liv 4H 23
Garth, The CH43: Oxton 2C 20
Garth Blvd. CH63: Hghr B 1E 29
Garth Rd. CH65: Ell P 2D 50
Gascoyne St. L3: Liv 2E 15
Gateacre Cl. CH65: Ell P 5F 43
Gateway, The CH62: Brom . . .2C 36
Gautby Rd. CH41: Birke 4C 12
Gawsworth Cl. CH43: Oxton . .4D 20
Gawsworth Rd.
   CH66: Gt Sut 2E 49
Gaybeech Cl. CH43: Bid 5H 11
GAYTON 4D 32
Gayton Av. CH45: New B 3F 5
   CH63: Hghr B 1C 28
Gayton Farm Rd.
   CH60: Hesw 6C 32
Gayton La. CH60: Hesw 5D 32
Gayton Mill Cl.
   CH60: Hesw 4D 32
Gayton Parkway
   CH60: Hesw 6E 33

Gayton Rd. CH60: Hesw 5B 32
Gaytree Cl. CH43: Bid 6A 12
Gaywood Cl. CH43: Bid 6A 12
Gelling St. L8: Liv 2H 23
Gem St. L5: Liv 6E 7
Geneva Rd. CH44: Wall 3H 13
George Rd. CH47: Hoy 1E 17
George's Dock Gates
   L3: Liv 4D 14
Georges Dock Way L3: Liv . .4D 14
George St. CH41: Birke 6A 14
   CH65: Ell P 1A 50
   L3: Liv 3E 15
Georgia Av. CH62: Brom 6C 30
Geraint St. L8: Liv 1H 23
Gerald Rd. CH43: Oxton 3E 21
Gerard Av. CH45: Wall 4E 5
Gerard Rd. CH45: Wall 5D 4
   CH48: W Kir 4D 16
Gerard St. L3: Liv 3G 15
Gerrard Av. CH66: Gt Sut 3C 48
Gertrude St. CH41: Birke 1B 22
Gibbs Ct. CH61: Irby 3B 26
Gibraltar Row L3: Liv 3D 14
Gibson Cl. CH61: Pens 6B 26
Gibson Ct. CH65: Ell P 1G 43
Gibson Rd. L8: Liv 6H 15
Gibson Ter. CH44: Wall 6H 5
   (off Royden Av.)
Gilbert Cl. CH63: Spit 1F 35
Gilbert St. L1: Liv 5F 15
Gildarts Gdns. L3: Liv 1E 15
Gildart St. L3: Liv 3H 15
Gillbrook Sq. CH41: Birke 5D 12
Gills La. CH61: Barn, Pens . . .5C 26
Gill St. L3: Liv 3H 15
Gilman St. L4: Walt 4H 7
Gilmartin Gro. L6: Liv 2H 15
Gilmour Mt. CH43: Oxton 3F 21
Gilroy Nature Pk. 3E 17
Gilroy Rd. CH48: W Kir 4E 17
Gilwell Av. CH46: More 6E 11
Gilwell Cl. CH46: More 6E 11
Ginnel, The CH42: Port S 4H 29
Girton Av. L20: Boot 1G 7
Girton Cl. CH65: Ell P 3B 50
Girton Rd. CH65: Ell P 3B 50
Girtrell Cl. CH49: Upton 2D 18
Girtrell Rd. CH49: Upton 2D 18
Girvan Dr. CH64: Lit N 1D 44
Glacier Bldg. L3: Liv 3G 23
Glade, The CH47: Meols 4F 9
Glade Dr. CH66: Lit Sut 1H 47
Gladstone Cl. CH41: Birke . . .1H 21
Gladstone Ct. L8: Liv 6H 15
   (off Up. Parliament St.)
Gladstone Hall Rd.
   CH62: Port S 5H 29
Gladstone Rd.
   CH42: Rock F 4B 22
   CH44: Wall 2H 13
   CH64: Nest 5C 38
Gladstone St. L3: Liv 2E 15
Gladstone Ter. CH64: Will 5B 40
   (off Neston Rd.)
Gladstone Theatre 5H 29
Glaisher St. L5: Liv 5H 7
Glamis Cl. CH43: Noct 4B 20
Glasier Rd. CH46: More 4C 10
Gleaston Cl. CH62: Brom 2B 36
Gleave Cres. L6: Liv 1H 15
Glebe Hey Rd.
   CH49: Woodc 4G 19
Glebelands Rd. CH46: More . .5E 11
Glebe Rd. CH45: Wall 5E 5
Glebeway Way CH65: Ell P . . .2D 50
Gleggside CH48: W Kir 5E 17
Glegg St. L3: Liv 1D 14
Glen, The CH63: Spit 6A 30
Glenalmond Rd.
   CH44: Wall 1H 13
Glenathol Rd. CH66: Gt Sut . .3C 48
Glenavon Rd. CH43: Pren 6E 21
Glenburn Av. CH62: East 1G 41
Glenburn Rd. CH44: Wall 2H 13
Glencoe Rd. CH45: Wall 5F 5
   CH66: Gt Sut 3C 48
Glendale Cl. L8: Liv 4H 23
Glendale Gro. CH63: Spit 1H 35
Glendower St. L20: Boot 2E 7

Glendyke Rd. CH66: Gt Sut . . .3C 48
Gleneagles Cl. CH61: Pens . . .5B 26
Gleneagles Rd.
   CH66: Gt Sut 2C 48
Glenesk Rd. CH66: Gt Sut 3C 48
Glenfield Cl. CH43: Bid 5A 12
   CH46: More 4B 10
Glenham Cl. CH47: Meols 5G 9
Glenmarsh Cl.
   CH63: Hghr B 4D 28
Glenmaye Rd. CH66: Gt Sut . .3C 48
Glenmore Rd. CH43: Oxton . . .3E 21
Glen Pk. Rd. CH45: Wall 4E 5
Glen Rd. CH66: Gt Sut 2C 48
Glen Ronald Dr. CH49: Grea . .2D 18
Glenton Pk. CH64: Lit N 1D 44
Glentree Cl. CH49: Grea 2D 18
Glenwood Cl. CH66: Lit Sut . .1C 48
Glenwood Dr. CH61: Irby 2A 26
Glenwood Gdns.
   CH66: Lit Sut 1C 48
Glenwood Rd.
   CH66: Lit Sut 1C 48
Globe St. L4: Walt 4G 7
Gloucester Cl. CH66: Gt Sut . .6A 48
Gloucester Pl. L6: Liv 2H 15
   (off Gilmartin Gro.)
Gloucester Rd. CH45: Wall . . .5C 4
Glover St. CH42: Tran 3G 21
Glyn Av. CH62: Brom 4C 36
Glyn Rd. CH44: Wall 6F 5
Golden Gro. L4: Walt 2H 7
Goldie St. L4: Walt 4H 7
Goldsmith Rd. CH43: Pren . . .6D 20
Goldsmith Way CH43: Pren . .6D 20
Golf Links Rd. CH42: Tran 6F 21
Gonville Rd. L20: Boot 1F 7
Goodakers Ct.
   CH49: Woodc 5G 19
   (off Childwall Grn.)
Goodakers Mdw.
   CH49: Woodc 5G 19
Goodall Pl. L4: Kirkd 3G 7
Goodall St. L4: Kirkd 2G 7
Goodison Av. L4: Walt 3H 7
Goodison Pk. 3H 7
Goodison Rd. L4: Walt 2H 7
Goodwood Dr. CH46: Leas . . .2F 11
Goodwood Gro.
   CH66: Gt Sut 4D 48
Goodwood St. L5: Liv 6F 7
Goose Green, The
   CH47: Meols 4F 9
Goostrey Cl. CH63: Spit 2H 35
Gordon Av. CH49: Grea 4E 19
   CH62: Brom 4C 36
Gordon Ct. CH49: Grea 4E 19
Gordon Dr. CH45: New B 4G 5
Gordon St. CH41: Birke 1G 21
Gordon Ter. CH64: Will 5B 40
   (off Neston Rd.)
Goree L2: Liv 4E 15
Goree Piazza L2: Liv 4E 15
   (off The Strand)
Gore St. L8: Liv 1G 23
Gorsebank St. CH44: Wall . . .2G 13
Gorse Cres. CH44: Wall 3G 13
Gorsedale Pk. CH44: Wall . . .3H 13
Gorsedale Rd. CH44: Wall . . .3F 13
Gorsefield Av. CH62: Brom . .6B 36
Gorsefield Cl. CH62: Brom . . .6B 36
Gorsefield Rd. CH42: Tran . . .4G 21
Gorsehill Rd. CH45: New B . . .4E 5
   CH60: Hesw 2C 32
Gorse La. CH48: W Kir 6G 17
Gorse Rd. CH47: Meols 5F 9
Gorsey La. CH44: Wall 3F 13
Gorseyville Cres.
   CH63: Hghr B 4E 29
Gorseyville Rd.
   CH63: Hghr B 4E 29
Gorstons La. CH64: Lit N 1E 45
Gorst St. L4: Walt 4H 7
Goschen St. L5: Liv 4H 7
Gosford St. L8: Liv 3H 23
Gotham Rd. CH63: Spit 1G 35
Gothic St. CH42: Rock F 5B 22
Gourleys La. CH48: W Kir 6F 17
Government Rd. CH47: Hoy . . .6D 8

Gower St.—Hampstead Rd.

Gower St. L3: Liv 5E 15
Gowy Ct. CH66: Ell P 5E 43
Grace Cl. CH45: Wall 6F 5
Grace Rd. CH65: Ell P 1H 49
Grace St. L8: Liv 3H 23
Gradwell St. L1: Liv 4F 15
Grafton Cres. L8: Liv 1G 23
Grafton Dr. CH49: Upton 3G 19
Grafton Gro. L8: Liv 3G 23
Grafton Rd. CH45: New B 4F 5
CH65: Ell P 2G 43
Grafton St. CH43: Oxton 2F 21
L8: Liv 4H 23
(Beresford Rd.)
L8: Liv 1F 23
(Stanhope St., not continuous)
Grafton Wlk. CH48: W Kir 5E 17
Graham Av. CH66: Gt Sut 2D 48
Graham Rd. CH48: W Kir 4C 16
Grainger Av. CH43: Pren 5D 20
CH48: W Kir 3D 16
Grain Ind. Est. L8: Liv 3G 23
Grammar School La.
CH48: W Kir 6F 17
Grampian Av. CH46: More 5F 11
Grampian Way CH46: More 5E 11
CH62: East 6C 36
CH64: Lit N 2C 44
Granary Way L3: Liv 1F 23
Granby Cres. CH63: Spit 1G 35
Grand Central *L3: Liv 4G 15*
(off Hilbre St.)
GRANGE 5E 17
Grange, The CH42: Rock F 6B 22
CH44: Wall 1G 13
Grange Av. CH45: Wall 5F 5
Grange Ct. CH43: Oxton 4E 21
Grange Cres. CH66: Hoot 4A 42
Grange Cross Cl.
CH48: W Kir 6G 17
Grange Cross Hey
CH48: W Kir 6G 17
Grange Cross La.
CH48: W Kir 6G 17
Grange Dr. CH60: Hesw 1B 32
CH63: Thorn H 4A 34
Grange Farm Cres.
CH48: W Kir 4G 17
Grange Mt. CH43: Oxton 2G 21
CH48: W Kir 5F 17
CH60: Hesw 2B 32
Grange Old Rd.
CH48: W Kir 5E 17
Grange Pl. CH41: Birke 1G 21
Grange Pct. CH41: Birke 1A 22
Grange Rd. CH41: Birke 1H 21
(not continuous)
CH48: W Kir 5C 16
CH60: Hesw 1B 32
CH65: Ell P 2A 50
Grange Rd. E. CH41: Birke 1A 22
Grange Road Sports Cen. 2F 21
Grange Rd. W. CH41: Birke 1F 21
CH43: Oxton 1F 21
Grange Vw. CH43: Oxton 2G 21
Grange Wlk. CH48: W Kir 6F 17
Grange Wood CH48: W Kir 6F 17
Grantham Cl. CH61: Pens 5A 26
Granton Rd. L5: Liv 5H 7
Grant Rd. CH46: Leas 2H 11
Granville Cl. CH45: Wall 5C 4
Granville Ct. CH45: Wall 5C 4
Granville Dr. CH66: Lit Sut 6B 42
Grappenhall Rd.
CH65: Gt Sut 3F 49
Grappenhall Way CH43: Bid 6A 12
Grasmere Av. CH43: Noct 2A 20
Grasmere Ct. *CH41: Birke 2G 21*
(off Penrith St.)
Grasmere Dr. CH45: Wall 5F 5
Grasmere Rd. CH64: Nest 1C 44
CH65: Ell P 5A 50
Grassmoor Cl. CH62: Brom 3C 36
Grasswood Rd.
CH49: Woodc 5H 19
Grasville Rd. CH42: Tran 4A 22
Gratrix Rd. CH62: Brom 3B 36
Graylands Rd. CH62: Port S 3A 30
Grayson M. *CH41: Birke 6B 14*
(off John St.)
Grayson St. L1: Liv 5F 15
GREASBY 4D 18
Greasby Dr. CH66: Gt Sut 3E 49
Greasby Hill Rd.
CH48: W Kir 6E 17
Greasby Rd. CH44: Wall 1E 13
CH49: Grea 4C 18
Gt. Charlotte St. L1: Liv 4F 15
(Elliot St.)
L1: Liv 4F 15
(Roe St.)
Gt. Crosshall St. L3: Liv 3E 15
Gt. George Pl. L1: Liv 6G 15
Gt. George Sq. L1: Liv 5G 15
Gt. George's Sq. *L1: Liv 5G 15*
(off Grenville St. Sth.)
Gt. George St. L1: Liv 5G 15
Gt. Homer St. L5: Liv 5G 7
Gt. Homer St. Shop. Cen.
L5: Liv 6G 7
Gt. Howard St. L3: Liv 2D 14
L5: Liv 5D 6
GREAT MEOLS 4G 9
Gt. Mersey St. L5: Kirkd 5F 7
(not continuous)
Gt. Nelson St. L3: Liv 1F 15
Gt. Newton St. L3: Liv 3H 15
Gt. Orford St. L3: Liv 4H 15
Gt. Richmond St. L3: Liv 2G 15
GREAT SUTTON 3D 48
Gt. Western Ho.
CH41: Birke 6B 14
Greaves St. L8: Liv 2H 23
Grecian Ter. L5: Liv 6H 7
Greek St. L3: Liv 3G 15
Green, The CH48: Caldy 2B 24
CH62: Brom 4B 30
CH63: Raby 1G 39
CH64: Lit N 1D 44
CH64: Nest 5B 38
CH64: Will 5B 40
CH65: Whit 5H 49
Greenacre Dr. CH63: Brom 4A 36
Greenacres Cl. CH43: Bid 5A 12
Greenacres Ct. CH43: Bid 5A 12
Green Bank CH63: Brim 1A 34
Greenbank Av. CH45: New B 4F 5
CH66: Lit Sut 6C 42
Greenbank Dr. CH61: Pens 6B 26
Greenbank Rd. CH42: Tran 4G 21
CH48: W Kir 3D 16
Greencroft Hey CH63: Spit 1H 35
Greencroft Rd. CH44: Wall 2G 13
Greendale Rd.
CH62: Port S 3G 29
Greenfield La. CH60: Hesw 1G 31
Greenfield Rd.
CH66: Lit Sut 6B 42
GREENFIELDS 5A 12
Greenfields Av.
CH62: Brom 4A 36
Greenfields Cl. CH64: Lit N 2D 44
Greenfields Cres.
CH62: Brom 4A 36
Greenfields Cft. CH64: Lit N 2C 44
Greenfields Dr. CH64: Lit N 3C 44
Greenfield Way CH44: Wall 1F 13
Greengables Cl. L8: Liv 2H 23
Greengates Cres.
CH64: Lit N 2C 44
Green Haven CH43: Noct 2B 20
Greenheath Way
CH46: Leas 2F 11
Greenheys Rd. CH44: Wall 2F 13
CH61: Irby 4G 25
Greenhow Av. CH48: W Kir 4D 16
Greenland St. L1: Liv 6F 15
Green La. CH41: Tran 3A 22
CH45: Wall 6A 4
(not continuous)
CH62: East 3D 36
CH63: Beb 4F 29
CH65: Ell P 3A 50
CH66: Gt Sut 3C 48
(not continuous)
L3: Liv 4G 15
Green Lane Station (Rail) 3B 22
Green Lawn CH42: Rock F 6B 22
Green Lawn Gro.
CH42: Rock F 6B 22
Green Lawns Dr.
CH66: Gt Sut 6A 48
Greenlea Cl. CH63: Beb 3F 29
CH65: Whit 5H 49
Greenleas Cl. CH45: Wall 5B 4
Greenleas Rd. CH45: Wall 5B 4
Green Mt. CH49: Upton 2G 19
Greenock St. L3: Liv 2D 14
Greens Health & Fitness
Liverpool 4H 23
Greenside L6: Liv 2H 15
Green St. L5: Liv 1E 15
Greenville Cl. CH63: Beb 4F 29
Greenville Rd. CH63: Beb 4F 29
Greenway CH49: Grea 3E 19
CH61: Pens 5A 26
CH62: Brom 6B 30
CH64: Park 3A 38
Greenway Rd. CH42: Tran 4H 21
Greenways Ct. CH62: Brom 5A 36
Greenwood La. CH44: Wall 6G 5
Greenwood Rd. CH47: Meols 5G 9
CH49: Woodc 4G 19
Greetham St. L1: Liv 5F 15
Gregson Ct. CH45: New B 3G 5
Gregson St. L6: Liv 2H 15
Grenfell Cl. CH64: Park 4A 38
Grenfell Ct. CH64: Park 5A 38
Grenfell Pk. CH64: Park 4A 38
Grennan, The CH45: New B 3F 5
Grennan Ct. *CH45: New B 3F 5*
(off The Grennan)
Grenville Cres. CH63: Brom 4A 36
Grenville Dr. CH61: Pens 6A 26
Grenville Rd. CH42: Tran 4B 22
CH64: Nest 4C 38
Grenville St. Sth. L1: Liv 5F 15
Grenville Way CH42: Tran 4B 22
Gresford Av. CH43: Pren 5E 21
CH48: W Kir 4E 17
Greystoke Cl. CH49: Upton 3F 19
Greystones CH66: Gt Sut 3D 48
Grey St. L8: Liv 1H 23
Griffin Av. CH46: More 5E 11
Griffiths Cl. CH49: Grea 4C 18
Griffiths St. L1: Liv 5G 15
Grimshaw St. L20: Boot 1D 6
Grindley Gdns. CH65: Ell P 5A 50
Grinshill Cl. L8: Liv 1H 23
Grisedale Rd. CH62: Brom 3D 36
Grosvenor Av. CH48: W Kir 5D 16
Grosvenor Ct. CH43: Oxton 2F 21
CH47: Hoy 1D 16
Grosvenor Dr. CH45: New B 3F 5
Grosvenor Pl. CH43: Oxton 2E 21
Grosvenor Rd. CH43: Oxton 1E 21
CH45: New B 3F 5
CH47: Hoy 1D 16
L4: Walt 1H 7
Grosvenor St. CH44: Wall 6F 5
L3: Liv 2F 15
Grosvenor Wharf Rd.
CH65: Ell P 2H 43
Grove, The CH43: Oxton 4F 21
CH44: Wall 2G 13
CH63: Beb 4G 29
Grove Av. CH60: Hesw 2B 32
Grovedale Dr. CH46: More 4G 11
Groveland Av. CH45: Wall 5B 4
CH47: Hoy 6D 8
Groveland Rd. CH45: Wall 5B 4
Grovelands *L7: Liv 5H 15*
(off Falkner St.)
Grove Pl. CH47: Hoy 6D 8
L4: Kirkd 4G 7
Grove Rd. CH42: Rock F 5B 22
CH45: Wall 5C 4
CH47: Hoy 6D 8
Groves, The CH43: Oxton 2F 21
CH66: Whit 6B 48
L7: Liv 5H 15
(off Grove St.)
Groveside CH48: W Kir 5C 16
L7: Liv 5H 15
Grove Sq. CH62: New F 2G 29
Grove St. CH62: New F 2H 29
L7: Liv 5H 15
Grove Ter. CH47: Hoy 6D 8
Grove Way L7: Liv 5H 15
Grovewood Ct. CH43: Oxton 4F 21
Grundy St. L5: Kirkd 5D 6
Guardian Ct. CH48: W Kir 6D 16
Guernsey Dr. CH65: Ell P 6A 50
Guffitts Cl. CH47: Meols 4G 9
Guffitt's Rake CH47: Meols 4G 9
Guildford St. CH44: Wall 1H 13
Guinea Gap CH44: Wall 2A 14
Guinea Gap Baths & Recreation Cen.
. . . . 2A 14
Gulls Way CH60: Hesw 3H 31
Gunn Gro. CH64: Nest 5D 38
Gurnall St. L4: Walt 4H 7
Guy Cl. CH41: Tran 3A 22
Gwendoline Cl.
CH61: Thing 4C 26
Gwendoline St. L8: Liv 1H 23
Gwent St. L8: Liv 1H 23
Gwladys St. L4: Walt 2H 7
Gwydir St. L8: Liv 2H 23
Gym, The 4E 15
(off One Park W.)

H

Hackins Hey L2: Liv 3E 15
Hackthorpe St. L5: Liv 4G 7
Haddock St. L20: Kirkd 2D 6
Haddon Dr. CH61: Pens 5B 26
Haddon Ho. *CH64: Nest 5C 38*
(off Churchill Way)
Haddon La. CH64: Ness 3F 45
(not continuous)
Haddon Rd. CH42: Rock F 5C 22
Hadfield Av. CH47: Hoy 6E 9
Hadley Av. CH62: Brom 2A 36
Hadlow La. CH64: Will 6B 40
Hadlow Rd. CH64: Will 2B 46
Hadlow Road Station Mus. 6C 40
Hadlow Ter. CH64: Will 6B 40
Hahnemann Rd. L4: Walt 1G 7
Haig Av. CH46: More 5F 11
Haigh St. L3: Liv 1H 15
(not continuous)
Halcyon Rd. CH41: Birke 3G 21
Haldane Av. CH41: Birke 6D 12
Haldane Rd. L4: Walt 1H 7
Hale Rd. CH45: Wall 5G 5
L4: Walt 2G 7
Hale St. L2: Liv 3E 15
Half Crown St. L5: Kirkd 5E 7
Half-Tide Wharf L3: Liv 6E 15
Halkyn Dr. L5: Liv 6H 7
Hall Dr. CH49: Grea 4C 18
Hallfield Pk. CH66: Gt Sut 3D 48
Hallville Rd. CH44: Wall 2G 13
Hallwood Ct. CH64: Nest 6C 38
Hallwood Dr. CH66: Led 3F 47
Hallwood Wlk. CH65: Ell P 6H 43
Halsall Grn. CH63: Spit 2H 35
Halsbury Rd. CH45: Wall 5F 5
Halstead Rd. CH44: Wall 2G 13
Halton Cres. CH49: Grea 4B 18
CH66: Gt Sut 5F 49
Halton Rd. CH45: Wall 5E 5
CH66: Gt Sut 6E 49
Halton Way CH66: Gt Sut 6E 49
Hambledon Cl.
CH66: Lit Sut 1A 48
Hambledon Dr. CH49: Grea 3C 18
Hamil Cl. CH47: Meols 4G 9
Hamilton Cl. CH64: Park 3A 38
Hamilton Ct. CH64: Nest 5D 38
Hamilton Ho. *L3: Liv 3E 15*
(off Pall Mall)
Hamilton La. CH41: Birke 6A 14
Hamilton Plaza *CH41: Birke 1B 22*
(off Duncan St.)
Hamilton Rd. CH45: New B 3E 5
L5: Liv 6H 7
Hamilton Sq. CH41: Birke 6B 14
Hamilton Square Station (Rail)
. . . . 6B 14
Hamilton St. CH41: Birke 1A 22
(not continuous)
Hamlet Rd. CH45: Wall 5D 4
Hampden Gro. CH42: Tran 3A 22
Hampden Rd. CH42: Tran 3H 21
Hampden St. L4: Walt 1H 7
Hampstead Rd. CH44: Wall 2G 13

Hampton Chase—Hillside Dr.

Hampton Chase CH43: Noct . . . 4B 20
Hampton Cl. CH64: Nest 1C 44
Hampton Cres. CH64: Nest . . . 1C 44
Hampton Gdns. CH65: Ell P . . . 2G 49
Hampton St. L8: Liv 6H 15
Handa Dr. CH65: Ell P 6H 49
Handfield Pl. L5: Liv 6H 7
Handfield St. L5: Liv 6H 7
Handford Av. CH62: East 6D 36
Hankin St. L5: Liv 6F 7
Hannah Cl. CH61: Pens 6A 26
Hanns Hall Rd.
CH64: Nest, Will 5G 39
Hanover Cl. CH43: Clau 1D 20
Hanover St. L1: Liv 4F 15
Hanson Pk. CH43: Oxton 2C 20
Hans Rd. L4: Walt 2H 7
Hapton St. L5: Liv 5G 7
Harborne Dr. CH63: Spit 1F 35
Harcourt Av. CH44: Wall 2A 14
Harcourt St. CH41: Birke 6G 13
L4: Kirkd 4F 7
Hardie Av. CH46: More 4C 10
Harding Av. CH63: Beb 5F 29
Hardknott Rd. CH62: Brom 2C 36
Hardman St. L1: Liv 5G 15
Hardy Cl. CH66: Gt Sut 4F 49
Hardy St. L1: Liv 6G 15
(not continuous)
Harebell St. L5: Kirkd 4F 7
Harewood Av. CH66: Gt Sut . . . 3B 48
Harewood Rd. CH45: New B 4E 5
Harfield Gdns. CH66: Lit Sut . . . 2C 48
Hargrave Av. CH43: Oxton 4C 20
Hargrave Cl. CH43: Oxton 4C 20
Hargrave Dr. CH66: Gt Sut 2E 49
Hargrave La. CH64: Will 6F 35
Harker St. L3: Liv 2G 15
Harland Rd. CH42: Tran 3H 21
Harlech Ct. CH63: Beb 5F 29
CH65: Ell P 4B 50
Harlech St. CH44: Wall 3A 14
L4: Kirkd, Walt 2G 7
Harlech Way CH65: Ell P 4B 50
Harley Av. CH63: Hghr B 1C 28
Harlian Av. CH46: More 6D 10
Harlow St. L8: Liv 3G 23
Harn, The CH66: Gt Sut 4C 48
Harper St. L6: Liv 3H 15
Harpur Cl. CH66: Gt Sut 3D 48
Harrington Av. CH47: Hoy 6E 9
Harrington Rd. L3: Liv 3G 23
Harrington St. L2: Liv 4E 15
(not continuous)
Harrington Vw. *CH44: Wall 6H 5*
(off Greenwood La.)
Harris Cl. CH63: Spit 1G 35
Harrison Dr. CH45: Wall 4B 4
Harrisons Ter. CH66: Lit Sut . . . 1C 48
Harrison's Yd. CH62: East 5D 36
Harrison Way L3: Liv 3G 23
Harrock Wood Cl.
CH61: Irby 3A 26
Harrogate Cl. CH62: East 1F 41
Harrogate Dr. L5: Liv 6H 7
Harrogate Rd. CH42: Rock F . . . 1G 29
CH62: East 1F 41
Harrogate Wlk.
CH42: Rock F 1G 29
Harrowby Rd. CH42: Tran 3G 21
CH44: Wall 1A 14
Harrowby Rd. Sth.
CH42: Tran 3G 21
Harrowby St. L8: Liv 6H 15
Harrow Cl. CH44: Wall 6D 4
Harrow Gro. CH62: Brom 3C 36
Harrow Rd. CH44: Wall 6D 4
CH65: Ell P 3B 50
Hartford Cl. CH43: Oxton 4D 20
Hartford Dr. CH65: Whit 3F 49
Harthill M. CH43: Bid 4A 12
Hartington Av. CH41: Birke 6F 13
Hartington Rd. CH44: Wall 1F 13
Hartismere Rd. CH44: Wall . . . 2H 13
Hartley Cl. L4: Walt 4H 7
Hartley Quay L3: Liv 5E 15
Hartnup St. L5: Liv 5H 7
(Herschell St.)
L5: Liv 5H 7
(Towson St.)
Hartnup Way CH43: Bid 6A 12
Hartor Cl. L5: Liv 5G 7
(not continuous)
Hart St. L3: Liv 3G 15
Harvest Ct. CH46: More 4E 11
Harvester Way CH49: Grea 3C 18
Harvest La. CH46: More 4D 10
Harvey Av. CH49: Grea 4D 18
Harvey Rd. CH45: Wall 5E 5
CH46: Leas 3G 11
Hassal Rd. CH42: Rock F 1G 29
Hatchmere Cl. CH43: Oxton . . . 4D 20
Hatherley St. CH44: Wall 3A 14
L8: Liv 6H 15
Hatton Av. CH62: East 2G 41
Hatton Cl. CH60: Hesw 2H 31
Hatton Gdn. L3: Liv 3E 15
Hatton Gdn. Ind. Est.
L3: Liv 3E 15
(off Johnson St.)
Hawarden Av. CH43: Oxton . . . 1G 21
CH44: Wall 1G 13
Hawarden Ct. CH63: Beb 5F 29
Hawarden Gdns.
CH65: Ell P 5B 50
Hawick Cl. CH66: Lit Sut 2A 48
Hawke St. L3: Liv 4G 15
Hawkhurst Cl. L8: Liv 3H 23
Hawkhurst Dr.
CH42: Rock F 6C 22
Hawkins Rd. CH64: Nest 4C 38
Hawkshead Rd.
CH62: Brom 2C 36
Hawksmore Cl.
CH49: Upton 1D 18
Hawks Way CH60: Hesw 3A 32
Hawthorn Dr. CH48: W Kir 5G 17
CH61: Hesw 6B 26
Hawthorne Dr. CH64: Will 4D 40
Hawthorne Gro. CH44: Wall . . . 3A 14
Hawthorne Rd. CH42: Tran 4H 21
L20: Boot 1F 7
Hawthornes, The
CH42: Rock F 6C 22
Hawthorn La. CH62: Brom 3B 36
Hawthorn Rd. CH64: Park 3A 38
CH66: Lit Sut 1C 48
Hawthorns, The CH66: Ell P . . . 6F 43
Haycroft Cl. CH66: Gt Sut 5D 48
Haydock Rd. CH45: Wall 4G 5
Hayfield Pl. CH46: More 5G 11
Hayfield St. L4: Walt 4H 7
Haylock Cl. L8: Liv 3H 23
Hazel Cl. CH66: Gt Sut 6F 49
Hazel Ct. *L8: Liv 3H 23*
(off Byles St.)
L20: Boot 1E 7
Hazeldene Av. CH45: Wall 6E 5
CH61: Thing 3D 26
Hazeldene Way
CH61: Thing 3D 26
Hazel Gro. CH61: Irby 2H 25
CH63: Hghr B 5E 29
Hazel Rd. CH41: Birke 2H 21
CH47: Hoy 6E 9
Hazelwood CH49: Grea 2D 18
Headington Rd.
CH49: Upton 2D 18
Headland Cl. CH48: W Kir 6D 16
Head St. L8: Liv 1G 23
Hearts Health Club
Wallasey 1E 13
(off Wallasey Rd.)
Heath Av. CH65: Whit 6G 49
Heathbank Av. CH44: Wall 2E 13
CH61: Irby 2G 25
Heathbank Rd. CH42: Tran 4H 21
Heath Cl. CH48: W Kir 1A 24
Heathcote Gdns. CH63: Beb . . . 4F 29
Heathcote Rd. L4: Walt 1H 7
Heath Ct. CH66: Lit Sut 6B 42
Heathdale CH63: Beb 6F 29
Heath Dr. CH49: Upton 2G 19
CH60: Hesw 2B 32
Heather Bank CH63: Hghr B . . . 3D 28
Heather Brow CH43: Clau 6D 12
Heather Cl. CH66: Gt Sut 4E 49
L4: Walt 3H 7
Heather Ct. *L4: Walt 3H 7*
(off Tetlow St.)
Heatherdale Cl. CH42: Tran . . . 3G 21
Heather Dene CH62: Brom 6B 30
Heatherdene Rd.
CH48: W Kir 4D 16
Heatherfield Ct. *CH42: Tran . . . 3G 21*
(off Victoria Flds.)
Heatherleigh CH48: Caldy 3B 24
Heather Rd. CH60: Hesw 2C 32
CH63: Hghr B 5D 28
Heathfield CH62: Brom 1B 36
Heathfield Ct. CH65: Ell P 2H 49
Heathfield Ho. CH61: Thing . . . 3C 26
Heathfield Rd. CH43: Oxton . . . 3G 21
CH63: Beb 4F 29
CH65: Ell P 2H 49
Heathfield St. L1: Liv 4G 15
(not continuous)
Heath Gro. CH66: Lit Sut 6B 42
Heathlands, The
CH46: Leas 1E 11
Heathlands Rd.
CH66: Lit Sut 1B 48
Heath La. CH64: Will 4E 41
CH66: Chil T, Lit Sut 6F 41
Heathmoor Rd. CH46: More . . . 4D 10
Heath Rd.
CH63: Beb, Hghr B 4E 29
Heathside CH60: Hesw 2G 31
Heathway CH60: Hesw 4D 32
Heatley Cl. CH43: Bid 6A 12
Helena St. CH41: Birke 2A 22
L9: Walt 1H 7
Helen Ho. *L8: Liv 6H 15*
(off Birley Ct.)
Helmingham Gro.
CH41: Tran 3A 22
Helsby Av. CH62: East 2H 41
Helton Cl. CH43: Noct 4C 20
Hemingford Cl.
CH66: Gt Sut 4D 48
Hemingford St. CH41: Birke . . . 1H 21
Hemsworth Av.
CH66: Lit Sut 2C 48
Henderson Cl. CH49: Upton . . . 1D 18
Hendon Wlk. CH49: Grea 4C 18
Henglers Cl. L6: Liv 2H 15
Henley Cl. CH63: Spit 1G 35
CH64: Nest 1C 44
Henley Rd. CH64: Nest 1C 44
Henry Edward St. L3: Liv 2F 15
Henry St. CH41: Birke 1A 22
L1: Liv 5F 15
Henthorne Rd.
CH62: New F 1H 29
Henthorne St. CH43: Oxton . . . 2G 21
Herberts La. CH60: Hesw 3B 32
Herculaneum Ct. L8: Liv 4H 23
Herculaneum Rd. L8: Liv 3G 23
Hereford Av. CH49: Upton 1E 19
CH66: Gt Sut 6A 48
Heriot St. L5: Kirkd 5F 7
(not continuous)
Hermitage, The *CH60: Hesw . . . 4B 32*
(off School Hill)
Herm Rd. L5: Liv 6E 7
Heron Ct. CH64: Park 6A 38
Heronpark Way CH63: Spit 1H 35
Heron Rd. CH47: Meols 6H 9
CH48: W Kir 6H 9
Hero St. L20: Boot 1F 7
Herschell St. L5: Liv 5H 7
Hertford Dr. CH45: Wall 5G 5
Hertford Rd. L20: Boot 1E 7
Hesketh Av. CH42: Rock F 6H 21
Hesketh Dr. CH60: Hesw 2C 32
Hesketh Wlk. CH62: Brom 6A 30
Hesketh Way CH62: Brom 6A 30
Hessle Dr. CH60: Hesw 4B 32
Hesslewell Ct. CH60: Hesw . . . 2C 32
HESWALL 3C 32
Heswall Av. CH63: Hghr B 1C 28
Heswall Dales Local Nature Reserve
. . . . 2A 32
Heswall Mt. CH61: Thing 4C 26
Heswall Point CH60: Hesw 3C 32
Heswall Rd. CH66: Gt Sut 3D 48
Heswall Station (Rail) 3F 33
Hewitts Pl. *L2: Liv 3E 15*
(off Vernon St.)
Heyes Dr. CH45: Wall 1A 12
Heyes St. L5: Liv 6H 7
Heyfield Pk. Rd.
CH66: Lit Sut 6B 42
Heygarth Dr. CH49: Grea 3D 18
Heygarth Rd. CH62: East 6C 36
Heys, The CH62: East 6D 36
Heys Av. CH62: Brom 3B 36
Heythrop Dr. CH60: Hesw 3E 33
Heyville Rd. CH63: Hghr B 3E 29
Heywood Blvd. CH61: Thing . . . 3C 26
Heywood Cl. CH61: Thing 3C 26
Heywood Rd. CH66: Gt Sut 2C 48
Heyworth St. L5: Liv 6H 7
Hickmans Rd. CH41: Birke 4F 13
Highacre Rd. CH45: New B 4E 5
Higham Sq. L5: Liv 1G 15
High Bank Cl. CH43: Noct 2B 20
Highcroft, The CH63: Beb 4G 29
Highcroft Av. CH63: Beb 4G 29
Highcroft Grn. CH63: Beb 4G 29
HIGHER BEBINGTON 2D 28
Higher Bebington Rd.
CH63: Hghr B 3D 28
Highfield Cl. CH44: Wall 2E 13
CH64: Nest 5C 38
Highfield Cres.
CH42: Rock F 6B 22
Highfield Dr. CH49: Grea 3D 18
Highfield Gdns. CH43: Clau . . . 1D 20
Highfield Gro.
CH42: Rock F 6B 22
Highfield Rd. CH42: Rock F . . . 5B 22
CH64: Nest 5C 38
CH65: Ell P 2A 50
CH66: Lit Sut 1B 48
Highfield Rd. Nth.
CH65: Ell P 1A 50
Highfields CH60: Hesw 2B 32
Highfield Sth. CH42: Rock F . . . 2F 29
Highfield St. L3: Liv 2E 15
(not continuous)
Highgate Cl. CH60: Hesw 1B 32
Highgreen Rd. CH42: Tran 4G 21
High Mt. CH60: Hesw 3B 32
Highpark Rd. CH42: Tran 4G 21
High Pk. St. L8: Liv 2H 23
High St. CH62: Brom 2C 36
CH64: Nest 5C 38
L2: Liv 3E 15
Higson Ct. L8: Liv 4H 23
Hilary Dr. CH49: Upton 1G 19
Hilary Mans. *CH44: Wall 1E 13*
(off Colville Rd.)
Hilbre Av. CH44: Wall 1E 13
CH60: Hesw 5A 32
Hilbre Ct. CH48: W Kir 6C 16
Hilbre Dr. CH65: Ell P 6A 50
Hilbre Rd. CH48: W Kir 6D 16
Hilbre St. CH41: Birke 5H 13
L3: Liv 4G 15
Hilbre Vw. CH48: W Kir 5E 17
Hillaby Cl. L8: Liv 1H 23
Hillam Rd. CH45: Wall 5B 4
Hillary Rd. CH62: East 6B 36
Hill Bark Rd. CH48: Frank 5A 18
Hillburn Dr. CH41: Birke 4C 12
Hill Cl. CH64: Ness 2F 45
Hill Ct. CH64: Ness 2F 45
Hill Crest L20: Boot 1G 7
Hillcrest Ct. CH44: Wall 2E 13
Hillcrest Dr. CH49: Grea 4C 18
CH66: Lit Sut 1A 48
Hillcrest Rd.
CH66: Lit Sut 1B 48
Hillcroft Rd. CH44: Wall 2G 13
Hillfield Dr. CH61: Hesw 1B 32
Hillfield Rd. CH66: Lit Sut 6D 42
Hillfoot Cl. CH43: Bid 5A 12
Hill Gro. CH46: More 6E 11
Hillhead Rd. L20: Boot 1G 7
Hillingdon Av.
CH61: Hesw 1B 32
Hill Ridge CH43: Noct 2B 20
Hill Rd. CH43: Clau 6C 12
Hillsdown Way
CH66: Gt Sut 5C 48
Hillside Cl. CH41: Tran 3A 22
L20: Boot 1G 7
Hillside Ct. CH41: Tran 3A 22
Hillside Dr. CH66: Ell P 5E 43

Hillside Rd. CH41: Tran 3A 22
  CH43: Bid 5B 12
  CH44: Wall 1C 12
  CH48: W Kir 5F 17
  CH60: Hesw 4C 32
Hillside St. L6: Liv 2H 15
Hillside Vw. CH43: Oxton 4E 21
Hillsmore Way L5: Liv 5H 7
Hill St. L8: Liv 1F 23
  (not continuous)
Hill St. Bus. Cen. L8: Liv 1F 23
  (off Hill St.)
Hill Top La. CH64: Ness 2F 45
Hilltop La. CH60: Hesw 3D 32
Hillview Av. CH48: W Kir 4D 16
Hillview Cl. CH43: Bid 4A 12
Hill Vw. Dr. CH49: Upton 1G 19
Hillview Rd. CH61: Irby 2G 25
Hillwood Cl. CH63: Spit 2G 35
Hilton Cl. CH41: Birke 1G 21
Hilton Gro. CH48: W Kir 4C 16
Himalayan Birch Cl.
  CH66: Ell P 1E 49
HINDERTON 4F 39
Hinderton Cl. CH41: Birke 3A 22
Hinderton Dr. CH48: W Kir . . .6G 17
  CH60: Hesw 5B 32
Hinderton Grn. CH64: Nest . . .5D 38
Hinderton La. CH64: Nest 4E 39
Hinderton Rd. CH41: Birke . . .2A 22
  CH64: Nest 5D 38
Hind St. CH41: Birke 2A 22
Hinson St. CH41: Birke 1A 22
Hobhouse Ct. CH43: Clau 1F 21
Hoblyn Rd. CH43: Bid 5C 12
Hockenhall All. L2: Liv 3E 15
Hockenhull Cl. CH63: Spit 1G 35
Hodder Rd. L5: Liv 5H 7
Hodder St. L5: Liv 5H 7
Hodson Pl. L6: Liv 1H 15
Hogarth Dr. CH43: Noct 4B 20
Hogarth Wlk. L4: Kirkd 3F 7
Holborn Hill CH41: Tran 3A 22
Holborn Sq. CH41: Tran 3A 22
Holborn Sq. Ind. Est.
  CH41: Tran 3A 22
Holborn St. L6: Liv 3H 15
Holcombe Cl. CH49: Grea 3D 18
Holland Gro. CH60: Hesw 2B 32
Holland Rd. CH45: Wall 4G 5
Holly Av. CH63: Beb 6F 29
Hollybank Cl. CH41: Birke 2H 21
Hollybank Rd. CH41: Birke . . .2H 21
Hollyfield Rd. CH65: Ell P 1H 49
Hollygro. CH42: Tran 3A 22
Hollyhurst Cl. L8: Liv 2H 23
Holly Pl. CH46: More 6F 11
Holly Rd. CH65: Ell P 2A 50
Holm Cotts. CH43: Oxton 5D 20
Holmes Ct. CH42: Tran 4G 21
Holme St. L5: Kirkd 5E 7
Holmesway CH61: Pens 5B 26
Holmfield CH43: Oxton 5D 20
Holmfield Dr. CH66: Gt Sut . . .4D 48
Holm Hey Rd. CH43: Pren 5D 20
Holm Hill CH48: W Kir 6E 17
Holmlands Cres.
  CH43: Oxton 5C 20
Holmlands Dr. CH43: Oxton . . .5C 20
Holmlands Way
  CH43: Oxton 5D 20
Holm La. CH43: Oxton 5D 20
Holm Oak Way
  CH66: Gt Sut 6A 48
Holmside Cl. CH46: More 5F 11
Holmside La. CH43: Oxton . . .5D 20
Holm Vw. Cl. CH43: Oxton . . .4E 21
Holmville Rd.
  CH63: Hghr B 4E 29
Holmway CH63: Hghr B 4F 29
Holmwood Av. CH61: Thing . . .4E 27
Holmwood Dr. CH61: Thing . . .4E 27
  CH65: Whit 4H 49
Holmwood Gdns.
  CH48: W Kir 6G 17
Holt Av. CH46: More 5E 11
Holt Hey CH64: Ness 2E 45
Holt Hill CH41: Birke 3A 22
Holt Hill Ter. CH42: Tran 2A 22
Holt Rd. CH41: Tran 3A 22

Holy Cross Cl. L3: Liv 2F 15
Holywell Cl. CH64: Park 4A 38
Homecrofts CH64: Lit N 2C 44
Home Farm Cl.
  CH49: Woodc 5A 20
Home Farm Rd.
  CH49: Woodc 5H 19
Homerton Cl. CH65: Ell P 3B 50
Homestead M. CH48: W Kir . . .5D 16
Honeysuckle Cl.
  CH66: Gt Sut 6A 48
Hood St. CH44: Wall 2H 13
  L1: Liv 3F 15
Hookstone Dr. CH66: Lit Sut . .1C 48
Hoole Rd. CH49: Woodc 4H 19
Hoose Ct. CH47: Hoy 6E 9
Hope Cotts. CH66: Chil T 5A 42
  (off New Rd.)
Hope Cft. CH66: Gt Sut 5F 49
Hope Farm Pct.
  CH66: Gt Sut 5F 49
Hope Farm Rd.
  CH66: Gt Sut 6E 49
Hope Pl. L1: Liv 5G 15
Hope St. CH41: Birke 6H 13
  CH45: New B 3F 5
  L1: Liv 5H 15
Hope Way L8: Liv 5H 15
Hopfield Rd. CH46: More 5F 11
Hopwood St. L5: Liv 6F 7
Horace Black Gdns.
  CH65: Ell P 1A 50
Horatio St. CH41: Birke 1H 21
Horbury Gdns.
  CH66: Lit Sut 2C 48
Hornbeam Av. CH66: Gt Sut . .6F 49
Hornbeam Cl. CH46: More 5B 10
Hornby Av. CH62: Brom 2A 36
Hornby Rd. CH62: Brom 2B 36
Hornby St. CH41: Birke 1B 22
Hornby Wlk. L5: Liv 1E 15
Hornet Cl. L6: Liv 6H 7
Horseman Pl. CH44: Wall 3A 14
Horsfall Gro. L8: Liv 3G 23
Horsfall St. L8: Liv 3G 23
Horstone Cres.
  CH66: Gt Sut 5F 49
Horstone Gdns.
  CH66: Gt Sut 5G 49
Horstone Rd. CH66: Gt Sut . . .5F 49
Hoscote Pk. CH48: W Kir 5C 16
Hose Side Rd. CH45: Wall 4E 5
Hotham St. L3: Liv 3G 15
Hothfield Rd. CH44: Wall 2H 13
Hotspur St. L20: Boot 3E 7
Houghton La. L1: Liv 4F 15
Houghton Rd.
  CH49: Woodc 3H 19
Houghton St. L1: Liv 4F 15
Houghton Way L1: Liv 4F 15
  (off St John's Cen.)
Houlgrave Rd. L5: Liv 6E 7
Hourd Way CH66: Gt Sut 6A 48
Howard Av. CH62: Brom 2A 36
Howard Ct. CH64: Nest 4D 38
Howards Rd. CH61: Thing 3D 26
Howards Way CH64: Lit N 1E 45
Howbeck Cl. CH43: Clau 1D 20
Howbeck Ct. CH43: Oxton 2D 20
Howbeck Dr. CH43: Clau 1D 20
Howbeck Rd. CH43: Oxton . . .2D 20
Howell Dr. CH49: Grea 5D 18
Howell Rd. CH62: New F 2G 29
Howells Av. CH66: Gt Sut 4C 48
Howe St. L20: Boot 2D 6
Howgill Cl. CH66: Lit Sut 1H 47

Howson St. CH42: Rock F 5B 22
HOYLAKE 6D 8
Hoylake Rd. CH41: Birke 3B 12
  CH46: More 6B 10
Hoylake Station (Rail) 1D 16
Hoyle Ct. Rd. CH47: Hoy 5D 8
Hoyle Rd. CH47: Hoy 5D 8
Huddleston Cl.
  CH49: Woodc 4H 19
Hudson Pl. CH49: Upton 1E 19
Hudson Rd. CH46: Leas 1G 11
Hughes La. CH43: Oxton 4F 21
Hughson St. L8: Liv 2G 23
Hulme Cl. CH62: Brom 5A 30
Hulme Wlk. CH62: Brom 5A 30
Hulmewood CH63: Beb 2G 29
Humber Cl. L4: Kirkd 3G 7
Humber Rd. CH66: Gt Sut 5F 49
Humber St. CH41: Birke 4D 12
Hume Ct. CH47: Meols 5E 9
Hunstanton Cl.
  CH49: Upton 6G 11
Hunter St. L3: Liv 3F 15
Hunters Way CH64: Park 5A 38
Huntington Cl. CH46: More . . .5B 10
Hurford Av. CH65: Gt Sut 4D 48
Hurrell Rd. CH41: Birke 4B 12
Hurst Bank CH42: Rock F 1F 29
Hurst St. L1: Liv 5G 15
Huskisson St. L8: Liv 6H 15
Hutchinson Cl. CH43: Bid 1H 19
Huxley Cl. CH46: More 5B 10
Huxley Ct. CH66: Ell P 5F 43
Hyacinth Gro. CH46: More 3G 11
Hyde Cl. CH65: Gt Sut 3A 49
Hydro Av. CH48: W Kir 6D 16
Hylton Av. CH44: Wall 1E 13
Hylton Ct. CH65: Ell P 5C 50
Hyslop St. L8: Liv 1G 23

Iffley Cl. CH49: Upton 2D 18
Ikin Cl. CH43: Bid 4A 12
Ilchester Rd. CH41: Birke 4D 12
  CH44: Wall 2H 13
Ilford Av. CH44: Wall 3F 13
Ilford St. L3: Liv 3H 15
Iliad St. L5: Liv 1G 15
Ilsley Cl. CH49: Upton 3F 19
Imison St. L9: Walt 1H 7
Imison Way L9: Walt 1G 7
Imperial Av. CH45: Wall 5G 5
Imperial Chambers L1: Liv 3E 15
  (off Davies St.)
Imperial Ct. L2: Liv 3E 15
  (off Exchange St. E.)
Imperial M. CH65: Ell P 1H 49
Imrie St. L4: Walt 1H 7
Ince Av. CH62: East 2G 41
Ince Cl. CH43: Oxton 3D 20
Ince Gro. CH43: Oxton 3D 20
Inchcape Rd. CH45: Wall 6B 4
Index St. L4: Walt 2H 7
Indigo Rd. CH65: Ell P 2D 50
Ingestre Ct. CH43: Oxton 4E 21
Ingestre Rd. CH43: Oxton 4E 21
Ingleborough Rd.
  CH42: Tran 5H 21
Ingleby Rd. CH44: Wall 2E 13
  CH62: New F 1H 29
Inglefield Ct. CH42: Rock F 6C 22
  (off The Hawthornes)
Inglegreen CH60: Hesw 3D 32
Inglemere Rd.
  CH42: Rock F 5A 22
Ingleton Cl. CH49: Grea 3D 18
Inglewood Av. CH46: More 6D 10
Inley Cl. CH63: Spit 1G 35
Inley Rd. CH63: Spit 1F 35
Inman Rd. CH49: Upton 1E 19
Innisfree Cl. CH66: Gt Sut 2C 48
Intake Cl. CH64: Will 5C 40
International Slavery Mus. . . .5E 15
Inverisk Ct. CH43: Noct 1C 20
Inward Way CH65: Ell P 6H 43
Ionic Ct. CH42: Rock F 5B 22
IRBY 3H 25
Irby Av. CH44: Wall 1E 13

Irby Cl. CH66: Gt Sut 3E 49
IRBY HEATH 3G 25
IRBY HILL 1G 25
Irby Rd.
  CH61: Hesw, Irby, Pens
   . . . . .4H 25
Irbyside Rd. CH48: Frank 6B 18
Ireton St. L4: Walt 1H 7
Iris Av. CH41: Birke 5D 12
Irlam Ho. L20: Boot 1D 6
  (off Church Wlk.)
Irlam Rd. L20: Boot 1D 6
Ironbridge Vw. L8: Liv 3H 23
Irvine Rd. CH42: Tran 5H 21
Irvine Ter. CH62: New F 1A 30
Irwell Chambers L3: Liv 3E 15
  (off Fazakerley St.)
Irwell Cl. L3: Liv 4E 15
Irwell St. L3: Liv 3H 23
Isaac St. L8: Liv 3H 23
Islay Cl. CH65: Ell P 6A 50
Islington L3: Liv 3G 15
Islington Sq. L3: Liv 2H 15
Islip Cl. CH61: Irby 2H 25
Ismay Dr. CH44: Wall 6H 5
Ismay St. L4: Walt 2H 7
Ivanhoe Rd. CH44: Wall 6G 5
Ivy Av. CH63: Hghr B 4E 29
Ivydale Rd. CH42: Tran 4A 22
Ivy Farm Dr. CH64: Lit N 1D 44
Ivy La. CH46: More 3E 11
Ivy St. CH41: Birke 1B 22

J

Jack McBain Ct. L3: Liv 1E 15
Jackson Cl. CH63: Hghr B 1F 29
Jackson St. CH41: Birke 2A 22
Jacks Wood Av. CH65: Ell P . . .6H 43
Jacks Wood Grn.
  CH65: Ell P 1H 49
Jacob St. L8: Liv 3H 23
Jamaica St. L1: Liv 6F 15
James Av. CH66: Gt Sut 4C 48
Jamesbrook Cl.
  CH41: Birke 5E 13
James Clarke St. L5: Liv 1E 15
James Dunne Av. L5: Liv 6E 7
James Hopkins Way
  L4: Kirkd 4F 7
James Larkin Way L4: Kirkd . . .4F 7
James St. CH43: Oxton 3G 21
  CH44: Wall 3A 14
  L2: Liv 4E 15
James Street Station (Rail)
   . . . . .4E 15
Jarrow Cl. CH43: Oxton 3F 21
Jasmine Cl. CH49: Upton 6D 10
  L5: Liv 1H 15
Jasmine M. L17: Aig 4H 23
Jason St. L5: Liv 5G 7
Jason Wlk. L5: Liv 5G 7
Jedburgh Av.
  CH66: Lit Sut 1H 47
Jeffreys Dr. CH49: Grea 2D 18
Jellicoe Cl. CH48: Caldy 3B 24
Jenkinson St. L3: Liv 2G 15
Jenner Dr. CH46: Leas 3G 11
Jersey Av. CH65: Ell P 6A 50
Jessamine Rd. CH42: Tran 4A 22
Jessop Ct. CH66: Lit Sut 1C 48
  (off Black Lion La.)
Joan Av. CH46: More 5D 10
  CH49: Grea 3E 19
Joan Bartlett Cl. CH65: Ell P . . .1F 49
Jocelyn Cl. CH63: Spit 6G 29
John Bagot Cl. L5: Liv 6G 7
John Lennon Statue 4E 15
  (off Mathew St.)
John Moores University
  Aquinas Building 4G 15
  Blackburne Pl. 5H 15
    (off Blackburne Pl.)
  Brownlow Hill 4G 15
  Dean Walters Building
   . . . . .5G 15
  Design Academy 4H 15
  Haigh Building 5G 15
    (off Maryland St.)
  Hope St. 5G 15

John Moores University
   Joe H Makin Drama Cen.
   . . . . .5G 15
     (off Hope Pl.)
Josephine Butler House
Mount Pleasant Campus
   . . . . .4G 15
     (off Rodney St.)
Mount St. 5G 15
     (off Rodney St.)
Myrtle St. 5H 15
Rice St. 5H 15
Roscoe St. 5G 15
     (off Rodney St.)
John Nicholas Cres.
  CH65: Ell P 1A 50
Johnson Rd. CH43: Pren . . .6D 20
Johnson St. L3: Liv 3F 15
John St. CH41: Birke 6B 14
  CH65: Ell P 1H 49
  L3: Liv 2G 15
John Willis Ho.
  CH42: Rock F 5C 22
John Yeoman Cl.
  CH64: Lit N 4C 38
Jonson Rd. CH64: Nest . . .4C 38
Jordan St. L1: Liv 6F 15
Joseph Groome Towers
  CH65: Ell P 1A 50
Josephine Butler Sq.
  L6: Liv 2H 15
     (off Shaw St.)
Joshua Cl. L5: Liv 5G 7
Jubilee Cres.
  CH62: Port S 4H 29
Jubilee Dr. CH48: W Kir . . .3C 16
Jubilee Grn. CH65: Ell P . .3A 50
Jugglers Yd. L3: Liv 2E 15
     (off Marlborough St.)
Juliet Av. CH63: Hghr B . . .2E 29
Junction Eight Bus. Cen.
  CH65: Ell P 1G 49
Junction One Retail Pk.
  CH44: Wall 2B 12
June Av. CH62: Brom 3C 36
Juniper Cl. CH49: Grea . . .5C 18
Juniper Dr. CH66: Gt Sut . .6E 49
Juniper Gro. CH66: Gt Sut . .6F 49
Juniper St. L20: Kirkd 3E 7
Juvenal Pl. L3: Liv 1G 15
Juvenal St. L3: Liv 2F 15

K

Kaber Ct. L8: Liv 3G 23
Kale Cl. CH48: W Kir 6D 16
Karen Way CH66: Gt Sut . .4D 48
Karslake Rd. CH44: Wall . . .2H 13
Kearsley Cl. L4: Walt 4G 7
Kearsley St. L4: Walt 4G 7
Keats Cl. CH66: Gt Sut . . .6A 48
Keble Dr. CH45: Wall 5B 4
Keble Rd. L20: Boot 2E 7
Keegan Dr. CH44: Wall . . .3A 14
Keele Cl. CH43: Bid 3A 12
Keel Hey CH64: Will 4D 40
Keel Wharf L3: Liv 6E 15
Keepers La. CH63: Store . .4B 28
Keighley Av. CH45: Wall . . .6C 4
Keightley St. CH41: Birke . .6H 13
Keith Av. L4: Walt 2H 7
Keith Dr. CH63: East 6A 36
Kelby Cl. L8: Liv 3H 23
Kellet's Pl. CH42: Rock F . .4B 22
Kellett Rd. CH46: Leas . . .2H 11
Kelmscott Cl. CH66: Gt Sut . .5D 48
Kelmscott Dr. CH44: Wall . . .1C 12
Kelsall Av. CH62: East 2G 41
Kelsall Cl. CH43: Oxton . . .4D 20
  CH62: East 2G 41
Kelvin Cl. CH44: Wall 4A 14
Kelvin Pk. CH41: Birke 4A 14
Kelvin Rd. CH41: Tran 3A 22
  CH44: Wall 4A 14
Kelvinside CH44: Wall 4H 13
Kempson Ter. CH63: Beb . . .5F 29
Kempston St. L3: Liv 3G 15
Kempton Rd. CH62: New F . .1H 29

Kendal Cl. CH63: Beb 3F 29
  CH66: Gt Sut 5D 48
Kendal Dr. CH66: Gt Sut . . .5D 48
Kendal Rd. CH44: Wall 3E 13
Kendal St. CH41: Birke 1A 22
Kenilworth Ct. CH65: Ell P . .5C 50
Kenilworth Dr. CH61: Pens . .4A 26
Kenilworth Gdns.
  CH49: Upton 1E 19
Kenilworth Rd. CH44: Wall . .2H 13
  CH64: Nest 1C 44
Kenmore Rd. CH43: Pren . . .6C 20
Kennet Rd. CH63: Hghr B . . .4D 28
Kensington Gdns.
  CH46: More 5E 11
Kensington Rd. CH65: Ell P . .2G 49
Kent Cl. CH63: Brom 3H 35
Kentmere Dr. CH61: Pens . .6B 26
Kent M. CH43: Oxton 3F 21
     (off Kent St.)
Kentridge Dr. CH66: Gt Sut . .4D 48
Kent Rd. CH44: Wall 2E 13
Kent St. CH43: Oxton 3F 21
  L1: Liv 5E 15
Kenwick Cl. CH66: Gt Sut . . .4C 48
Kenwyn Rd. CH45: Wall 6F 5
Kenyon Ct. L8: Liv 1H 23
     (off Park Rd.)
Kenyons Steps L1: Liv 4F 15
     (off Paradise St.)
Kenyon Ter. CH43: Oxton . . .2F 21
Keppel St. L20: Boot 2D 6
Kerry Cft. CH66: Gt Sut 6E 49
Kestrel Av. CH49: Upton . . .1D 18
Kestrel Cl. CH49: Upton . . .1D 18
Kestrel Rd. CH46: More 4C 10
  CH60: Hesw 4E 33
Keswick Av. CH63: East . . .6A 36
Keswick Gdns. CH63: Brom . .6A 36
Keswick Pl. CH43: Bid 4C 4
Keswick Rd. CH45: Wall 4C 4
Kevelioc Cl. CH63: Spit 6F 29
Kew St. L5: Liv 6F 7
Keys Cl. L4: Walt 4F 15
Kiddman St. L9: Walt 1H 7
Kilburn Av. CH63: East 5C 36
Killarney Gro. CH44: Wall . . .2E 13
Killington Way L4: Kirkd . . .3G 7
Kilmalcolm Cl. CH43: Oxton . .3D 20
Kiln Rd. CH49: Woodc 4G 19
Kimberley Rd. CH45: Wall . . .5F 5
Kindale Rd. CH43: Pren 6C 20
Kinder St. L6: Liv 2H 15
King Edward Dr.
  CH62: Port S 3H 29
King Edward Ind. Est.
  L3: Liv 2D 14
     (off Gibraltar Row)
King Edward Pde. L3: Liv . . .3D 14
     (off Brook St.)
King Edward St. L3: Liv 3D 14
Kingfisher Ho. CH41: Birke . .1C 22
Kingfisher Way
  CH49: Upton 1D 18
King George Dr. CH44: Wall . .5H 5
King George's Dr.
  CH62: Port S 3H 29
King George's Way
  CH43: Bid 6C 12
Kingham Cl. CH46: Leas . . .2H 11
Kinglake Rd. CH44: Wall . . .1H 13
Kinglass Rd. CH63: Spit . . .6H 29
Kingsbrook Way
  CH63: Hghr B 1D 28
King's Brow CH63: Hghr B . .3D 28
Kingsbury CH48: W Kir 4F 17
Kings Cl. CH63: Hghr B 2D 28
Kings Ct. CH43: Oxton 3F 21
  CH47: Hoy 6C 8
  CH63: Hghr B 2D 28
Kingsdale Av. CH42: Tran . . .5H 21
Kings Dock St. L1: Liv 6F 15
Kingsdown St. CH41: Tran . .3A 22
King's Dr. CH8: Caldy 2A 24
  CH61: Pens 4B 26
King's Dr. Nth. CH48: W Kir . .6F 17
King's Gap, The CH47: Hoy . .6C 8
Kingsland Rd. CH42: Tran . .3G 21
King's La. CH63: Hghr B . . .2D 28

Kingsley Av. CH62: East 2G 41
Kingsley Cl. CH61: Pens 6C 26
Kingsley Rd. CH44: Wall 2F 13
  CH65: Ell P 2A 50
Kingsley St. CH41: Birke . . .5E 13
Kingsmead Gro.
  CH43: Oxton 2D 20
Kingsmead Rd.
  CH43: Oxton 2D 20
  CH46: More 3F 11
Kingsmead Rd. Nth.
  CH43: Oxton 2D 20
Kingsmead Rd. Sth.
  CH43: Oxton 2D 20
Kings M. CH66: Lit Sut 6C 42
Kings Mt. CH43: Oxton 3F 21
Kings Pde. CH45: New B 2E 5
  CH45: Wall, New B 3B 4
  L3: Liv 6E 15
Kings Rd. CH63: Hghr B . . .1D 28
  CH66: Lit Sut 6C 42
  L20: Boot 1E 7
Kings Sq. CH41: Birke 1B 22
Kings Ter. L20: Boot 2E 7
Kingston Cl. CH46: More 5E 11
King St. CH42: Rock F 6C 22
  CH44: Wall 6H 5
  CH65: Ell P 1A 50
Kingsville Rd.
  CH63: Hghr B 4E 29
Kings Wlk. CH47: Rock F . . .6C 22
  CH48: W Kir 5E 17
Kingsway CH45: Wall 5E 5
  CH60: Hesw 5E 33
  CH63: Hghr B 2D 28
  L3: Liv 2E 15
Kingsway Cl. L3: Liv 1F 15
Kingsway Pk. L3: Liv 1F 15
Kingsway Tunnel App.
  CH44: Wall 2C 12
Kings Wharf CH41: Birke . . .4B 14
Kingswood Blvd.
  CH63: Hghr B 1E 29
Kingswood Rd. CH44: Wall . .6G 5
Kington Rd. CH48: W Kir . . .4C 16
Kinloss Rd. CH49: Grea 4C 18
Kinmel Cl. CH41: Birke 6H 13
Kinnaird Rd. CH45: Wall 5E 5
Kinnerley Rd. CH65: Whit . . .4G 49
Kinnerton Cl. CH46: More . . .5B 10
Kinnington Way CH1: Back . .6A 48
Kinross Rd. CH45: Wall 5B 4
Kinsey Rd. CH65: Ell P 6B 50
Kintore Cl. CH63: East 1E 41
Kintyre Cl. CH65: Ell P 6A 50
Kipling Av. CH42: Rock F . . .6B 22
Kirby Cl. CH48: W Kir 6E 17
Kirby Mt. CH48: W Kir 1A 24
Kirby Pk. CH48: W Kir 6E 17
Kirby Pk. Mans.
  CH48: W Kir 6D 16
Kirkburn Cl. L8: Liv 3H 23
Kirk Cotts. CH45: Wall 4F 5
KIRKDALE 3G 7
Kirkdale Station (Rail) 2F 7
Kirkdale Va. L4: Walt 4G 7
Kirket Cl. CH63: Beb 5G 29
Kirket La. CH63: Beb 5F 29
Kirkfield Gro. CH42: Rock F . .6C 22
Kirkland Av. CH42: Tran 5H 21
Kirkland Rd. CH45: New B . . .3G 5
Kirklands, The CH48: W Kir . .6E 17
Kirkmount CH49: Upton 2G 19
Kirk St. L5: Liv 5G 7
Kirkway CH45: Wall 4F 5
  CH49: Grea 3E 19
  CH49: Upton 2F 19
  CH63: Hghr B 2D 28
Kitchen St. L1: Liv 5G 15
Knap, The CH60: Hesw 5C 32
Knaresborough Rd.
  CH44: Wall 1D 12
Knightsbridge Ct.
  CH43: Noct 4B 20
Knight St. L1: Liv 5G 15
Knoll, The CH43: Oxton . . .4E 21
Knottingley Dr.
  CH66: Gt Sut 2C 48
Knowe, The CH64: Will 5C 40

Knowle Cl. CH66: Gt Sut . . .4E 49
Knowles St. CH41: Birke . . .6G 13
Knowsley Cl. CH42: Rock F . .6C 22
Knowsley Ct. CH42: Rock F . .6C 22
Knowsley Rd. CH42: Rock F . .6C 22
  CH45: Wall 5E 5
Knowsley St. L4: Walt 1H 7
Knox Cl. CH62: Port S 3H 29
Knox St. CH41: Birke 1B 22
Knutsford Grn. CH46: More . .4F 11
Knutsford Rd. CH46: More . . .4E 11
Kronsbec Av. CH66: Lit Sut . .1D 48
Kylemore Av. CH61: Pens . . .6A 26
Kylemore Cl. CH61: Pens . . .6A 26
Kylemore Dr. CH61: Pens . . .6A 26
Kylemore Rd. CH43: Oxton . .3E 21
Kylemore Way CH61: Pens . .6A 26

L

Laburnum Farm Cl.
  CH64: Ness 2E 45
Laburnum Gro. CH61: Irby . .3H 25
  CH66: Whit 6B 48
Laburnum Rd. CH43: Oxton . .3G 21
  CH45: New B 4F 5
Lace St. L3: Liv 3F 15
Ladies Wlk. CH64: Nest 5C 38
Ladybower Cl. CH49: Upton . .1E 19
Lady Chapel Cl. L1: Liv . . .6G 15
Lady Chapel Sq. L1: Liv . . .6G 15
     (off Lady Chapel Cl.)
Ladyewood Rd. CH44: Wall . .2G 13
Ladyfield CH43: Bid 6A 12
Lady Lever Art Gallery 3H 29
Lagan Ho. CH46: Leas 1E 11
Laird Cl. CH41: Birke 5D 12
Lairdside Technical Pk.
  CH41: Tran 3B 22
Lairds Pl. L3: Liv 1F 15
Laird St. CH41: Birke 5D 12
Lake Ent. Pk. CH62: Brom . .1C 36
Lakeland Cl. L1: Liv 5F 15
Lake Pl. CH47: Hoy 6D 8
Lake Rd. CH47: Hoy 6D 8
Lakeside Cl. CH45: New B . . .3G 5
Lake St. L4: Walt 4H 7
Lambert St. L3: Liv 3G 15
     (Kempston St.)
  L3: Liv 3G 15
     (off Lambert Way)
Lambert Way L3: Liv 3G 15
Lambeth Rd. L4: Kirkd 4F 7
  L5: Kirkd 4F 7
Lambeth Wlk. L4: Kirkd 4F 7
     (not continuous)
Lambourne Cl.
  CH66: Gt Sut 6A 48
Lambrigg Row L5: Liv 4H 7
Lamport St. L8: Liv 1G 23
Lancaster Av. CH45: Wall . . .6F 5
Lancaster Cl. CH62: Port S . .3H 29
  L5: Kirkd 5F 7
Lancaster Gdns.
  CH65: Ell P 4B 50
Lancaster St. L5: Kirkd 5F 7
Lance Cl. L5: Liv 6H 7
Lancelots Hey L3: Liv 3D 14
     (off Union St.)
Lancelyn Ct. CH63: Spit . . .6G 29
Lancelyn Pct. CH63: Spit . . .6G 29
     (off Spital Rd.)
Lancelyn Ter. CH63: Beb . . .5F 29
Lancers Cft. CH66: Gt Sut . .6E 49
Lancing Rd. CH65: Ell P . . .3B 50
LANDICAN 1E 27
Landican Cemetery & Crematorium
  CH49: Woodc 6H 19
Landican La. CH49: Woodc . .6A 20
  CH63: Store 3G 27
Landican Rd. CH49: Woodc . .2D 26
Landor Cl. L5: Liv 6E 7
Landsdowne Ho.
  CH41: Birke 1C 22
Landseer Av. CH64: Lit N . . .6D 38
Landseer Rd. L5: Liv 6H 7
Langdale Av. CH61: Pens . . .5B 26
Langdale Cl. CH41: Birke . . .5F 13
Langdale Rd. CH45: Wall . . .4D 4
  CH63: Beb 5E 29

Langfield Gro. CH62: Brom . . .6B **36**
Langham Ct. L4: Walt 3H **7**
Langham St. L4: Walt 3H **7**
Langham St. Ind. Est.
   L4: Walt 3H **7**
   (off Langham St.)
Lang La. CH48: W Kir 4D **16**
Lang La. Sth. CH48: W Kir . . .4E **17**
Langley Ct. CH63: Spit 1G **35**
Langley Ct. CH65: Ell P 4C **50**
Langley Rd. CH63: Spit 1G **35**
Langley St. L8: Liv 1G **23**
Langrove St. L5: Liv 6G **7**
Langsdale St. L3: Liv 2G **15**
   (not continuous)
Langstone Av. CH49: Grea 4C **18**
Langtry Cl. L4: Kirkd 3F **7**
Langtry Rd. L4: Kirkd 3F **7**
Lansdowne Cl. CH41: Birke . . .5E **13**
Lansdowne Ct. CH43: Bid 5D **12**
Lansdowne Pl. CH43: Bid 5D **12**
   L5: Liv 5H **7**
Lansdowne Rd.
   CH41: Birke 5D **12**
   CH43: Bid 5D **12**
   CH45: Wall 3D **4**
Lanyork Rd. L3: Liv 2D **14**
Lapwing Ri. CH60: Hesw 5B **32**
Lapworth Cl. CH40: More 5B **10**
Lapworth St. L5: Kirkd 5F **7**
Larchdale Cl. CH66: Whit 6A **48**
Larch Gro. CH43: Bid 5C **12**
Larch Rd. CH42: Tran 2G **21**
Larchwood Cl. CH61: Pens . . .6B **26**
Larchwood Dr.
   CH63: Hghr B 2F **29**
Larcombe Av. CH49: Upton . . .2F **19**
Larkhill Av. CH49: Upton 6G **11**
Larkhill Way CH49: Upton 6G **11**
Larkin Cl. CH62: New F 2G **29**
Larksway CH60: Hesw 3D **32**
Larton Farm Cl.
   CH48: W Kir 5G **17**
Larton Rd. CH48: W Kir 4G **17**
Lartonwood CH48: W Kir 4G **17**
Latchford Rd. CH60: Hesw . . .5D **32**
Latham St. L5: Kirkd 5F **7**
   (not continuous)
Latham Way CH63: Spit 1H **35**
Lathom Av. CH44: Wall 1F **13**
Latimer St. L5: Liv 5F **7**
Laund, The CH45: Wall 6D **4**
Laurel Av. CH60: Hesw 2B **32**
   CH63: Hghr B 5E **29**
Laurelbanks CH60: Hesw 2A **32**
Laurel Dr. CH64: Will 4D **40**
   CH65: Whit 5H **49**
Laurelhurst Av. CH61: Pens . . .6E **27**
Laurel Rd. CH42: Tran 3H **21**
Laurels, The CH46: Leas 2E **11**
Laurelwood Dr.
   CH66: Gt Sut 6E **49**
Laurence Deacon Ct.
   CH41: Birke 6H **13**
Lavrock Bank L8: Liv 3G **23**
Lawford Dr. CH60: Hesw 3E **33**
Lawns, The CH43: Bid 6B **12**
Lawns Av. CH63: Raby M 5H **35**
Lawnside Cl. CH42: Rock F . . .6B **22**
Lawrence Cl. CH42: Rock F . . .1G **29**
Lawton St. L1: Liv 4G **15**
Laxey St. L8: Liv 1G **23**
Laxton Cl. CH66: Gt Sut 6A **48**
Layton Av. CH43: Pren 5D **20**
Lazonby Cl. CH43: Bid 5A **12**
Leach Way CH61: Irby 3G **25**
Lea Cl. CH43: Noct 3C **20**
Leadenhall Cl. L5: Liv 5H **7**
Leafield Cl. CH61: Irby 3B **26**

Leahurst University of Liverpool
   Veterinary Field Station
   . . . .**5H 39**
Leamington Cl. CH64: Nest . . .1C **44**
Leander Rd. CH45: Wall 6E **5**
Lea Rd. CH44: Wall 6G **5**
Leas, The CH45: Wall 4C **4**
   CH61: Thing 3D **26**
Leas Cl. CH66: Gt Sut 2C **48**
LEASOWE **1H 11**
Leasowe (Park & Ride) **3G 11**

Leasowe Av. CH45: Wall 5C **4**
Leasowe Gdns. CH46: Leas . . .2E **11**
Leasowe Lighthouse **2C 10**
Leasowe Recreation Cen. . . .**2G 11**
Leasowe Rd. CH44: Wall 1F **11**
   CH45: Wall 1F **11**
   CH46: Leas 2D **10**
Leasoweside CH46: Leas 1G **11**
Leasowe Station (Rail) **3F 11**
Leas Pk. CH47: Hoy 3C **16**
Leather La. L2: Liv 3E **15**
   (off Tempest Hey)
Leaway CH49: Grea 3D **18**
Leawood Gro. CH46: More 5F **11**
Ledbury Cl. CH43: Oxton 5C **20**
LEDSHAM **6H 47**
Ledsham Cl. CH43: Noct 3C **20**
Ledsham Ct. CH66: Lit Sut 1C **48**
Ledsham Hall La.
   CH66: Led 2G **47**
Ledsham La. CH66: Led 3G **47**
Ledsham Pk. Dr.
   CH66: Lit Sut 1A **48**
Ledsham Rd.
   CH66: Lit Sut 2H **47**
Ledsham Village
   CH66: Led 6H **47**
Leece St. L1: Liv 5G **15**
Leeds St. L3: Liv 2D **14**
Lee Rd. CH47: Hoy 6E **9**
Lees Av. CH42: Rock F 5B **22**
Lees La. CH64: Lit N, Nest 1E **45**
   CH65: Ell P 3B **50**
Leeswood Rd.
   CH40: Woodc 4G **19**
Legh Rd. CH62: New F 2H **29**
Legion La. CH62: Brom 2B **36**
Leigh Bri. Way *L5: Liv* 6E **7**
   (off New Hedley Gro.)
Leigh Pl. *L1: Liv* 4F **15**
   (off Leigh St.)
Leigh Rd. CH48: W Kir 4D **16**
Leigh St. L1: Liv 4F **15**
   (not continuous)
Leighton Av. CH47: Meols 5G **9**
Leighton Chase CH64: Nest . . .4B **38**
Leighton Ct. CH64: Nest 5B **38**
Leighton Pk. CH64: Nest 5B **38**
Leighton Rd. CH41: Tran 3A **22**
   CH64: Nest 2A **38**
Leightons, The CH64: Nest . . .5B **38**
Leighton St. L4: Kirkd 2G **7**
Leison St. L4: Kirkd 4F **7**
   L5: Kirkd 5F **7**
Leiston Cl. CH61: Irby 2A **26**
Lemon St. L5: Kirkd 5F **7**
Lennox Av. CH45: New B 4F **5**
Lennox La. CH43: Bid 4A **12**
Lenthall St. L4: Walt 1H **7**
Leominster Rd. CH44: Wall . . .1F **13**
Leonard Ho. CH41: Birke 3B **14**
Leonora St. L8: Liv 3H **23**
Leopold St. CH44: Wall 2A **14**
Leslie Av. CH49: Grea 4D **18**
Lester Cl. L4: Kirkd 4G **7**
Lester Dr. CH61: Irby 2G **25**
Lestock St. L8: Liv 6G **15**
Leta St. L4: Walt 2H **7**
   (not continuous)
Lethbridge Cl. L5: Kirkd 5E **7**
Letitia St. L8: Liv 2H **23**
Levens Hey CH46: More 5D **10**
Leven St. L4: Kirkd 3G **7**
Leven Wlk. CH66: Ell P 5G **43**
Lever Av. CH44: Wall 3A **14**
Lever C'way.
   CH63: Hghr B, Store 4A **28**
Lever Ct. L1: Liv 5F **15**
Leverhulme Ct. CH63: Beb . . .5G **29**
Lever Ter. *CH42: Tran* 4A **22**
   (off Summerford Cl.)
Lewis Cl. CH65: Ell P 6A **50**
Lewisham Rd.
   CH62: Port S 3A **30**
Leyburn Rd. CH45: Wall 5D **4**
Liberton St. *L5: Liv* 5H **7**
   (off St Domingo Va.)
Lichfield Dr. CH66: Gt Sut 6E **49**
Lichfield St. CH45: New B 4G **5**
Liddell Ct. CH45: Wall 6B **4**

Liege Ho. *CH49: Upton* 1F **19**
   (off Manorside Cl.)
Lifestyles
   Alsop **1H 7**
   Everton **5G 7**
   Millennium **3F 15**
   (off Victoria St.)
   Park Road **2H 23**
Lifestyles Toxteth Sports Cen.
   . . . .**1H 23**
Liffey Ct. *L3: Liv* 3H **15**
   (off London Rd.)
Lightbody St. L5: Liv 6D **6**
Light Cinema, The **2F 5**
Lightfoot Cl. CH60: Hesw 4D **32**
Lightfoot La. CH60: Hesw 4D **32**
Lighthouse Rd. CH47: Hoy . . .1D **16**
Lilac Gro. CH66: Whit 6B **48**
Lillie Cl. CH43: Bid 5A **12**
Lillyfield CH60: Hesw 5B **32**
Limbo La. CH61: Irby 1H **25**
Lime Av. CH63: Hghr B 5D **28**
Limehurst Gro. CH62: Brom . .5B **36**
Limekiln La. CH44: Wall 3E **13**
   L3: Liv 1F **15**
   L5: Liv 6F **7**
Limes, The CH49: Upton 2F **19**
Lime St. CH65: Ell P 6H **43**
   L1: Liv 3F **15**
Lime St. Chambers *L1: Liv* . .3G **15**
   (off Lime St.)
Lime Street Station (Rail) . . .**4G 15**
Lime Tree Cl. CH66: Whit 6B **48**
Lime Tree Gro. CH60: Hesw . .3E **33**
Linacre Ho. L20: Boot 1E **7**
Lincoln Dr. CH45: Wall 5G **5**
Lincoln Rd. CH66: Gt Sut 4D **48**
Lincoln St. CH41: Birke 4E **13**
Lindale Cl. CH46: More 4G **11**
Linden Cl. CH66: Gt Sut 6A **48**
Linden Dr. CH43: Pren 6C **20**
Linden Gro. CH45: Wall 4F **5**
Lindens, The CH43: Oxton 2G **21**
Lindeth Av. CH44: Wall 3F **13**
Lindfield Cl. L8: Liv 3H **23**
Lindisfarne Av. CH65: Ell P . . .6A **50**
Lind St. L4: Walt 2H **7**
Lindwall Cl. CH43: Bid 4A **12**
Linear Pk. CH46: More 4C **10**
Lingdale Av. CH43: Clau 1D **20**
Lingdale Ct. CH43: Clau 6D **12**
   CH48: W Kir 5B **16**
Lingdale Rd. CH43: Clau 6D **12**
   CH48: W Kir 4C **16**
Lingdale Rd. Nth.
   CH41: Birke 6D **12**
Lingham Cl. CH46: More 4D **10**
Lingham La. CH46: More 2C **10**
   (not continuous)
Links, The CH43: Oxton 2D **20**
Links Av. CH66: Lit Sut 6C **42**
Links Cl. CH45: Wall 4D **4**
   CH48: W Kir 6F **17**
   CH63: Raby M 5H **35**
Links Hey Rd. CH48: Caldy . . .3C **24**
Linkside CH63: Hghr B 2D **28**
Linkside Way CH66: Gt Sut . . .6A **48**
Links Vw. CH43: Oxton 2C **20**
   CH45: Wall 3D **4**
Linkside Ct. CH44: Wall 6C **42**
Linkway CH45: Wall 4D **4**
Linnets Way CH60: Hesw 3A **32**
Linton St. L4: Walt 2H **7**
Linwood Rd. CH42: Tran 4A **22**
Lions Cl. CH43: Clau 1D **20**
Lipton Cl. L20: Boot 1E **7**
LISCARD **6F 5**
Liscard Cres. CH44: Wall 6F **5**
Liscard Gro. CH44: Wall 1E **13**
Liscard Ho. CH44: Wall 1F **13**
Liscard Rd. CH44: Wall 1F **13**
   (not continuous)
Liscard Village CH45: Wall 6F **5**
Liscard Way CH44: Wall 1F **13**
Lister Av. CH46: Leas 3G **11**
Liston St. L4: Walt 1H **7**
Litcham Cl. CH49: Upton 6G **11**
Litherland Av. CH46: More 4D **10**
Lithou Cl. L5: Liv 6F **7**

Little Birches CH65: Ell P 1G **43**
Lit. Canning St. L8: Liv 6H **15**
Lit. Catharine St. L8: Liv 6H **15**
Little Ct. L3: Liv 1E **15**
Littledale Rd. CH44: Wall 2H **13**
Little Green CH66: Gt Sut 4D **48**
Lit. Hardman St. L1: Liv 5G **15**
Lit. Howard St. L3: Liv 1D **14**
Lit. Huskisson St. L8: Liv 6H **15**
Little La. CH64: Park 4A **38**
Littlemore Cl. CH49: Upton . . .2D **18**
LITTLE NESTON **2C 44**
Little St Bride St. L8: Liv 5H **15**
LITTLE STANNEY **6C 50**
Lit. Stanney La.
   CH2: Lit Stan, Stoak 6C **50**
Lit. Storeton La.
   CH63: Store 3A **28**
LITTLE SUTTON **1C 48**
Little Sutton Station (Rail) . . .1C **48**
Littleton Cl. CH43: Noct 3C **20**
Little Whissage
   CH66: Gt Sut 5F **49**
Lit. Woolton St. L7: Liv 4H **15**
LIVERPOOL **4F 15**
Liverpool Arts Village
   L1: Liv 5F **15**
   (off Henry St.)
Liverpool Cathedral Church of Christ
   . . . .**6G 15**
Liverpool Empire Theatre . . .**3G 15**
Liverpool FC (Anfield) **4H 7**
Liverpool John Moores University
   Avril Robarts Cen. **3E 15**
   Byrom St. **2F 15**
   The Henry Cotton Campus
   . . . .**3F 15**
   (off Webster St.)
   William Brown St. **3F 15**
Liverpool Metropolitan
   Cathedral of Christ the King (RC)
   . . . .**4H 15**
Liverpool One L1: Liv 4E **15**
Liverpool Parish Church **4D 14**
   (off Old Church Yd.)
Liverpool Playhouse **4F 15**
Liverpool Rd. CH66: Nest 5C **38**
   (not continuous)
LIVERPOOL UNIVERSITY
   DENTAL HOSPITAL **3H 15**
Liverpool Waters **6C 6**
LIVERPOOL WOMEN'S HOSPITAL
   . . . .**5H 15**
Liversidge Rd. CH42: Tran . . .3H **21**
Liver St. L1: Liv 5E **15**
Livingstone Gdns.
   CH41: Birke 6G **13**
Livingstone Rd. CH46: Leas . . .1G **11**
   CH65: Ell P 2G **43**
Livingstone St. CH41: Birke . .6G **13**
Llandaff Cl. CH66: Gt Sut 6E **49**
Llanrwst Cl. L8: Liv 2G **23**
Lloyd Av. CH41: Birke 6F **13**
Lloyd Cl. L6: Liv 1H **15**
Lloyd Dr. CH49: Grea 4C **18**
   CH65: Ell P 6A **50**
Lochinvar St. L9: Walt 1H **7**
Lochinver Av. CH66: Lit Sut . . .1H **47**
Locker Pk. CH49: Grea 3C **18**
Lockfields Vw. L3: Liv 6E **7**
Lockington Cl. L8: Liv 3H **23**
Lock Rd. CH62: East 3E **37**
Loddon Cl. CH49: Upton 6H **11**
Lodge, The CH43: Noct 1B **20**
Lodge La. CH62: Port S 3H **29**
Lodwick St. L20: Kirkd 2D **6**
Logan Rd. CH41: Birke 4F **13**
Lois Ct. CH45: Wall 5G **5**
Lombard Rd. CH46: More 3F **11**
Lombardy Av. CH49: Grea 5B **18**
Lomond Gro. CH46: More 5F **11**
   CH66: Gt Sut 4F **49**
London Rd. L3: Liv 3G **15**
   (not continuous)
Longacre Cl. CH45: Wall 6B **4**
Longacre Rd. CH64: Nest 3C **38**
Long Acres CH49: Grea 2D **18**
Longfellow Dr. CH62: New F . .2G **29**
Longfield Cl. CH49: Grea 3D **18**
Long Hey Rd. CH48: Caldy . . .2C **24**

Longland Rd. CH45: Wall 5F **5**
Longlooms Rd. CH65: Ell P . .6B **50**
Longlooms Rd. E.
　　CH65: Ell P 6B **50**
Long Meadow CH60: Hesw . . .5B **32**
Longridge Av. CH49: Upton . . .1E **19**
Longridge Wlk. L4: Kirkd 3G **7**
Longview Av. CH45: Wall 6E **5**
Longville St. L8: Liv 2G **23**
Lonsboro Rd. CH44: Wall 2G **13**
Lonsdale Av. CH45: Wall 5E **5**
Lonsdale Vs. CH45: Wall 5E **5**
　　　　　　　　　(off Seaview Rd.)
Looms, The CH64: Park 3A **38**
Loomsway CH61: Irby 3G **25**
Loraine St. L5: Liv 6H **7**
Lord Nelson St. L1: Liv 3G **15**
　　L3: Liv 3G **15**
Lords Av. CH43: Bid 5A **12**
Lord St. CH41: Birke 6A **14**
　　L2: Liv 4E **15**
Loretto Dr. CH49: Upton 1G **19**
Loretto Rd. CH44: Wall 6D **4**
Lorn Ct. CH41: Birke 1A **22**
Lorn Ct. CH43: Oxton 3F **21**
Lorne Rd. CH43: Oxton 3E **21**
Lorn St. CH41: Birke 1A **22**
Lothair Rd. L4: Walt 4H **7**
Lothian St. L8: Liv 1H **23**
Lough Grn. CH63: Spit 1G **35**
Love La. CH44: Wall 2E **13**
　　L3: Liv 1E **15**
Lowell St. L4: Walt 2H **7**
LOWER BEBINGTON 4G **29**
Lwr. Bank Vw. L20: Kirkd 2D **6**
Lwr. Castle St. L2: Liv 4E **15**
Lwr. Flaybrick Rd.
　　CH43: Bid 5C **12**
Lwr. Gill St. L3: Liv 3H **15**
Lower Grn. CH49: Woodc 4G **19**
Lwr. Mersey St. CH65: Ell P . .2G **43**
Lwr. Mersey Vw. L20: Kirkd . . .2D **6**
Lwr. New Hall Pl. L3: Liv 3D **14**
　　　　　　　　　　(off Union St.)
Lwr. Rd. CH62: Port S 3H **29**
Lwr. Thingwall La.
　　CH61: Thing 3E **27**
Lowfields Av. CH62: East 2F **41**
Lowfields Cl. CH62: East 2G **41**
Low Hill L6: Liv 2H **15**
Lowry Bank CH44: Wall 2A **14**
Lowther St. L8: Liv 6H **15**
Low Wood Gro. CH61: Barn . . .5E **27**
Lowwood Gro. CH41: Birke . . .2H **21**
Lowwood Rd. CH41: Birke . . .2H **21**
Loxdale Cl. L8: Liv 3H **23**
Loxdale Dr. CH65: Gt Sut 4F **49**
Lucerne Rd. CH44: Wall 3H **13**
Ludlow Ct. CH48: W Kir 6D **16**
Ludlow Dr. CH48: W Kir 6D **16**
　　CH65: Ell P 4C **50**
Ludlow Gro. CH62: Brom 2B **36**
Ludlow St. L4: Kirkd 2H **7**
Luke St. CH44: Wall 3A **14**
　　L8: Liv 1H **23**
Lumina CH62: Brom 1C **36**
Lumley Rd. CH44: Wall 4H **13**
Lundy Dr. CH65: Ell P 6A **50**
Lupus Way CH66: Gt Sut 4F **49**
Luton Gro. L4: Walt 3H **7**
Luton Rd. CH65: Ell P 2F **49**
Luton St. L5: Kirkd 5D **6**
Lutyens Cl. L4: Walt 3H **7**
Luxmore Rd. L4: Walt 2H **7**
Lycett Rd. CH44: Wall 6C **4**
Lyceum Pl. L1: Liv 4F **15**
　　　　　　　　　(off Ranelagh St.)
Lydbrook Cl. CH42: Rock F . . .4B **22**
Lydden Rd. CH65: Ell P 6H **43**
Lydia Ann St. L1: Liv 5F **15**
Lydiate, The CH60: Hesw 4B **32**
Lydiate La. CH64: Will 5A **40**
Lyle St. L5: Liv 6F **7**
Lymington Rd. CH44: Wall . . .1D **12**
Lymm Rd. CH43: Bid 6B **12**
Lynas St. CH41: Birke 5H **13**
Lyncroft Rd. CH44: Wall 3G **13**
Lyndale Av. CH62: East 1G **41**
Lyndhurst Av. CH61: Pens . . .6C **26**
Lyndhurst Cl. CH61: Thing . . .4C **26**

Lyndhurst Rd. CH45: Wall 5D **4**
　　CH47: Meols 4G **9**
　　CH61: Irby 4G **25**
Lyneal Av. CH66: Gt Sut 4C **48**
Lynnbank CH43: Oxton 3F **21**
Lynndene CH66: Lit Sut 6D **42**
Lynton Cl. CH60: Hesw 5D **32**
Lynton Dr. CH63: Beb 6G **29**
Lynton Rd. CH45: Wall 5C **4**
Lynwood Av. CH44: Wall 2E **13**
Lynwood Dr. CH61: Irby 3A **26**
Lyons Cl. CH46: More 4E **11**
Lyons Rd. CH46: More 4E **11**
Lytton Av. CH42: Rock F 6B **22**
Lytton St. L6: Liv 2H **15**

M

McAllester Lodge
　　CH43: Oxton 3D **20**
　　　　　　　　　(off Bidston Rd.)
Macalpine Cl. CH49: Upton . . .1G **19**
Macbeth St. L20: Kirkd 2E **7**
Macdona Dr.
　　CH48: W Kir . . .6D **16** & 1A **24**
Macdonald Dr. CH49: Grea . . .4D **18**
Macdonald Rd. CH46: More . . .5C **10**
McGarva Way CH65: Ell P . . .3A **50**
McGill Ct. CH41: Birke 6H **13**
　　　　　　　　　(off Cathcart St.)
Mackenzie Rd. CH46: Leas . . .2H **11**
McKeown Cl. L5: Liv 6F **7**
Maddock Rd. CH44: Wall 6H **5**
Maddock St. CH41: Birke 5G **13**
Maddrell St. L3: Liv 1D **14**
Madelaine St. L8: Liv 1H **23**
Madeley Cl. CH48: W Kir 6D **16**
Madeley Dr. CH48: W Kir 6D **16**
Madison Sq. L1: Liv 5G **15**
Maelor Cl. CH63: Brom 5A **36**
Magazine Av. CH45: New B . . .4F **5**
Magazine La. CH45: New B . . .4F **5**
Magazine Brow CH45: New B .4G **5**
Magazine Rd. CH62: Brom . . .6B **30**
Magazines Prom.
　　CH45: New B 3G **5**
Magazine Wlk. CH62: Brom . . .6B **30**
Magdalene Wlk.
　　CH65: Ell P 3C **50**
　　　　　　　　　(off Robinson Rd.)
Magdalen Ho. L20: Boot 1E **7**
Magnolia Cl. CH45: Gt Sut . . .6F **49**
Magnolia Wlk. CH49: Grea . . .5C **18**
Mahon Ct. L8: Liv 6H **15**
　　　　　　　　　(off Morpeth St.)
Maiden Gdns. CH65: Ell P . . .4B **50**
Main Rd. CH62: Port S 5H **29**
Mainwaring Rd. CH44: Wall . . .2H **13**
　　CH62: Brom 3B **36**
Maitland Rd. CH45: New B . . .3G **5**
Major St. L5: Liv 5F **7**
Makepeace Wlk. L8: Liv 1H **23**
　　　　　　　　　(off Thackeray Cl.)
Makin St. L4: Walt 1H **7**
Malcolm Cres. CH63: Brom . . .5A **36**
Malcolm Gro. L20: Kirkd 2F **7**
Maldwyn Rd. CH44: Wall 6F **5**
Mallaby Ct. CH41: Birke 5E **13**
　　　　　　　　　(off Mallaby St.)
Mallaby St. CH41: Birke 5E **13**
Mallard Way CH46: More 4C **10**
Mallory Rd. CH42: Tran 5H **21**
Mallowdale Cl. CH62: East . . .6D **36**
Malmesbury Cl. CH49: Grea . .3C **18**
Malpas Av. CH43: Pren 5E **21**
Malpas Dr. CH63: Hghr B 2E **29**
Malpas Gro. CH45: Wall 5E **5**
Malpas Rd. CH45: Wall 5D **4**
　　CH65: Gt Sut 3F **49**
Malta St. L8: Liv 2H **23**
Malta Wlk. L8: Liv 2H **23**
Malvern Av. CH65: Ell P 4A **50**
Malvern Gro. CH42: Tran 5H **21**
Malvern Rd. CH44: Wall 6B **4**
Malwood St. L8: Liv 3H **23**
Mandeville St. L4: Walt 1H **7**
Manesty's La. L1: Liv 4F **15**
Manfred St. L6: Liv 3H **15**

Manley Cl. CH43: Oxton 4D **20**
Manners La. CH60: Hesw 5A **32**
Mannington Cl. CH47: Meols . .5G **9**
Mann Island L3: Liv 4E **15**
Mann St. L8: Liv 1G **23**
Manor Cl. CH64: Park 6A **38**
　　L20: Boot 1G **7**
Manor Ct. CH48: W Kir 4C **16**
　　　　　　　　　(off Bridge Rd.)
　　CH49: Grea 4C **18**
　　CH61: Irby 3H **25**
Manor Dr. CH49: Upton 6F **11**
　　　　　　　　　(off St John's Cen.)
MANOR GREEN 6A **12**
Manor Hill
　　CH43: Clau, Oxton 1E **21**
Manor Ho. CH62: Brom 3B **36**
　　CH66: Gt Sut 5D **48**
　　　　　　　　　(off Kelmscott Cl.)
Manor Ho., The
　　CH49: Upton 6F **11**
Manorial Rd. CH64: Park 5A **38**
Manorial Rd. Sth.
　　CH64: Park 5A **38**
Manor La. CH42: Rock F 5C **22**
　　CH45: Wall 6G **5**
　　CH65: Gt Sut 4D **48**
Manor M. CH45: Wall 6G **5**
Manor Pk. Cl. CH61: Thing . . .3C **26**
Manor Pk. Dr. CH66: Gt Sut . .5D **48**
Manor Pl. CH62: Brom 4B **30**
Manor Rd. CH44: Wall 6F **5**
　　CH45: Wall 6F **5**
　　CH47: Hoy 5E **9**
　　CH61: Irby 3H **25**
　　CH62: East 5B **36**
　　CH63: Thorn H 2H **33**
Manor Road Station (Rail) . . .6E **9**
Manorside CH49: Upton 1F **19**
Manor Way CH43: Bid 6A **12**
Mansfield Rd. CH65: Whit 5G **49**
Mansfield St. L3: Liv 2G **15**
Manville Rd. CH45: New B 4F **5**
Maple Av. CH66: Lit Sut 1C **48**
Maple Gro. CH62: Brom 3A **36**
　　CH66: Whit 6G **49**
Maples Ct. CH43: Oxton 4E **21**
Maple St. CH41: Birke 2H **21**
Mapleton Cl. CH43: Pren 6C **20**
Maple Tree Gro.
　　CH60: Hesw 3E **33**
Maplewood Gro. CH43: Bid . . .5C **12**
Marathon Cl. L6: Liv 1H **15**
Marble Cl. L20: Boot 1E **7**
Marbury Gdns. CH65: Ell P . . .1F **49**
Marchwiel Rd. CH65: Ell P . . .3B **50**
Marcus St. CH41: Birke 5H **13**
　　　　　　　　　(not continuous)
Mare Hall La. CH64: Nest 5F **39**
Marfords Av. CH63: Brom 4A **36**
Margaret Rd. L4: Walt 1G **7**
Margaret's La. CH66: Chil T . .6H **41**
Margaret St. L6: Liv 1H **15**
Marian Dr. CH46: More 5E **11**
Maria Rd. L9: Walt 1H **7**
Marina Dr. CH65: Ell P 3H **49**
Marina Wlk. CH65: Ell P 3A **50**
　　　　　　　　(within The Port Arcades)
Marine Dr. CH60: Hesw 4H **31**
Marine Pk. CH48: W Kir 3D **16**
Marine Pk. Mans.
　　CH45: New B 2F **5**
Marine Point CH45: New B 2F **5**
Marine Prom. CH45: New B . . .2F **5**
Marine Rd. CH47: Hoy 6C **8**
Mariners Pk. CH44: Wall 5H **5**
Mariners Rd. CH45: New B 2F **5**
Mariners Wharf CH65: Ell P . . .2H **43**
　　　　　　　　(off Grosvenor Wharf Rd.)
　　L3: Liv 1E **23**
Marine Ter. CH45: Wall 6E **5**
Marion St. CH41: Birke 1A **22**
Maritime Ct. CH49: Woodc . . .6H **19**
　　　　　　　　　(off Childwall Grn.)
Maritime Grange
　　CH44: Wall 3A **14**
Maritime Gro. CH43: Oxton . . .2F **21**
Maritime Lodge L5: Liv 5H **7**
　　　　　　　　　(off Towson St.)
Maritime Pk. CH43: Oxton 2G **21**
Maritime Pl. L3: Liv 2G **15**

Maritime Vw. CH42: Tran 4H **21**
Maritime Way L1: Liv 5F **15**
Marius Cl. L4: Walt 3H **7**
Mark Av. CH66: Gt Sut 3C **48**
Markden M. L8: Liv 6H **15**
Market Pl. Sth. CH41: Birke . .1B **22**
Market Sq. CH65: Ell P 3A **50**
　　L1: Liv 4F **15**
　　　　　　　　　(off St John's Cen.)
Market St. CH41: Birke 1A **22**
　　CH47: Hoy 1D **16**
Market Way L1: Liv 4F **15**
　　　　　　　　　(off St John's Cen.)
Markham Gro. CH43: Bid 5D **12**
Mark Rake CH62: Brom 2B **36**
Mark St. CH44: Wall 3A **14**
　　L5: Liv 4G **7**
Marksway CH61: Pens 5C **26**
Marlborough Gro.
　　CH43: Oxton 3G **21**
Marlborough Pl. L3: Liv 2E **15**
Marlborough Rd.
　　CH45: New B 4G **5**
　　CH65: Ell P 4B **50**
Marlborough St. L3: Liv 2E **15**
Marlborough Wlk.
　　CH65: Ell P 4B **50**
Marlfield La. CH61: Pens 5C **26**
Marline Av. CH63: Brom 5A **36**
Marlowe Rd. CH44: Wall 1E **13**
　　CH64: Nest 5C **38**
Marlston Av. CH61: Irby 3B **26**
Marlwood Av. CH45: Wall 6C **4**
Marmion Rd. CH47: Hoy 6D **8**
Marmonde St. L4: Walt 3G **7**
Marnell Cl. L5: Liv 6E **7**
Marple Cl. CH43: Oxton 4C **20**
Marquis St. CH41: Tran 3A **22**
　　CH62: New F 2H **29**
　　L3: Liv 3G **15**
Marram Cl. CH46: More 3G **11**
Marsden Cl. CH44: Wall 6H **5**
Marsden Ct. CH45: New B 4F **5**
Marsden St. L6: Liv 2H **15**
Marshall Pl. L3: Liv 1E **15**
Marshall St. CH41: Birke 5G **13**
Marsham Cl. CH49: Upton 6G **11**
Marshfield Ct. CH46: Leas . . .2E **11**
Marshlands Rd. CH45: Wall . . .5C **4**
　　CH64: Lit N 2B **44**
Marsh La. CH63: Hghr B 2C **28**
Marshside Cl. L8: Liv 2H **23**
Marsh St. L20: Kirkd 2F **7**
Marston Cl. CH43: Oxton 4D **20**
　　CH62: East 2G **41**
Marston Gdns. CH65: Ell P . . .1F **49**
Marsworth Dr. L6: Liv 1H **15**
Marten Av. CH63: Brom 4A **36**
Martin Cl. CH61: Irby 3G **25**
Martindale Rd. CH62: Brom . . .2C **36**
Martin's La. CH44: Wall 1C **13**
Martlesham Cres.
　　CH49: Grea 4B **18**
Marwood Towers L5: Liv 5G **7**
　　　　　　　　　(off Boundary St.)
Marybone L3: Liv 3F **15**
Marybone Apartments
　　L3: Liv 2E **15**
　　　　　　　　　(off Marybone)
Marybone Student Village
　　L3: Liv 3F **15**
　　　　　　　　　(off Marybone)
Maryland La. CH46: More 4D **10**
Maryland St. L1: Liv 5G **15**
Marymount Cl. CH44: Wall . . .2F **13**
Maryport Cl. L5: Liv 5H **7**
Maryville Cl. CH65: Ell P 1A **50**
Maryville Wlk. CH65: Ell P . . .1A **50**
Masefield Cl. CH62: New F . . .2G **29**
Mason Cl. CH66: Gt Sut 5D **48**
Mason St. CH45: New B 3F **5**
Massey Pk. CH45: Wall 6E **5**
Massey St. CH41: Birke 5H **13**
Mather Ct. CH43: Oxton 2F **21**
Mather Rd. CH43: Oxton 2F **21**
Mathew St. L2: Liv 4E **15**
Matterhorn Rd. CH66: Ell P . . .6F **43**
Matthew Cl. CH44: Wall 3A **14**
Matthew St. CH44: Wall 3A **14**
Maud St. L8: Liv 1H **23**

Maurice Jones Ct.
CH46: More 4E **11**
Mavis Dr. CH49: Woodc 4G **19**
Maxwell Cl. CH47: Upton . . .1G **19**
CH65: Whit 5G **49**
Maxwell Cl. CH42: Tran 4G **21**
May Av. CH44: Wall 3H **13**
Maybank Rd. CH42: Tran . . .3H **21**
Mayer Av. CH63: Beb 5F **29**
Mayew Rd. CH61: Irby 3B **26**
Mayfair Ct. CH43: Oxton . . .4F **21**
(off The Grove)
Mayfield Dr. CH62: East 5F **37**
Mayfield Gdns.
CH64: Nest 4C **38**
Mayfield Rd. CH45: Wall 6D **4**
CH63: Beb 6G **29**
Mayfields CH66: Ell P 6F **43**
L4: Kirkd 3G **7**
Mayfields Ho. CH62: New F . . .2H **29**
(off Mayfields Nth.)
Mayfields Nth.
CH62: New F 2H **29**
Mayfields Sth.
CH62: New F 2H **29**
May Rd. CH60: Hesw 3C **32**
May St. L3: Liv 4G **15**
Mazenod Ct. L3: Liv 2F **15**
(off Addison Way)
Mazzini Cl. L5: Liv 6G **7**
Meadfoot Rd. CH46: More . . .4D **10**
Meadow, The CH49: Woodc . . .4H **19**
(not continuous)
Meadowbank Dr.
CH66: Lit Sut 1A **48**
Meadowbrook Rd.
CH46: More 6D **10**
Meadow Cl. CH64: Nest 1C **44**
CH64: Will 5B **40**
Meadow Cres.
CH49: Woodc 5G **19**
Meadow Cft. CH64: Will 5A **40**
Meadowcroft CH60: Hesw . . .2E **33**
Meadowcroft Rd.
CH47: Meols 4G **9**
Meadowfield Cl.
CH42: Rock F 5B **22**
Meadowgate CH48: Caldy . . .4B **24**
Meadow La. CH42: Rock F . . .5B **22**
CH64: Will 4A **40**
CH65: Ell P 1A **50**
Meadow La. Ind. Pk.
CH65: Ell P 2B **50**
Meadow La. Works
CH65: Ell P 1B **50**
Meadow Pk. CH42: Rock F . . .5B **22**
Meadow Rd. CH48: W Kir . . .4H **17**
Meadows, The CH41: Birke . . .6H **13**
(off Conway St.)
CH62: Brom 4B **36**
CH64: Lit N 1D **44**
Meadowside CH46: Leas . . .1H **11**
Meadowside Rd.
CH62: Brom 4B **36**
Meadow St. CH45: New B . . .3E **5**
Meadow Wlk. CH61: Pens . . .6A **26**
Meadway CH45: Wall 6E **5**
CH49: Upton 1H **19**
CH60: Hesw 5B **32**
CH62: Spit 1A **36**
CH66: Lit Sut 6B **42**
Mealor's Weint CH64: Park . . .4A **38**
Mecca Bingo
Birkenhead 1H **21**
Ellesmere Port 3A **50**
Meddowcroft Rd. CH45: Wall . . .5D **4**
Medea Cl. L5: Liv 5G **7**
Medlock Ct. CH43: Oxton . . .2E **21**
Medlock St. L4: Kirkd 3G **7**
Mega Centre, The 1E **15**
Melbourne St. CH45: New B . . .3E **5**
Melda Cl. L6: Liv 2H **15**
Melford Dr. CH43: Pren 6C **20**
Melksham Dr. CH61: Irby 2H **25**
Melling Ct. CH45: New B 4G **5**
Melling Rd. CH45: New B 4G **5**
Mellock Cl. CH64: Lit N 1D **44**
Mellock La. CH64: Lit N 6D **38**
Melloncroft Dr. CH48: Caldy . . .1A **24**

Melloncroft Dr. W.
CH48: Caldy 2A **24**
Mellor Rd. CH42: Tran 5G **21**
Melrose Av. CH46: More 4G **11**
Melrose Av. CH47: Hoy 6D **8**
Melrose Dr. CH66: Gt Sut 6A **48**
Melrose Gdns.
CH43: Pren 1H **27**
Melrose Rd. L4: Kirkd 3F **7**
Melton Cl. CH49: Upton . . .2E **19**
Melville CH62: New F 6D **22**
Melville Av. CH42: Rock F . . .6C **22**
Melville Pl. L7: Liv 5H **15**
Melville Rd. CH63: Hghr B . . .4E **29**
Melville St. L8: Liv 2H **23**
Menai St. CH41: Birke 1G **21**
Mendell Cl. CH62: Brom 3C **36**
Mendip Cl. CH42: Tran 6G **21**
CH66: Gt Sut 4E **49**
Mendip Rd. CH42: Tran 6G **21**
Menlo Av. CH61: Irby 3B **26**
Menlo Cl. CH43: Oxton 3C **20**
MEOLS 5G **9**
Meols Cl. CH66: Gt Sut 3E **49**
Meols Ct. CH47: Hoy 1C **16**
Meols Dr. CH47: Hoy 4C **16**
CH48: W Kir 4C **16**
Meols Pde. CH47: Meols 5D **8**
Meols Station (Rail) 5G **9**
Mercer Dr. L4: Kirkd 4G **7**
Mercer Rd. CH43: Bid 5C **12**
Mercer Wlk. CH65: Ell P 3A **50**
(within The Port Arcades)
Merchants Ct. L1: Liv 4E **15**
(off Lord St.)
Mercury Ct. L2: Liv 3E **15**
Mere Av. CH63: Raby M 5H **35**
Merebank CH43: Oxton 3C **20**
Mere Cl. CH66: Gt Sut 5D **48**
Merecroft Av. CH44: Wall 3G **13**
Mere Farm Gro.
CH43: Oxton 3D **20**
Mere Farm Rd. CH43: Oxton . . .3C **20**
Mere Grn. L4: Walt 2H **7**
Mereheath CH46: Leas 2E **11**
Mereheath Gdns.
CH46: Leas 2E **11**
(off Mereheath)
Mere La. CH45: Wall 4C **4**
CH60: Hesw 1A **32**
L5: Liv 6H **7**
Mere Pk. CH49: Grea 4C **18**
Mereworth CH48: Caldy 3B **24**
Meriden Av. CH63: Spit 2G **35**
Merlin Av. CH49: Upton . . .1D **18**
Merlin Cl. CH49: Upton 1D **18**
Merlin Rd. CH42: Tran 4G **21**
Merlin St. L8: Liv 1H **23**
Merrills La. CH49: Upton . . .2G **19**
Merrilox Rd. CH41: Birke 5F **13**
Merseybank Ho.
CH62: New F 1H **29**
(off New Ferry Rd.)
Merseybank Rd.
CH62: New F 1H **29**
Mersey Ct. CH44: Wall 3A **14**
(off Borough Rd. E.)
Mersey La. Sth.
CH42: Rock F 5C **22**
Mersey Rd. CH42: Rock F . . .5C **22**
Mersey St. CH44: Wall 3A **14**
Mersey Ter. CH65: Ell P 2G **43**
(off Lwr. Mersey Rd.)
Merseyton Rd. CH65: Ell P . . .5H **43**
Merseyton Rd. Workshops
CH65: Ell P 2G **43**
(off Merseyton Rd.)
Mersey Tunnel - Toll
L3: Liv 2B **14**
(not continuous)
Mersey Vw. CH41: Tran 3D **21**
(off Marquis St.)
CH63: Hghr B 3D **28**
Mersey Wlk. CH42: Tran 4A **22**
Merton Cl. CH64: Nest 2C **44**
Merton Dr. CH49: Woodc . . .4G **19**
Merton Ho. L20: Boot 1E **7**
Merton Pl. CH43: Oxton 1G **21**

Merton Rd. CH45: Wall 6E **5**
CH65: Hoot 2B **42**
CH66: Gt Sut 4F **49**
L20: Boot 1E **7**
Mesham Cl. CH49: Upton . . .2E **19**
Methuen St. CH41: Birke 5E **13**
Metquarter L1: Liv 4F **15**
Mews Ct. CH64: Will 5B **40**
Micawber Cl. L8: Liv 2H **23**
Michael Dragonette Ct.
L3: Liv 1E **15**
Midghall St. L3: Liv 2E **15**
Midland St. CH43: Oxton . . .2G **21**
Mile End L5: Liv 1F **15**
Miles Cl. CH49: Grea 4C **18**
Miles La. CH49: Grea 5C **18**
Miles St. L8: Liv 3H **23**
Milford St. L5: Kirkd 5E **7**
Mill Bank CH64: Ness 2E **45**
Mill Bank Rd. CH44: Wall . . .2E **13**
Millbrook Rd. CH41: Birke . . .3F **13**
Mill Brow CH63: Hghr B 3D **28**
Millbutt Cl. CH63: Hghr B . . .3D **28**
Mill Cl. CH42: Tran 3H **21**
Mill Ct. CH65: Ell P 1F **49**
Mill Cft. CH64: Nest 4C **38**
Millcroft Pk. CH49: Grea 4B **18**
Millennium Ct. CH64: Nest . . .4C **38**
Millers Bri. L20: Boot 1D **6**
Millers Bri. Ind. Est.
L20: Boot 1D **6**
Millers Cl. CH46: More 6B **10**
Millersdale Cl. CH62: East . . .6D **36**
Millers Way CH46: More 5C **10**
Millfield CH64: Nest 4C **38**
Millfield Cl. CH63: Hghr B . . .4D **28**
Millfield Ter. CH66: Lit Sut . . .6C **42**
Mill Grn. CH64: Will 5B **40**
Mill Hey Rd. CH48: Caldy . . .3B **24**
Mill Hill CH43: Oxton 4E **21**
Mill Hill Rd. CH61: Irby 1G **25**
Millhouse Cl. CH46: More . . .4B **10**
Millhouse La. CH46: More . . .4B **10**
Millington Cl. CH43: Pren . . .6C **20**
Mill La. CH44: Wall 2E **13**
CH49: Grea 4C **18**
CH60: Hesw 3D **32**
CH64: Burt 6G **45**
CH64: Ness 4A **40**
CH64: Will 4A **40**
CH66: Ell P, Gt Sut 3D **48**
L3: Liv 3F **15**
Mill La. Ind. Est.
CH2: Lit Stan 6D **50**
Mill Pk. Dr. CH62: East 2G **41**
Mill Rd. CH61: Thing 3C **26**
CH62: Brom 6B **30**
CH63: Hghr B 2D **28**
L6: Liv 1H **15**
(not continuous)
Mill St. CH42: Tran 3H **21**
CH64: Nest 5B **38**
L8: Liv 1G **23**
Mill Ter. CH63: Hghr B 4D **28**
Millthwaite Ct. CH44: Wall . . .1D **12**
Millthwaite Rd. CH44: Wall . . .1D **12**
Mill Vw. L8: Liv 2G **23**
Mill Vw. Dr. CH63: Hghr B . . .3D **28**
Millwood CH63: Hghr B 3D **28**
Mill Yd. CH61: Thing 3D **26**
Milman Rd. L4: Walt 2H **7**
Milman Way CH49: Upton . . .3F **19**
Milner Cop CH60: Hesw 6C **32**
Milner Rd. CH60: Hesw 3C **32**
Milner St. CH41: Birke 5E **13**
Milnthorpe Cl. L4: Kirkd 3G **7**
Milton Cl. CH65: Ell P 3B **50**
Milton Cres. CH60: Hesw . . .2C **32**
Milton Grn. CH61: Thing 3D **26**
Milton Pavement
CH41: Birke 1H **21**
Milton Rd. CH42: Tran 3G **21**
CH44: Wall 3H **13**
CH48: W Kir 4C **16**
CH65: Ell P 3B **50**
L4: Walt 1G **7**
Milton Rd. E. CH42: Tran . . .3H **21**
Miranda Av. CH63: Hghr B . . .2E **29**
Miranda Pl. L20: Kirkd 2F **7**
Miranda Rd. L20: Boot 2F **7**

Miranda Rd. Sth. L20: Kirkd . . .2F **7**
Miriam Pl. CH41: Birke 5D **12**
Miskelly St. L20: Kirkd 3E **7**
Miston St. L20: Kirkd 3E **7**
Mitchell Ct. CH41: Birke 2H **21**
Mitchell Pl. L1: Liv 4F **15**
Mitylene St. L5: Liv 5G **7**
Mobberley Cl. CH63: Spit 6G **29**
Mobberley Way CH63: Spit . . .6G **29**
Mockbeggar Dr. CH45: Wall . . .4B **4**
Mockbeggar Wharf
CH45: Wall 4C **4**
Modred St. L8: Liv 2H **23**
Moelwyn Dr. CH66: Ell P 6F **43**
Moira Sephton Ct.
CH43: Noct 3B **20**
(off Sandalwood Dr.)
Mollington Link
CH41: Birke 2A **22**
Mollington Rd. CH44: Wall . . .2G **13**
Mollington St. CH41: Birke . . .2A **22**
Molyneux Cl. CH49: Upton . . .2F **19**
Molyneux Dr. CH45: New B . . .3F **5**
Monarchs Quay L3: Liv 6E **15**
Mona St. CH41: Birke 6D **12**
Monk Rd. CH44: Wall 1F **13**
Monks Ferry CH41: Birke . . .1B **22**
Monks Gro. CH65: Ell P 1H **49**
Monk St. CH41: Birke 1B **22**
(off Cross St.)
L5: Liv 5H **7**
Monks Way CH48: W Kir 5D **16**
CH63: Beb 5F **29**
Monmouth Dr. CH44: Wall . . .1D **12**
Monro Cl. L8: Liv 3H **23**
Monro St. L8: Liv 3H **23**
Montgomery Hill
CH48: Caldy, Frank 1D **24**
Montpelier Dr. L8: Liv 3H **23**
Montpellier Ct. CH45: New B . . .3E **5**
(off Montpellier Cres.)
Montpellier Cres.
CH45: New B 3E **5**
Montpellier Ho.
CH45: New B 3E **5**
Montrose Av. CH44: Wall . . .4A **14**
Montrose Ct. CH47: Hoy 1D **16**
Monument Pl. L3: Liv 3H **15**
Moorcroft Rd. CH45: Wall . . .6B **4**
Moore Av. CH42: Rock F 5A **22**
Moore's Ho. L4: Walt 1H **7**
Moorfield Dr. CH64: Park . . .3A **38**
Moorfields L2: Liv 3E **15**
Moorfields Av. CH43: Noct . . .3B **20**
Moorfields Station (Rail) 3E **15**
Moorings, The CH41: Birke . . .2H **21**
CH60: Hesw 3G **31**
Moorings Cl. CH64: Park 4A **38**
Moorland Cl. CH60: Hesw . . .4C **32**
Moorland Pk. CH60: Hesw . . .4C **32**
Moorland Rd. CH42: Tran . . .4A **22**
CH66: Ell P 5E **43**
Moor La. CH60: Hesw 3B **32**
L4: Walt 1H **7**
Moor Pl. L3: Liv 3G **15**
MOORSIDE 6A **38**
Moorside Av. CH64: Park 5A **38**
Moorside La. CH64: Park 6A **38**
Moor St. L2: Liv 4E **15**
Moorway CH60: Hesw 3D **32**
Morecroft Rd.
CH42: Rock F 6C **22**
Morello Dr. CH63: Spit 1H **35**
MORETON 5E **11**
MORETON COMMON 1D **10**
Moreton Gro. CH45: Wall . . .5C **4**
Moreton Hills Golf Cen. . . .3D **10**
Moreton Rd. CH49: Upton . . .6F **11**
Moreton Station (Rail) 3E **11**
Morland Av. CH62: Brom 5B **36**
CH64: Lit N 6D **38**
Morley Av. CH41: Birke 5F **13**
Morley Rd. CH44: Wall 2E **13**
Morley St. L4: Walt 4G **7**
Mornington Av. CH65: Ell P . . .2A **50**
Mornington Rd. CH45: New B . . .5F **5**
Mornington St. L8: Liv 2G **23**
Morpeth Cl. CH46: More 5B **10**
Morpeth Rd. CH47: Hoy 2C **16**
Morpeth St. L8: Liv 6H **15**

Morpeth Walkway
   CH41: Birke 5A **14**
Morpeth Wharf CH41: Birke . .5A **14**
Morris Ct. CH43: Oxton 2D **20**
Mortar Mill Quay
   CH41: Birke 4H **13**
Mortimer St. CH41: Birke 1B **22**
Morton St. L8: Liv 2H **23**
   (not continuous)
Mortuary Rd. CH45: Wall 5F **5**
Morval Cres. L4: Walt 1G **7**
Mosedale Rd. CH62: Brom . . .1C **36**
Moseley Av. CH45: Wall 1E **13**
Moseley Rd. CH63: Spit 2G **35**
Moses St. L8: Liv 3H **23**
Moss Cl. CH64: Will 5C **40**
Mossdene Rd. CH44: Wall . . .1D **12**
Moss Gro. CH42: Tran 5F **21**
Mosshey Ct. CH63: Spit 6G **29**
Mosslands Cl. CH66: Gt Sut . .5E **49**
Mosslands Dr. CH44: Wall . . .6C **4**
   CH45: Wall 6C **4**
Moss La. CH42: Tran 5F **21**
Mossley Av. CH42: Brom 3B **36**
Mossley Rd. CH42: Tran 4A **22**
Moss St. L6: Liv 1F **15**
Mossvale CH66: Lit Sut 5D **42**
Mossy Bank Rd. CH44: Wall . .1H **13**
Moston Way CH66: Gt Sut . . .4F **49**
   CH60: Hesw 3G **31**
Mostyn Av. CH48: W Kir 6D **16**
   CH60: Hesw 3G **31**
Mostyn Cl. L4: Kirkd 4G **7**
Mostyn Gdns. CH46: Park . . .4A **38**
Mostyn Sq. CH64: Park 4A **38**
Mostyn St. CH44: Wall 2F **13**
Mould St. L5: Liv 5F **7**
Mounsey Rd. CH42: Tran 2H **21**
Mount, The CH44: Wall 1G **13**
   CH60: Hesw 3B **32**
   CH63: Hghr B 2D **28**
Mount Cl. CH45: Wall 3E **5**
   CH60: Hesw 3B **32**
Mount Dr. CH63: Hghr B 2D **28**
Mt. Farm Way CH66: Gt Sut . .5C **48**
Mount Gro. CH41: Birke 2G **21**
Mount Gro. Pl. CH41: Birke . .2G **21**
   (off Mount Gro.)
Mt. Haven Cl. CH49: Upton . .2G **19**
Mount Olive CH43: Oxton . . .4E **21**
Mount Pk. CH63: Hghr B 2D **28**
Mt. Pleasant CH43: Oxton . . .4F **21**
   L3: Liv 4G **15**
Mt. Pleasant Cl.
   CH45: New B 4F **5**
Mt. Pleasant Rd.
   CH45: New B, Wall 5E **5**
Mount Rd. CH42: Tran 6G **21**
   CH45: Wall 3E **5**
   CH48: W Kir 6E **17**
   CH49: Upton 2G **19**
   CH63: Hghr B, Spit 1E **35**
Mount St. L1: Liv 5G **15**
Mt. Vernon Rd. L7: Liv 3H **15**
Mt. Vernon St. L7: Liv 3H **15**
Mountview Cl. L8: Liv 2H **23**
Mount Way CH63: Hghr B . . .2D **28**
Mountwood Rd. CH42: Tran . .1C **28**
Mourne Cl. CH66: Lit Sut 1A **48**
Mowbray Ct. L20: Kirkd 2E **7**
Mr Hardman's Photographic Studio
   . . . . .5G **15**
Mudhouse La. CH64: Burt . . .5A **46**
Mulberry Cl. L7: Liv 5H **15**
   (off Mulberry St.)
Mulberry Gro. CH44: Wall . . .2H **13**
Mulberry Pl. L7: Liv 5H **15**
Mulberry Rd. CH42: Rock F . .5B **22**
Mulberry St. L7: Liv 5H **15**
Mulgrave St. L8: Liv 6H **15**
Mull Cl. CH65: Ell P 6A **50**
Mulveton Rd. CH63: Spit 6F **29**
Mumfords Gro. CH47: Meols . .4G **9**
Mumfords La. CH47: Meols . . .4F **9**
   (not continuous)
Muncaster Cl. CH62: Brom . . .2B **36**
Muriel St. L4: Walt 3H **7**
Murrayfield Dr. CH46: Leas . .1F **19**
Murrayfield Spire Hospital
   . . . . .4F **27**

Murray Gro. CH48: W Kir 4C **16**
Museum of Liverpool 4D **14**
Mycroft Cl. L5: Liv 5H **7**
Mynsule Rd. CH63: Spit 6F **29**
Myrtle Gro. CH44: Wall 2A **14**
Myrtle Pde. L7: Liv 5H **15**
Myrtle St. CH65: Ell P 2G **43**
   L7: Liv 5H **15**
Myrtle Way CH49: Woodc . . .3H **19**

N

Naburn Gro. CH46: More 6E **11**
Nairn Cl. CH63: East 1F **41**
Nansen Gro. L4: Walt 2H **7**
Nant Pk. Ct. CH45: New B . . .3G **5**
Nantwich Cl. CH49: Woodc . .5G **19**
Nantwich Rd. CH66: Gt Sut . .4F **49**
Napier Dr. CH46: More 5F **11**
Napier Rd. CH62: New F 1H **29**
Napier St. L20: Boot 2D **6**
Naples Rd. CH44: Wall 2H **13**
Napps Way CH61: Hesw 1C **32**
Naseby Cl. CH43: Noct 3A **20**
Naseby St. L4: Walt 1H **7**
National Conservation Cen.
   . . . . .3F **15**
National Waterways Mus. . . .2H **43**
Navigation Wharf L3: Liv 1F **23**
Naylor Cl. CH65: Ell P 5F **43**
Naylor Ct. CH66: Ell P 1E **49**
Naylor Cres. CH65: Ell P 5F **43**
Naylor Grn. CH66: Ell P 5F **43**
Naylor Pl. CH66: Ell P 5F **43**
Naylor Rd. CH43: Bid 5C **12**
   CH66: Ell P 6F **43**
Naylor St. L3: Liv 2E **15**
Naylor Wlk. CH66: Ell P 6F **43**
Neale Dr. CH49: Grea 4E **19**
Needham Cres. CH43: Noct . .3B **20**
Needwood Dr. CH63: Beb 6F **29**
Nelson Ct. CH42: Rock F 6C **22**
   CH45: New B 2F **5**
Nelson Dr. CH61: Pens 5A **26**
Nelson Ho. CH42: Rock F 6C **22**
Nelson Memorial 3E **15**
   (off Exchange Pas. E.)
Nelson Rd. CH42: Rock F 6C **22**
   CH65: Ell P 2G **43**
Nelson's Cft. CH63: Beb 6G **29**
Nelson St. CH45: New B 4G **5**
   L1: Liv 6F **15**
   (not continuous)
   L20: Boot 1D **6**
Neptune St. CH41: Birke 5H **13**
Neptune Theatre 4F **15**
NESS 2E **45**
Ness Acre La. CH64: Will 5A **40**
Ness Botanical Gdns. 4E **45**
Ness Botanical Gdns. Vis. Cen.
   . . . . .3E **45**
Nesse Ho. CH64: Nest 5C **38**
   (off Churchill Way)
NESSHOLT 2D **44**
NESTON 5C **38**
Neston Gdns. CH41: Birke . . .5F **13**
   (off Churchview Rd.)
Neston Grn. CH66: Gt Sut . . .3D **48**
   (not continuous)
Neston Recreation Cen. 4D **38**
Neston Rd. CH63: Thorn H . . .1D **38**
   CH64: Burt, Ness 2D **44**
   CH64: Nest 1D **38**
   CH64: Will 5A **40**
Neston Station (Rail) 5C **38**
Neston St. L4: Walt 2H **7**
Netherby St. L8: Liv 4H **23**
Netherfield Cl. CH43: Noct . . .3A **20**
Netherfield Rd. Nth. L5: Liv . .5G **7**
Netherfield Rd. Sth.
   L5: Liv 1G **15**
Netherpool Rd. CH66: Ell P . .6F **43**
Netherton Rd. CH66: More . . .5E **11**
Netley St. L4: Kirkd 3G **7**
Nettle Hill CH48: W Kir 4C **16**
Neva Av. CH46: More 5D **10**
Neville Cl. CH43: Noct 3A **20**
Neville Rd. CH44: Wall 1E **13**
   CH62: Brom 4C **36**

Nevin St. L6: Liv 2H **15**
New Acres Cl. CH43: Bid 5A **12**
Newark Cl. CH43: Noct 3A **20**
Newark St. L4: Walt 2H **7**
New Bird St. L1: Liv 6F **15**
Newbold Cres. CH48: W Kir . .4G **17**
Newbridge Cl.
   CH49: Woodc 3H **19**
New Bri. Ct. CH65: Ell P 3D **50**
Newbridge Rd.
   CH2: Lit Stan 4D **50**
   CH65: Ell P 3D **50**
NEW BRIGHTON 2F **5**
New Brighton Station (Rail) . .3E **5**
Newburn CH43: Oxton 2F **21**
Newburns La. CH43: Oxton . .4F **21**
Newburn St. L4: Walt 1H **7**
Newbury Way CH46: Leas . . .2F **11**
Newby St. L4: Walt 3H **7**
New Chester Rd.
   CH41: Birke, Tran 2B **22**
   CH42: Rock F, Tran 3B **22**
   CH62: Brom, East, New F, Port S
   . . . . .5C **22**
   CH66: Hoot 3A **42**
Newdales Cl. CH43: Bid 5A **12**
Newell Rd. CH44: Wall 6F **5**
New Extension Quay
   CH65: Ell P 5H **43**
NEW FERRY 2H **29**
New Ferry By-Pass
   CH62: New F, Port S 1H **29**
New Ferry Rd.
   CH62: New F 6D **22**
New Grosvenor Rd.
   CH65: Ell P 6H **43**
New Hall La. CH47: Hoy 1D **16**
New Hall Mnr. CH64: Nest . . .5G **33**
New Hall Pl. L3: Liv 3D **14**
Newhall St. L1: Liv 6F **15**
Newhaven Rd. CH45: New B . .4G **5**
New Hedley Gro. L5: Liv 6E **7**
New Henderson St.
   L8: Liv 1G **23**
New Heyes CH64: Nest 4C **38**
New Hey La. CH64: Will 6B **40**
New Hey Rd. CH49: Woodc . .3H **19**
Newhope Rd. CH41: Birke . . .6G **13**
New Houses La.
   CH64: Lit N 3C **44**
Newington L1: Liv 4G **15**
New Islington L3: Liv 3G **15**
Newland Dr. CH44: Wall 1E **13**
Newlands Rd. CH63: Beb 5H **29**
Newling St. CH41: Birke 6G **13**
Newlyn Cl. CH47: Meols 4G **9**
Newlyn Rd. CH47: Meols 4G **9**
Newman St. L4: Kirkd 4F **7**
Newnham Dr. CH65: Ell P . . .3A **50**
New Palace Amusement Pk. . .2F **5**
Newport Av. CH45: Wall 4B **4**
Newport Cl. CH43: Noct 3A **20**
Newport Ct. L5: Liv 6E **7**
New Quay L3: Liv 3D **14**
New Quay Ter. L3: Liv 3D **14**
   (off New Quay)
New Rd. CH66: Chil T 5A **42**
New School La.
   CH66: Chil T 5B **42**
Newsham St. L5: Liv 6F **7**
New St. CH44: Wall 3A **14**
   CH64: Lit N 2C **44**
NEWTON 5G **17**
Newton Ct. CH42: Rock F . . .6C **22**
   (off New Chester Rd.)
Newton Cross La.
   CH48: W Kir 5G **17**
Newton Dr. CH48: W Kir 5G **17**
Newton Pk. Rd.
   CH48: W Kir 5G **17**
Newton Rd. CH44: Wall 1E **13**
   CH47: Hoy 6E **9**
   CH65: Ell P 2A **50**
Newton St. CH41: Birke 6H **13**
Newton Way CH49: Upton . . .2F **19**
   L3: Liv 4H **15**
New Tower Ct. CH45: New B . .3G **5**
Newtown CH64: Lit N 1D **44**
New Way Bus. Cen.
   CH44: Wall 3H **13**

NHS WALK-IN CENTRE
   Liverpool City Centre . . .4F **15**
   Wirral 2F **13**
   (within Victoria Central Hospital)
   Wirral Arrowe Park 6G **19**
   (within Arrowe Park Hospital)
Nicholas St. L3: Liv 2F **15**
Nicholls Dr. CH61: Pens 5B **26**
Nickleby Cl. L8: Liv 2H **23**
Nicola Ct. CH45: Wall 5G **5**
Nigel Rd. CH60: Hesw 3E **33**
Nimrod St. L4: Walt 2H **7**
Nixon St. L4: Walt 1H **7**
NOCTORUM 3B **20**
Noctorum Av. CH43: Noct . . .2A **20**
Noctorum Dell CH43: Noct . .3B **20**
Noctorum La.
   CH43: Noct, Oxton 1B **20**
Noctorum Rd. CH43: Noct . . .2B **20**
Noctorum Way
   CH43: Noct 3B **20**
Nook, The CH43: Oxton 1F **21**
   CH48: Frank 5B **18**
Norbury Av. CH63: Hghr B . . .4E **29**
Norbury Cl. CH63: Hghr B . . .4F **29**
Norfolk Cl. CH43: Noct 3A **20**
Norfolk Dr. CH48: W Kir 6E **17**
Norfolk Rd. CH65: Ell P 2A **50**
Norfolk St. L1: Liv 6F **15**
Norgate St. L4: Walt 4H **7**
Norlands Ct. CH42: Rock F . . .6A **22**
Norley Av. CH62: East 2G **41**
   CH65: Ell P 1F **49**
Norman Cl. CH66: Gt Sut 6A **48**
Norman Rd. CH44: Wall 3A **14**
Normanston Cl.
   CH43: Oxton 3F **21**
Normanston Rd.
   CH43: Oxton 3F **21**
Norman St. CH41: Birke 5D **12**
   L3: Liv 3H **15**
   (off London Rd.)
Norris Cl. CH43: Noct 3A **20**
Nth. Brooke Way
   CH49: Woodc 4G **19**
Northbrook Rd. CH44: Wall . .2H **13**
Northbrook St. L8: Liv 6H **15**
Northbury Rd. CH66: Gt Sut . .6E **49**
Nth. Cheshire Trad. Est.
   CH43: Pren 1G **27**
North Cl. CH62: Brom 1A **36**
Northcote Cl. L5: Liv 1H **15**
Northcote Rd. CH45: Wall . . .5B **4**
   (not continuous)
North Dr. CH45: Wall 3D **4**
   CH60: Hesw 4C **32**
Northern Ri. CH66: Gt Sut . . .4E **49**
Nth. Hill St. L8: Liv 2H **23**
Nth. John St. L2: Liv 4E **15**
Northop Rd. CH45: Wall 5D **4**
North Pde. CH47: Hoy 6C **8**
   CH64: Park 3A **38**
   (off Boathouse Pde.)
North Pk. Ct. CH44: Wall 2A **14**
   (off Demesne St.)
Northridge Rd. CH61: Pens . .4C **26**
North Rd. CH42: Tran 4G **21**
   CH48: W Kir 5C **16**
   CH65: Ell P 1C **42**
   (not continuous)
North St. L3: Liv 3F **15**
North Ter. CH47: Meols 4F **9**
Northumberland Gro.
   L8: Liv 2F **23**
Northumberland St. L8: Liv . .2G **23**
Northumberland Ter.
   L5: Liv 5G **7**
North Vw. CH66: Lit Sut 1C **48**
   (off Station Rd.)
Nth. Wallasey App.
   CH45: Wall 5A **4**
Nth. Wall Terminal
   CH65: Ell P 1G **43**
Northway CH60: Hesw 2F **33**
Northways CH62: Brom 6B **30**
Nth. William St.
   CH44: Wall 3A **14**
North Wirral Coastal Pk. 3H **9**
Northwood Rd. CH43: Pren . .5D **20**

Norton Ct. CH44: Wall 2A **14**
   (off Borough Rd.)
Norton Dr. CH61: Irby 2G **25**
Norton Rd. CH48: W Kir 4C **16**
Norton St. L3: Liv 3G **15**
Norville CH66: Lit Sut 6D **42**
Norwich Dr. CH49: Upton 6G **11**
  CH66: Gt Sut 6A **48**
Norwood Ct. CH49: Grea 4D **18**
Norwood Rd. CH44: Wall 3F **13**
  CH49: Grea 3D **18**
Nowshera Av. CH61: Pens 4B **26**
Nuffield Cl. CH49: Upton 3F **19**
Nun Cl. CH43: Oxton 4F **21**
Nurse Rd. CH61: Thing 3D **26**
Nursery Cl. CH43: Oxton 4F **21**

O

Oak Av. CH49: Upton 1D **18**
Oak Bank CH41: Birke 2G **21**
Oakbank St. CH44: Wall 2G **13**
Oak Cl. CH46: More 6D **10**
Oakdale Av. CH44: Wall 3H **13**
Oakdale Dr. CH49: Grea 5C **18**
Oakdale Rd. CH44: Wall 3H **13**
Oakdene Av. CH66: Gt Sut 2C **48**
Oakdene Cl. CH62: Brom 6B **36**
Oakdene Rd. CH42: Tran 4G **21**
Oakenholt Rd. CH46: More 4E **11**
Oakes St. L3: Liv 3H **15**
Oakfield Rd. CH62: Brom 3A **36**
  CH66: Chil T 5G **41**
Oakfield Ter.
  CH66: Chil T 5G **41**
Oak Gro. CH65: Whit 4G **49**
Oakham Dr. CH46: More 4B **10**
Oakham St. L8: Liv 1F **23**
Oakland Dr. CH49: Upton 1G **19**
Oaklands CH62: Brom 5B **36**
Oaklands Bus. Cen.
  CH66: Hoot 3G **41**
Oaklands Dr. CH61: Hesw 2C **32**
  CH63: Beb 3G **29**
Oaklands Ter. CH61: Hesw 1C **32**
Oakland Va. CH45: New B 3G **5**
Oakleaf M. CH43: Noct 2B **20**
Oaklea Rd. CH61: Irby 3B **26**
Oakleigh Gro. CH63: Beb 3F **29**
Oakley Ct. CH65: Ell P 3A **50**
Oakmere Cl. CH46: Leas 1E **11**
Oakmere Dr. CH49: Grea 3C **18**
  CH66: Gt Sut 6F **49**
Oakridge Cl. CH62: Spit 1A **36**
Oakridge Rd. CH62: Spit 1A **36**
Oak Rd. CH63: Hghr B 2F **29**
  CH66: Hoot 4G **41**
Oaks, The CH62: Brom 3A **36**
Oaks La. CH61: Pens 5C **26**
Oak St. CH65: Ell P 2G **43**
OakswAy CH60: Hesw 5D **32**
Oaktree Ct. Bus. Cen.
  CH64: Ness 1H **45**
Oaktree Pl. CH42: Rock F 4B **22**
Oakwood Cl. CH66: Gt Sut 6D **48**
Oakwood Dr. CH43: Bid 5C **12**
Oakwood Pk. CH43: Bid 5C **12**
  CH62: Brom 6B **36**
Oakworth Dr. CH62: New F 2A **30**
Oarside Dr. CH45: Wall 5E **5**
Oatlands, The CH48: W Kir 6E **17**
Oban Dr. CH60: Hesw 3C **32**
Oberon St. L20: Boot 2E **7**
Observatory Rd. CH43: Bid 5C **12**
Ocean Pk. CH41: Wall 4H **13**
O'Connell Rd. L3: Liv 1F **15**
Odeon Cinema
  Bromborough **6C 30**
  Liverpool **4E 15**
Odyssey Cen. CH41: Birke 5G **13**
Oil Sites Rd. CH65: Ell P 1H **43**
Oil St. L3: Liv 1D **14**
Old Barn La. CH64: Will 5B **40**
Old Barn Rd. CH44: Wall 2E **13**
Old Bidston Rd. CH41: Birke . . .5F **13**
Old Chester Rd. CH41: Tran . . .3A **22**
  CH42: Rock F, Tran 3A **22**
  CH63: Beb, Hghr B 6B **22**
  CH66: Gt Sut 2D **48**

Old Church Cl. CH65: Ell P 1A **50**
Old Churchyard L2: Liv 4D **14**
Old Clatterbridge Rd.
  CH63: Spit 1E **35**
Old Court Ho. Rd.
  CH62: Brom 4B **30**
Old Farm Cl. CH64: Will 5C **40**
Oldfield Cl. CH60: Hesw 1A **32**
Oldfield Dr. CH60: Hesw 1H **31**
Oldfield Gdns.
  CH60: Hesw 2H **31**
Oldfield La. CH48: W Kir 3A **18**
Oldfield Rd. CH45: Wall 5D **4**
  CH60: Hesw 1H **31**
  CH65: Ell P 2H **49**
Oldfield Way CH60: Hesw 1H **31**
Old Greasby Rd.
  CH49: Upton 2F **19**
Old Hall Dr. CH65: Whit 3H **49**
Old Hall Rd. CH62: Brom 2C **36**
Old Hall St. L3: Liv 3D **14**
Oldham Pl. L1: Liv 4G **15**
Oldham St. L1: Liv 5G **15**
Old Haymarket L1: Liv 3F **15**
  (not continuous)
Old La. CH60: Hesw 3F **33**
Old Leeds St. L3: Liv 3D **14**
Old Maryland La.
  CH46: More 4E **11**
Old Meadow Rd.
  CH61: Pens 5A **26**
Old Mill, The
  CH66: Lit Sut 6C **42**
  (off Station Rd.)
Old Mill Cl. CH60: Hesw 4D **32**
Old Post Office Pl. L1: Liv 4F **15**
  (off School La.)
Old Pump La. CH49: Grea 4C **18**
Old Quay Cl. CH64: Park 6A **38**
Old Quay La. CH64: Park 6B **38**
Old Ropery L2: Liv 4E **15**
  (off Drury La.)
Old School Cl. CH45: Lit N 2D **44**
Old School Ho., The
  CH43: Oxton 2E **21**
  (off Beresford Rd.)
Old School Way
  CH41: Birke 6C **12**
Old Vicarage Rd.
  CH64: Will 5C **40**
Old Welsh Rd.
  CH66: Lit Sut 2H **47**
Old Wood Rd.
  CH61: Pens 5B **26**
Olinda St. CH62: New F 2H **29**
Olive Cres. CH41: Tran 3A **22**
Olive Dr. CH64: Nest 5G **38**
Olive Mt. CH41: Tran 3A **22**
Oliver Ho. CH66: Gt Sut 3D **48**
  (off Oliver La.)
Oliver La. CH41: Birke 1A **22**
  CH66: Gt Sut 3D **48**
Olive Rd. CH64: Nest 5C **38**
Oliver St. CH41: Birke 1H **21**
Oliver St. E. CH41: Birke 1A **22**
Olivia Cl. CH43: Noct 3A **20**
Olivia M. CH43: Noct 3A **20**
Olivia St. L20: Boot 2F **7**
Ollerton Cl. CH43: Noct 3A **20**
Olney St. L4: Walt 1H **7**
One Park W. L1: Liv 4E **15**
Onslow Rd. CH45: New B 3F **5**
  CH62: New F 1H **29**
Opal Ct. L3: Liv 3H **15**
Open Eye Gallery 4F **15**
  (off Wood St.)
Orchard, The CH45: Wall 4E **5**
Orchard Cl. CH66: Gt Sut 6F **49**
Orchard Ct. CH41: Tran 4B **12**
Orchard Dr. CH64: Lit N 2C **44**
Orchard Grange
  CH46: More 6C **10**
Orchard Haven
  CH66: Gt Sut 6E **49**
Orchard La. CH66: Chil T 5A **42**
Orchard Pl. CH62: Spit 1H **35**
Orchard Rd. CH46: More 4E **11**
  CH65: Whit 5G **49**

Orchard Wlk. CH64: Nest 5C **38**
Orchard Way CH63: Hghr B . . .3D **28**
Orchid Gro. L17: Aig 4H **23**
Orchil Cl. CH66: Lit Sut 1A **48**
O'Reilly Ct. L3: Liv 1E **15**
Oriel Cl. L2: Liv 4E **15**
  (off Water St.)
Oriel Ct. CH42: Tran 6F **21**
Oriel Cres. L20: Kirkd 2E **7**
Oriel Lodge L20: Boot 1E **7**
Oriel Rd. CH42: Tran 4A **22**
  L20: Boot 1E **7**
  L20: Kirkd 2E **7**
Oriel St. L3: Liv 2E **15**
Orkney Cl. CH65: Ell P 6A **50**
Orlando Cl. CH43: Noct 3A **20**
Orlando St. L20: Boot 2E **7**
Ormerod Cl. CH63: Beb 4G **29**
Ormesby Gro.
  CH63: Raby M 5H **35**
Ormiston Rd. CH45: New B 4F **5**
Ormond M. CH43: Noct 3A **20**
Ormond St. CH45: Wall 6F **5**
  L3: Liv 3E **15**
Ormond Way CH43: Noct 3A **20**
Orrell Rd. CH45: New B 4G **5**
Orret's Mdw. Rd.
  CH49: Woodc 4H **19**
Orrysdale Rd.
  CH48: W Kir 4C **16**
Orry St. L5: Liv 6F **7**
Orston Cres. CH63: Spit 1G **35**
Ortega Cl. CH62: New F 2A **30**
Orthes St. L3: Liv 4H **15**
Orwell Rd. L4: Kirkd 3F **7**
Osborne Av. CH45: New B 4F **5**
Osborne Ct. CH43: Oxton 1F **21**
  (off Osborne Rd.)
  CH62: Port S 3H **29**
Osborne Gro. CH45: New B 5F **5**
Osborne Rd. CH43: Oxton 2F **21**
  CH45: New B 4G **5**
Osborne Va. CH45: New B 4F **5**
Osbourne Cl. CH62: Brom 4C **36**
Osmaston Rd. CH42: Tran 5E **21**
Ossett Cl. CH43: Noct 3A **20**
Oteley Av. CH62: Brom 3B **36**
Othello Cl. L20: Kirkd 2E **7**
Otterburn Cl.
  CH46: More 5B **10**
Oulton Cl. CH43: Oxton 4C **20**
Oulton Way CH43: Oxton 5C **20**
Oundle Rd. CH46: More 4E **11**
Oval, The 2F **29**
Oval, The CH45: Wall 5D **4**
  CH65: Ell P 4A **50**
Overchurch Rd.
  CH49: Upton 1E **19**
Overdale Av. CH61: Barn 4F **27**
Overdale Rd. CH64: Will 4C **40**
Overgreen Gro.
  CH46: More 4D **10**
Overmarsh CH64: Ness 3E **45**
OVERPOOL **1E 49**
Overpool Gdns.
  CH66: Gt Sut 4F **49**
Overpool Rd.
  CH66: Ell P, Gt Sut, Whit
  . . . . .1F **49**
  (not continuous)
Overpool Station (Rail) 1E **49**
Overstrand CH48: W Kir 5C **16**
Overton Cl. CH43: Oxton 4D **20**
Overton Rd. CH44: Wall 1F **13**
Overton Way CH43: Oxton 4D **20**
Owen Rd. L4: Kirkd 3F **7**
Oxford Cl. CH66: Gt Sut 6A **48**
  (off St Asaph Rd.)
Oxford Dr. CH63: Thorn H 5H **33**
Oxford Ho. L20: Boot 1G **7**
  (off Fernhill Rd.)
Oxford Rd. CH44: Wall 1G **13**
Oxford St. CH65: Ell P 1A **50**
  (off Worcester St.)
  L7: Liv 4H **15**
  (not continuous)
Oxley Av. CH46: Leas 2H **11**
OXTON **3D 20**
Oxton Ct. CH43: Oxton 3F **21**
Oxton Grn. CH66: Gt Sut 3D **48**

Oxton Rd. CH41: Birke 2G **21**
  CH44: Wall 2F **13**
Oxton St. L4: Walt 3H **7**

P

Pacific Rd. CH41: Birke 6B **14**
Padbury St. L8: Liv 2H **23**
Paddington L7: Liv 4H **15**
Paddock, The CH46: More 6C **10**
  CH49: Upton 2H **19**
  CH60: Hesw 3E **33**
  CH66: Gt Sut 4D **48**
Paddock Dr. CH64: Park 3B **38**
Padstow Rd. CH49: Grea 4C **18**
Page Wlk. L3: Liv 2G **15**
  (not continuous)
Pagewood Cl. CH61: Noct 3A **20**
Paignton Rd. CH45: Wall 5D **4**
Painswick Rd.
  CH66: Gt Sut 5E **49**
Paisley Av. CH62: East 1G **41**
Paisley St. L3: Liv 2D **14**
Palace Hey CH64: Ness 2E **45**
Palatine Rd. CH44: Wall 3H **13**
  CH62: Brom 2A **36**
Palermo Cl. CH44: Wall 3H **13**
Paley Cl. L4: Walt 4H **7**
Pall Mall L3: Liv 2E **15**
Palmer Cl. CH43: Noct 4B **20**
Palmerston Rd. CH44: Wall 1D **12**
Palmerston St.
  CH42: Rock F 5B **22**
Palmer Vs. CH42: Rock F 6A **22**
Palm Gro. CH43: Oxton 1F **21**
  CH66: Whit 6G **49**
Palm Hill CH43: Oxton 3F **21**
Palmwood Cl. CH43: Pren 6C **20**
Paltridge Way CH61: Pens 5B **26**
Pansy St. L5: Kirkd 4F **7**
Parade, The CH64: Park 4A **38**
Paradise Island Bingo **2G 7**
Paradise Pl. L1: Liv 4F **15**
  (off Paradise St.)
Paradise St. L1: Liv 5F **15**
Park & Ride
  Leasowe **3G 11**
Park Av. CH44: Wall 2H **13**
Parkbridge Rd. CH42: Tran 4G **21**
Parkbury Ct. CH43: Oxton 4E **21**
Park Cl. CH41: Birke 1G **21**
Park Ct. CH48: W Kir 5C **16**
Parkdale CH48: Caldy 3B **24**
Park Dr. CH41: Birke 6E **13**
  (not continuous)
  CH43: Clau 6E **13**
  CH65: Whit 4H **49**
Parkend Rd. CH42: Tran 4G **21**
Parker St. L1: Liv 4F **15**
Parkfield Av. CH41: Birke 1H **21**
Parkfield Dr. CH44: Wall 1F **13**
  CH65: Whit 5G **49**
Parkfield Pl. CH41: Birke 1H **21**
Parkfield Rd. CH63: Beb 6G **29**
PARKGATE **4A 38**
Parkgate Ho. CH64: Park 3A **38**
  (off Greenway)
Parkgate Ho. Ct.
  CH64: Park 4A **38**
Parkgate La. CH64: Nest 6G **33**
Parkgate Rd. CH1: Woodb 6F **47**
  CH64: Nest 5B **38**
  CH66: Led 5E **47**
Park Gro. CH41: Birke 2H **21**
Parkhill Ct. L8: Liv 3H **23**
  (off Park Hill Rd.)
Park Hill Rd. L8: Liv 3H **23**
Parkhill Rd. CH42: Tran 4G **21**
Parkhurst Rd. CH42: Tran 5G **21**
Parkland Cl. L8: Liv 2H **23**
Parkland Ct. CH43: Bid 5A **12**
  CH49: Woodc 5G **19**
  (off Childwall Grn.)
Parklands CH66: Lit Sut 2C **48**
Parklands Dr. CH60: Hesw 5D **32**
Parklands Gdns.
  CH66: Lit Sut 1D **48**
Parklands Vw.
  CH66: Lit Sut 1D **48**

Park La. CH47: Meols 4H 9
  L1: Liv 5F 15
Park La. Cvn. Site
  CH47: Meols 3A 10
Parklea CH66: Lit Sut 1D 48
Park Pl. L8: Liv 1G 23
Park Rd. CH42: Tran 4A 22
  CH44: Wall 2G 13
  CH47: Meols 4G 9
  CH48: W Kir 5C 16
  CH60: Hesw 2D 32
  CH62: East 5D 36
  CH62: Port S 4H 29
  CH65: Will 5D 40
  CH65: Ell P 3A 50
    (not continuous)
  L8: Liv 1H 23
Park Rd. E. CH41: Birke 1G 21
Park Rd. Nth. CH41: Birke . . .6E 13
Park Rd. Sth. CH43: Clau . . .1F 21
Park Rd. W. CH43: Clau 6E 13
Parkside CH44: Wall 2G 13
Parkside Cl. CH63: Beb 3G 29
  CH64: Park 5B 38
Parkside Rd. CH42: Tran 4A 22
  CH63: Beb 3G 29
Parkside St. L6: Liv 2H 15
Parkstone Rd. CH42: Tran . . .4G 21
Park St. CH41: Birke 1H 21
    (not continuous)
  CH44: Wall 1G 13
  CH64: Nest 5C 38
  L8: Liv 2G 23
    (not continuous)
Park Vale CH64: Nest 6D 38
Parkvale Av. CH43: Pren 1G 27
Park Vw. CH62: Brom 3A 36
  CH62: New F 1H 29
Parkview CH49: Woodc 6G 19
Parkview Cl. CH41: Birke 6G 13
Parkview Ct. CH60: Hesw 3B 32
Park Way L8: Liv 6H 15
    (not continuous)
Parkway CH45: Wall 4C 4
  CH47: Meols 5G 9
  CH61: Irby 2B 26
Parkway Cl. CH61: Irby 2B 26
Park West CH60: Hesw 4H 31
Parkwood Cl. CH62: Brom 2C 36
Parliament Cl. L1: Liv 6G 15
Parliament Pl. L8: Liv 6H 15
Parliament St. L8: Liv 6F 15
Parliament Way
  CH66: Gt Sut 6A 48
Parnell Rd. CH63: Spit 1G 35
Parr Gro. CH49: Grea 3C 18
Parr's Rd. CH43: Oxton 4F 21
Parr St. L1: Liv 5F 15
Parry St. CH44: Wall 3H 13
Pasture Av. CH46: More 3E 11
Pasture Cres. CH46: More 4E 11
Pasture Rd. CH46: More 2D 10
Pastures, The CH48: W Kir 5H 17
Paterson St. CH41: Birke 1G 21
Patmos Cl. L5: Liv 5G 7
Paton Cl. CH48: W Kir 4F 17
Patricia Av. CH41: Birke 4D 12
Patten St. CH41: Birke 5F 13
Patterdale Rd. CH63: Beb 6F 29
Paul Orr Ct. L3: Liv 1E 15
Paulsfield Dr. CH46: More 6E 11
Paul St. L3: Liv 2E 15
Paulton Cl. L8: Liv 3H 23
Pavilions, The CH43: Oxton . . .3E 21
Peach St. L7: Liv 4H 15
Pearson Rd. CH42: Tran 2A 22
Pear Tree Cl. CH60: Hesw 2E 33
Peartree Way CH66: Gt Sut . . .6E 49
Peckforton Dr. CH66: Gt Sut . . .4E 49
Pecksniff Cl. L8: Liv 2H 23
Peebles Cl. CH66: Lit Sut 1H 47
Peel Av. CH42: Tran 4B 22
Peel Pl. L8: Liv 6H 15
Peerswood Ct. CH64: Lit N 2C 44
Pelham Rd. CH44: Wall 2E 13
Pelwood Dr. CH49: Woodc 4H 19
Pemberton Ct. CH64: Will 5C 40
Pemberton Rd.
  CH49: Woodc 4H 19
Pembridge Ct. CH65: Ell P 4C 50

Pembridge Gdns.
  CH65: Ell P 4C 50
    (off Rochester Dr.)
Pembroke Av. CH46: More 6E 11
Pembroke Dr. CH65: Whit 4G 49
Pembroke Gdns. L3: Liv 3H 15
Pembroke Pl. L3: Liv 3G 15
Pembroke Rd. L20: Boot 1E 7
Pembroke St. L3: Liv 3H 15
Pendennis Rd. CH44: Wall 2G 13
Pendle Cl. CH49: Upton 1E 19
  CH66: Lit Sut 1H 47
Pengwern St. L8: Liv 2H 23
Pengwern Ter. CH45: Wall 4G 5
    (off Holland Rd.)
Peninsula Cl. CH45: Wall 3C 4
Penistone Dr. CH66: Lit Sut . . .2B 48
Penkett Ct. CH45: Wall 5G 5
Penkett Gdns. CH45: Wall 5G 5
Penkett Gro. CH45: Wall 5G 5
Penkett Rd. CH45: Wall 5F 5
Penmon Dr. CH61: Pens 6B 26
Penn Gdns. CH65: Ell P 2H 49
Pennine Rd. CH42: Tran 6G 21
  CH44: Wall 1D 12
Pennine Wlk. CH66: Lit Sut 1B 48
Pennington Dr.
  CH66: Gt Sut 4C 48
Pennington St. L4: Walt 1H 7
Pennystone Cl.
  CH49: Upton 1D 18
Penrhos Rd. CH47: Hoy 1C 16
Penrhyd Rd. CH61: Irby 4H 25
Penrhyn Av. CH61: Thing 3C 26
Penrhyn St. L5: Liv 6F 7
Penrith St. CH41: Birke 2G 21
Penrose St. L5: Liv 5H 7
Pensall Dr. CH61: Hesw 1B 32
PENSBY 5C 26
Pensby Cl. CH61: Thing 4C 26
Pensby Dr. CH66: Gt Sut 3D 48
Pensby Hall La.
  CH61: Hesw 1B 32
Pensby Rd. CH60: Hesw 2C 32
  CH61: Hesw, Irby, Pens 2C 32
Pensby St. CH41: Birke 5G 13
Pentland Av. L4: Walt 2H 7
Penuel Rd. L4: Walt 1H 7
Peover St. L3: Liv 2F 15
Percival Rd. CH65: Ell P 1H 49
Percy Rd. CH44: Wall 3A 14
Percy St. L8: Liv 6H 15
Perrin Rd. CH45: Wall 6C 4
Perry St. L8: Liv 1F 23
Pershore Ho. CH42: Tran 6F 21
Peterborough Cl.
  CH66: Gt Sut 6A 48
Peter Ho. L3: Liv 3E 15
    (off Tithebarn St.)
Peterhouse M. L20: Boot 1F 7
Peter Price's La.
  CH63: Hghr B 5E 29
Peter Rd. L4: Walt 1G 7
    (not continuous)
Peters Arc. L1: Liv 4F 15
    (off Peter's La.)
Peter's La. L1: Liv 4F 15
Peter St. CH44: Wall 3A 14
  L1: Liv 3F 15
Peterwood CH42: Rock F 6C 22
Peveril St. L9: Walt 1H 7
Philharmonic Ct. L8: Liv 5H 15
    (off Catharine St.)
Philharmonic Hall 5H 15
Philip Leverhulme Lodge
  CH62: Port S 3H 29
Philips La. CH66: Gt Sut 3C 48
Phillips St. L3: Liv 2E 15
Phillips Way CH60: Hesw 3A 32
Pickerill Rd. CH49: Grea 4D 18
Pickmere Dr. CH62: East 2H 41
    (not continuous)
Pickop St. L3: Liv 3D 14
Pickwick St. L8: Liv 1H 23
Picton Cl. CH43: Oxton 3D 20
  CH62: East 2F 41
Picton Hall 3F 15
    (off Cuerden St.)

Pier Head L3: Liv 4D 14
Pikes Hey Rd. CH48: Caldy . . .2D 24
Pilgrim St. CH41: Birke 1H 21
  L1: Liv 5G 15
Pincroft Way L4: Kirkd 4F 7
    (off Fountains Rd.)
Pine Av. CH63: Beb 6F 29
Pine Ct. CH41: Birke 1H 21
  L8: Liv 3H 23
    (off Byles St.)
Pinedale Cl. CH43: Noct 3A 20
  CH66: Whit 6B 48
Pinefield Cl. L5: Liv 5H 7
Pine Gro. CH66: Whit 6G 49
Pine Hey CH64: Nest 4B 38
Pine M. L1: Liv 6G 15
Pineridge Cl. CH62: Spit 6A 30
Pine Rd. CH60: Hesw 2E 33
Pines, The CH63: Spit 6H 29
Pine Tree Av. CH43: Noct 3A 20
Pinetree Cl. CH46: More 5F 11
Pinetree Ct. CH44: Wall 6D 4
Pinetree Dr. CH48: W Kir 6F 17
Pinetree Gro. CH46: More 5F 11
Pine Vw. Dr. CH61: Hesw 1B 32
Pine Walks CH42: Tran 6F 21
  CH48: W Kir 6F 17
Pinewalks Ridge
  CH42: Tran 1C 28
Pine Way CH60: Hesw 1A 32
Pinewood Dr. CH60: Hesw 3D 32
Pinfold Ct. CH48: W Kir 3C 16
Pinfold La. CH48: W Kir 3C 16
Pioneer Pk. CH65: Ell P 5F 43
Pipers, The CH60: Hesw 2H 31
Piper's Cl. CH60: Hesw 3H 31
Piper's End CH60: Hesw 3H 31
Pipers La. CH60: Hesw 1G 31
    (not continuous)
  CH64: Pudd 6C 46
Pipistrelle Ri. CH43: Noct 3B 20
Pitch Cl. CH49: Grea 4D 18
Pitt St. L1: Liv 5F 15
Plane Tree Rd.
  CH63: Hghr B 5E 29
Plantation Bus. Pk.
  CH62: Brom 1D 36
Plantation St. CH62: Brom 1D 36
Plantation Dr. CH66: Ell P 6E 43
Plantation Rd. CH62: Brom 2D 36
Planters, The CH49: Grea 3C 18
Platt Gro. CH42: Rock F 1G 29
Plaza Blvd. L8: Liv 1F 23
Pleasant Hill St. L8: Liv 1F 23
Pleasant St. CH45: New B 4F 5
  L3: Liv 4G 15
  L20: Boot 1D 6
Pleasant Vw. CH42: Boot 1D 6
Pleasington Cl. CH43: Noct 3C 20
Pleasington Dr. CH43: Noct 3C 20
Pleck Rd. CH65: Whit 5G 49
Plemston Ct. CH66: Ell P 5F 43
Ploughmans Cl.
  CH66: Gt Sut 6A 48
Ploughmans Way
  CH66: Gt Sut 6A 48
Plumer St. CH41: Birke 5E 13
Plumpton St. L6: Liv 1H 15
Plymyard Av.
  CH62: Brom, East 5B 36
Plymyard Cl. CH62: Brom 6B 36
Plymyard Copse
  CH62: Brom 6B 36
Plymyard Ct. CH62: Brom 5A 36
    (off Plymyard Av.)
Poets Cnr. CH62: Port S 4H 29
Polden Cl. CH66: Lit Sut 1A 48
POLL HILL 1B 32
Poll Hill Rd. CH60: Hesw 2B 32
Pollitt Sq. CH62: New F 1H 29
Pomfret St. L8: Liv 1H 23
Pomona St. L3: Liv 4G 15
Pond Vw. Cl. CH60: Hesw 3E 33
Ponsonby Rd. CH45: Wall 6C 4
Pool Bank CH62: Port S 2H 29
Poolbank Rd. CH62: New F 2H 29
Poole Hall Ind. Est.
  CH66: Ell P 5F 43
Poole Hall La. CH66: Ell P 5E 43
Poole Hall Rd. CH65: Ell P 5F 43

Poole Rd. CH44: Wall 6H 5
Pool La. CH49: Woodc 5G 19
  CH62: Brom 4A 30
Pool St. CH41: Birke 6H 13
Pooltown Rd.
  CH65: Ell P, Whit 1F 49
Poolwood Rd.
  CH49: Woodc 3H 19
Poplar Av. CH49: Upton 2F 19
Poplar Cl. CH65: Whit 3H 49
Poplar Dr. CH63: Beb 5H 29
  L5: Liv 6H 7
Poplar Farm Cl.
  CH46: More 1C 18
Poplar Gro. CH42: Tran 3H 21
    (off Ash Rd.)
Poplar Rd. CH43: Oxton 3F 21
  CH45: New B 4F 5
Poplar Way L4: Kirkd 2F 7
Poplar Weint CH64: Nest 5C 38
Poppy Cl. CH46: More 3G 11
Porlock Cl. CH60: Hesw 5D 32
Portal M. CH61: Pens 6B 26
Portal Rd. CH61: Pens 6B 26
Port Arcades, The
  CH65: Ell P 2A 50
Portbury Cl. CH62: Port S 3A 30
Portbury Wlk. CH62: Port S 3H 29
Portbury Way CH62: Port S 3A 30
Port C'way. CH62: Brom 5A 30
Porter St. L3: Liv 1D 14
Portia Av. CH63: Hghr B 2E 29
Portia St. L20: Kirkd 2E 7
Portland Ct. CH45: New B 2E 5
Portland Gdns. L5: Liv 1E 15
    (off Green St.)
Portland Gate CH62: Port S 3A 30
    (off Portbury Cl.)
Portland Pl. L5: Liv 1G 15
Portland St. CH41: Birke 5E 13
  CH45: New B 2E 5
  L5: Liv 1E 15
Porto Hey Rd. CH61: Irby 4H 25
Portree Av. CH63: East 6B 36
Portside Bus. Pk.
  CH65: Ell P 5H 43
Portside Ind. Est.
  CH65: Ell P 1G 43
Portside Nth. CH65: Ell P 5H 43
Portside Sth. CH65: Ell P 1G 43
PORT SUNLIGHT 3H 29
Port Sunlight Driving Range
  . . . . .4A 30
Port Sunlight Station (Rail)
  . . . . .4H 29
POULTON
  CH44 . . . . .2F 13
  CH63 . . . . .1G 35
Poulton Bri. Rd.
  CH41: Birke 3D 12
  CH44: Wall 2E 13
Poulton Grn. Cl. CH63: Spit . . .2F 35
Poulton Hall Rd.
  CH44: Wall 2E 13
  CH63: Raby M 4G 35
Poulton Rd. CH44: Wall 2E 13
  CH63: Spit 2G 35
Poulton Royd Dr. CH63: Spit . . .1F 35
Poulton Vale CH44: Wall 3E 13
Pound Rd. CH66: Lit Sut 6C 42
Powerleague Soccer Cen.
  Liverpool 4G 7
Power Rd. CH42: Rock F 1G 29
  CH62: Brom 2D 36
Pownall Sq. L3: Liv 3E 15
Pownall St. L1: Liv 5E 15
Premier St. L5: Liv 6H 7
    (not continuous)
Prentice Rd. CH42: Rock F 6A 22
PRENTON 1H 27
Prenton Dell Av.
  CH43: Pren 1A 28
Prenton Dell Rd.
  CH43: Pren 6C 20
Prenton Farm Rd.
  CH43: Pren 1A 28
Prenton Hall Rd.
  CH43: Pren 6D 20
Prenton La. CH42: Tran 6F 21
Prenton Pk. 5G 21

Prenton Pk. Rd. CH42: Tran . . .4G **21**
Prenton Rd. E. CH42: Tran . . .5G **21**
Prenton Rd. W. CH42: Tran . . .5G **21**
Prenton Village Rd.
   CH43: Pren 6D **20**
Prenton Way CH43: Pren 6B **20**
Prenton Way Bus. Units
   CH43: Pren 6B **20**
Prentonwood Ct.
   CH42: Tran 1G **21**
Prescot St. CH45: New B 3E **5**
   L7: Liv 3H **15**
Prestbury Av. CH43: Oxton . . .5C **20**
Prestbury Cl. CH43: Oxton . . .5C **20**
Preston St. L1: Liv 3F **15**
Price's La. CH43: Oxton 3F **21**
Price St. CH41: Birke 5F **13**
   L1: Liv 5E **15**
Price St. Bus. Cen.
   CH41: Birke 5G **13**
Priestfield Rd. CH65: Ell P . . .2H **49**
Priestway La. CH64: Burt 6A **46**
Primrose Ct. CH45: New B 3F **5**
   (off Egerton St.)
Primrose Gro. CH44: Wall 3A **14**
Primrose Hill CH62: Port S . . .3G **29**
   L3: Liv 3F **15**
Primrose Rd. CH41: Birke 6D **12**
Primrose St. L4: Kirkd 4F **7**
Prince Albert M. L1: Liv 6G **15**
   (off Up. Frederick St.)
Prince Edward St.
   CH41: Birke 6G **13**
Prince Edwin St. L5: Liv 1G **15**
Prince Rupert's Tower 1H **15**
Princes Av. CH48: W Kir 5D **16**
   CH62: East 5C **36**
   L8: Liv 6H **15**
Princes Blvd. CH63: Hghr B . .1D **28**
Princes Gdns. L3: Liv 2E **15**
Princes Pde. L3: Liv 3D **14**
Princes Pavement
   CH41: Birke 1A **22**
Princes Rd. CH65: Ell P 1F **49**
   L8: Liv 6H **15**
Princess Rd. CH45: New B 4F **5**
Princess Ter. CH43: Oxton . . .2G **21**
Princes St. L2: Liv 3E **15**
   L20: Boot 2D **6**
Princesway CH45: Wall 5E **5**
Prince William St. L8: Liv 1G **23**
Priorsfield CH46: More 5E **11**
Priory, The CH64: Nest 4B **38**
Priory Cl. CH63: Beb 6G **29**
Priory M. CH41: Birke 1B **22**
Priory Rd. CH44: Wall 2A **14**
   CH48: W Kir 5E **17**
   L4: Walt 3H **7**
Priory St. CH41: Birke 1B **22**
Priory Wharf CH41: Birke 1B **22**
Pritt St. L3: Liv 2G **15**
Private Dr. CH61: Barn 4F **27**
Probyn Rd. CH45: Wall 6C **4**
Procter Rd. CH42: Rock F 6C **22**
Proctor Rd. CH47: Hoy 1E **17**
Progress Pl. L1: Liv 3E **15**
   (off Stanley St.)
Promenade Gdns. L17: Aig . . .4H **23**
Prophet Wlk. L8: Liv 2H **23**
Prospect Point L6: Liv 3H **15**
Prospect Rd. CH42: Tran 6F **21**
Prospect St. L6: Liv 3H **15**
Prospect Va. CH45: Wall 6D **4**
Proudman Dr. CH43: Bid 6A **12**
Providence Cres. L8: Liv 1G **23**
Prussia St. L3: Liv 3E **15**
   (not continuous)
Puddington La. CH64: Burt . . .6H **45**
   CH64: Pudd 6D **46**
Pudsey St. L1: Liv 3G **15**
Puffin Cl. CH65: Ell P 6A **50**
Pugin St. L4: Walt 4G **7**
Pulford Av. CH43: Pren 5E **21**
Pulford Rd. CH63: Beb 4F **29**
   CH65: Gt Sut 3F **49**
Pulford St. L4: Walt 4H **7**
Pullman Cl. CH60: Hesw 3F **33**
Pumpfields Rd. L3: Liv 2E **15**
Pump La. CH49: Grea 2B **18**
Purbeck Dr. CH61: Irby 2H **25**

Pye Rd. CH60: Hesw 3B **32**
Pym St. L4: Walt 1H **7**
Pyramids Shop. Cen., The
   CH41: Birke 1H **21**

Q

Quadrant, The CH47: Hoy 1D **16**
Quaker La. CH60: Hesw 2A **32**
Quakers All. L2: Liv 3E **15**
Quantock Cl. CH66: Lit Sut . . .1A **48**
Quarry Av. CH63: Beb 5F **29**
Quarry Bank CH41: Birke 2H **21**
Quarry Bank Flats
   CH41: Birke 2H **21**
   (off Quarry Bank)
Quarrybank St. CH41: Birke . .2G **21**
Quarrybank Workshops
   CH41: Birke 2G **21**
   (off Quarrybank St.)
Quarry Cl. CH61: Hesw 1B **32**
Quarry La. CH61: Thing 3C **26**
Quarry Rd. CH64: Nest 4F **39**
   L20: Boot 1F **7**
Quarry Rd. E. CH60: Hesw 2A **32**
   CH61: Hesw 2A **32**
   CH63: Beb 5G **29**
Quarry Rd. W.
   CH60: Hesw 2A **32**
Quayside CH64: Lit N 2B **44**
   CH65: Ell P 2B **49**
   (off Grosvenor Wharf Rd.)
Quebec Quay L3: Liv 1E **23**
Queen Anne Pde. L3: Liv 3D **14**
   (off Old Hall St.)
Queen Anne St. L3: Liv 2G **15**
Queen Av. L2: Liv 4E **15**
   (off Sweeting St.)
Queen Mary's Dr.
   CH62: Port S 3H **29**
Queens Av. CH47: Meols 5F **9**
   CH65: Whit 4G **49**
Queensberry St. L8: Liv 2H **23**
Queensbury CH48: W Kir 4F **17**
Queensbury Av.
   CH62: Brom 2C **36**
Queens Ct. CH67: Hoy 6D **8**
Queens Dock Commercial Cen.
   L1: Liv 6F **15**
Queens Dr. CH43: Pren 6E **21**
   CH60: Hesw 3A **32**
Queens Dr. Walton L4: Walt . . .1H **7**
Queens Gdns. CH65: Ell P . . .2H **49**
Queen Sq. L1: Liv 3F **15**
Queens Rd. CH42: Rock F 6C **22**
   CH44: Wall 1A **14**
   CH47: Hoy 6C **8**
   CH66: Lit Sut 6C **42**
   L6: Liv 6H **7**
   L20: Boot 1E **7**
Queen St. CH41: Tran 3A **22**
   CH45: Wall 6F **5**
   CH65: Ell P 2G **43**
Queen's Wlk. L1: Liv 6G **15**
   (off Lady Chapel Cl.)
Queensway CH41: Birke 5C **14**
   CH45: Wall 5E **5**
   CH60: Hesw 5E **33**
Queens Wharf L3: Liv 6E **15**
Queenswood Av.
   CH63: Hghr B 1E **29**
Quigley St. CH41: Tran 3B **22**
Quillet, The CH64: Nest 6D **38**
Quinesway CH49: Upton 2F **19**

R

RABY .1G **39**
Raby Av. CH63: Raby M 5H **35**
Raby Cl. CH60: Hesw 4B **32**
   CH63: Raby M 4G **35**
Raby Ct. CH65: Ell P 4B **50**
Raby Dell CH63: Raby M 5H **35**
Raby Dr. CH46: More 6D **10**
   CH63: Raby M 4G **35**
Raby Gdns. CH64: Nest 5C **38**
Raby Gro. CH63: Hghr B 1D **28**

Raby Hall Rd.
   CH63: Brom, Raby M 6E **35**
RABY MERE 4G **35**
Raby Mere Rd.
   CH63: Raby, Raby M 1G **39**
   (not continuous)
Raby Pk. Cl. CH64: Nest 5C **38**
Raby Pk. Rd. CH64: Nest 5C **38**
Raby Rd.
   CH63: Raby, Thorn H 5B **34**
   CH64: Nest 5C **38**
Rachel St. L5: Liv 1F **15**
Raddle Wharf CH65: Ell P 2G **43**
Radford Av. CH63: Spit 1H **35**
Radley Dr. CH63: Thorn H 5H **33**
Radley Rd. CH44: Wall 6D **4**
Radleys Ct. L8: Liv 2H **23**
   (off Up. Warwick St.)
Radnor Av. CH60: Hesw 2B **32**
Radnor Dr. CH45: Wall 5G **5**
Radnor Pl. CH43: Oxton 1G **21**
Radstock Rd. CH44: Wall 6C **4**
Radway Grn. CH66: Gt Sut . . .2E **49**
Raeburn Av. CH48: W Kir 4E **17**
   CH62: East 5B **36**
   CH64: Lit N 6D **38**
Raffles Rd. CH42: Tran 2G **21**
Raffles St. L1: Liv 6G **15**
Railside Cl. L5: Liv 6E **7**
Railway Cotts. CH66: Hoot 4F **41**
Raines Cl. CH49: Grea 3E **19**
Rainford Gdns. L2: Liv 4F **15**
   (off Mathew St.)
Rainford Sq. L2: Liv 4E **15**
Rake, The CH62: Brom 3A **36**
   CH64: Burt 6H **45**
Rake Cl. CH49: Upton 3G **19**
Rake Hey CH46: More 5B **10**
Rake Hey Cl. CH46: More 5C **10**
Rake La. CH2: Chor B 6C **50**
   CH45: New B, Wall 4F **5**
   CH49: Upton 3G **19**
Rake M. CH49: Upton 3G **19**
Rake Precinct, The
   CH62: Brom 2B **36**
Rakersfield Ct. CH45: New B . .3G **5**
Rakersfield Rd.
   CH45: New B 3G **5**
Raleigh Rd. CH46: Leas 1G **11**
   CH64: Nest 4D **38**
Raleigh St. L20: Boot 2D **6**
Ramsey Ct. CH48: W Kir 6D **16**
Ramsey Rd. CH65: Ell P 6A **50**
Randle Cl. CH63: Spit 1G **35**
Randle Mdw. CH66: Gt Sut . . .5F **49**
Randle Mdw. Ct.
   CH66: Gt Sut 5F **49**
   (off Randle Mdw.)
Randolph St. L4: Walt 4H **7**
Ranelagh Pl. L3: Liv 4G **15**
Ranelagh St. L1: Liv 4F **15**
Rankin St. CH44: Wall 3E **13**
Rankin Way CH62: Brom 2C **36**
Rannoch Cl. CH66: Gt Sut 4F **49**
Rappart Rd. CH44: Wall 2H **13**
Rashid Mufti Ct. L8: Liv 1H **23**
Rathmore Cl. CH43: Oxton . . .4E **21**
Rathmore Dr. CH43: Oxton . . .3E **21**
Rathmore Rd. CH43: Oxton . . .3E **21**
Ravendale Cl. CH43: Noct 3B **20**
Ravenhill Cres. CH46: Leas . . .1F **11**
Ravenscroft Rd.
   CH43: Oxton 2G **21**
Ravenstone Cl.
   CH49: Upton 6F **11**
Ravenswood Av.
   CH42: Rock F 1F **29**
Ravenswood Rd.
   CH61: Hesw 1C **32**
Rawcliffe Rd. CH42: Tran 2H **21**
Raymond Pl. L5: Liv 1F **15**
Raymond Rd. CH44: Wall 2G **13**
Raymond Way CH64: Lit N 6E **39**
Reach, The L3: Liv 2F **15**
Reade Cl. CH63: Spit 2G **35**
Reading Cl. L5: Kirkd 4F **7**
Reading St. L5: Kirkd 4F **7**
Reay Ct. CH44: Wall 2A **14**
Rectory Cl. CH42: Tran 3H **21**
   CH60: Hesw 4B **32**

Rectory La. CH1: Cap 6H **47**
   CH60: Hesw 4A **32**
Rectory Rd. CH48: W Kir 6D **16**
Redbrook Cl. CH62: Brom 5B **36**
Redburn Cl. L8: Liv 3H **23**
Redcap Cl. CH45: Wall 3C **4**
Redcar Dr. CH62: East 6B **36**
Redcar Rd. CH45: Wall 5C **4**
Redcote Cl. CH48: W Kir 6C **16**
Redcroft CH49: Grea 4C **18**
Red Cross St. L1: Liv 4E **15**
Redditch Cl. CH49: Grea 3C **18**
Redfern St. L20: Kirkd 3E **7**
Redfield Cl. CH44: Wall 1H **13**
Redford Cl. CH49: Grea 3C **18**
Redgrave St. L20: Boot 1E **7**
Red Hill Rd. CH63: Store 4B **28**
Redhills M. CH65: Ell P 1H **49**
Redhillswood Cl.
   CH65: Ell P 6H **43**
Redhouse Bank
   CH48: W Kir 4C **16**
Redhouse La. CH48: W Kir 4C **16**
Red Lion La. CH66: Lit Sut 6C **42**
Redmere Dr. CH60: Hesw 3F **33**
Redmont St. CH41: Tran 3A **22**
Red Pike CH66: Lit Sut 5D **42**
Red Rocks Marsh Nature Reserve
   . . . . .3B **16**
Redstone Cl. CH47: Meols 5F **9**
Redstone Dr. CH60: Hesw 2G **31**
Redstone M. CH47: Meols 5F **9**
Redstone Pk. CH45: Wall 3D **4**
Redstone Ri. CH43: Noct 1B **20**
Redvers Av. CH66: Hoot 3A **42**
Redwood Cl. CH43: Oxton 5D **20**
Redwood Ct. L8: Liv 3H **23**
   (off Byles St.)
Redwood Dr. CH66: Gt Sut 6F **49**
Reeds Av. E. CH46: Leas 2F **11**
Reeds Av. W. CH46: Leas 2F **11**
Reeds La.
   CH46: Leas, More 1F **11**
Reedville CH43: Oxton 2F **21**
Reedville Gro. CH46: Leas 3F **11**
Reedville Rd. CH63: Beb 4F **29**
Regal Cl. CH66: Gt Sut 4E **49**
Regal Wlk. L4: Walt 4H **7**
Regency Ct. CH42: Rock F 6C **22**
   (off Rock La. W.)
Regent Rd. CH45: Wall 5B **4**
   L3: Liv 1D **6**
   L5: Kirkd, Liv 1D **6**
   L20: Boot, Kirkd 1C **6**
Regents Cl. CH61: Thing 3D **26**
Regent St. CH65: Ell P 2F **49**
   L3: Liv 1D **14**
Regents Way CH63: Hghr B . . .1D **28**
Reid Ct. CH66: Lit Sut 6C **42**
Reins Cft. CH64: Nest 4C **38**
Rendal Cl. L5: Liv 6H **7**
Rendelsham Cl.
   CH49: Upton 2E **19**
Rendel St. CH41: Birke 6H **13**
Renfrew Av. CH62: East 6C **36**
Renshaw St. L1: Liv 4G **15**
Repton Rd. CH65: Ell P 3B **50**
Reservoir Rd. CH42: Tran 6F **21**
Reservoir Rd. Nth.
   CH42: Tran 5F **21**
Reservoir St. L6: Liv 1H **15**
Rest Hill Rd. CH63: Store 4B **28**
Rhodesway CH60: Hesw 4D **32**
Rhona Cl. CH63: East 1E **41**
Rhuddlan Ct. CH65: Ell P 5B **50**
Rhum Cl. CH65: Ell P 6A **50**
Rhyl St. L8: Liv 2H **23**
Rialto Cl. L8: Liv 6H **15**
Ribblesdale CH65: Whit 4H **49**
Ribblesdale Cl. CH62: East 6D **36**
Ribble St. CH41: Birke 4D **12**
Rice Hey Rd. CH44: Wall 6G **5**
Rice La. CH44: Wall 6G **5**
   (not continuous)
   L9: Walt 1H **7**
Richard Allen Way L5: Liv 1H **15**
   (off Netherfield Rd. Sth.)
Richard Chubb Dr.
   CH44: Wall 5H **5**

Richardson Rd.
CH42: Rock F 6A **22**
Richmond Cl. CH63: Beb 3G **29**
Richmond Ct. CH65: Ell P 4B **50**
Richmond Rd. CH63: Beb 3F **29**
Richmond Row L3: Liv 2G **15**
Richmond St. CH45: New B 2F **5**
L1: Liv 4F **15**
Richmond Way CH61: Hesw . .1B **32**
CH61: Thing 2C **26**
Rich Vw. CH43: Oxton 4F **21**
Rickaby Cl. CH63: Brom 3A **36**
Rickman St. L4: Kirkd 4F **7**
Riddings, The CH65: Whit . . .3H **49**
Ridge, The CH60: Hesw 1H **31**
Ridgefield Rd. CH61: Pens . .4B **26**
Ridgemere Rd. CH61: Pens . .4B **26**
Ridgeview Rd. CH43: Noct . .2B **20**
Ridgeway, The
CH47: Meols 6G **9**
CH60: Hesw 4D **32**
CH63: Hghr B 1D **28**
Ridgeway Cl. CH66: Gt Sut . .5C **48**
Ridgewood Dr.
CH61: Pens 5A **26**
Ridings, The CH43: Noct . . .2B **20**
Ridings Hey CH43: Noct . . .3B **20**
Riding St. L3: Liv 3H **15**
Ridley Gro. CH48: W Kir . . .4C **16**
Ridley St. CH43: Oxton 2G **21**
Rigby Dr. CH49: Grea 5D **18**
Rigby St. L3: Liv 3D **14**
Rimmer St. L3: Liv 3G **15**
Ring Rd. CH2: Lit Stan 6B **50**
CH66: Back 6A **48**
Ringway CH64: Nest 4D **38**
Ringways CH62: Brom 6B **30**
Ringwood CH43: Oxton . . .4E **21**
Ripon Av. CH66: Lit Sut 2C **48**
Ripon Rd. CH45: Wall 5C **4**
Ripon St. CH41: Tran 3A **22**
L4: Walt 2H **7**
Rishton Cl. L5: Liv 6H **7**
Rishton St. L5: Liv 6H **7**
(off Tynemouth Cl.)
Rivacre Brow CH66: Ell P . . .6E **43**
Rivacre Bus. Cen.
CH66: Ell P 6E **43**
Rivacre Pk. 4C **42**
CH62: East 6E **37**
CH66: Ell P 6E **43**
CH66: Ell P, Hoot 3C **42**
Rivacre Valley Country Pk. 5D **42**
Riva La. CH60: Hesw 1A **32**
Riveacre Rd. CH65: Hoot . .6E **37**
Riverbank Cl. CH60: Hesw . .5B **32**
Riverbank Rd. CH60: Hesw . .5A **32**
CH62: Brom 5C **30**
River Gro. CH62: New F . . .1H **29**
Riverpark Gdns. L8: Liv 1G **23**
(off Hyslop St.)
Riversdale Rd. CH44: Wall . .1H **13**
CH48: W Kir 5C **16**
Riverside CH48: W Kir 6D **16**
CH62: Port S 4H **29**
Riverside Bowl 2F **5**
Riverside Ct. CH62: New F . .6D **22**
Riverside Dr. L3: Liv 4G **23**
L17: Aig 4G **23**
Riverside Ho. CH41: Birke . .4B **14**
Riverside Wlk.
CH64: Lit N 2B **44**
L3: Liv 2F **23**
(Atlantic Way)
L3: Liv . . . .
(The Colonnades)
River St. CH41: Birke 1H **21**
River Vw. CH41: Tran 3A **22**
(off Marquis St.)
CH62: New F 1A **30**
Riverview CH49: Woodc . . .6G **19**
Riverview Gdns.
CH42: Rock F 5B **22**
Riverview Rd. CH44: Wall . .2A **14**
CH62: Brom 6D **30**
CH64: Lit N 2D **44**
Riverview Wlk. L8: Liv 3H **23**
(off Cockburn St.)
Riverwood Rd. CH62: Brom . .2D **36**

Riviera Dr. CH42: Rock F . . .6H **21**
Rivington Av. CH43: Noct . . .3C **20**
Rivington Rd. CH44: Wall . . .2H **13**
CH65: Ell P 2A **50**
Robert Dr. CH49: Grea 4E **19**
Robertson St. L8: Liv 2G **23**
Roberts St. L3: Liv 2D **14**
Robert St. CH41: Birke 6H **13**
Robins Cft. CH66: Gt Sut . .5F **49**
Robinson Rd. CH65: Ell P . . .3C **50**
Robin Way CH49: Woodc . .5H **19**
Robsart St. L5: Liv 6G **7**
Robson St. L5: Liv 6G **7**
Rochester Dr. CH65: Ell P . . .4B **50**
Rock Av. CH60: Hesw 2B **32**
Rock Bank CH49: Upton . . .2G **19**
Rock Cl. CH42: Rock F 5B **22**
Rockfarm Cl. CH64: Lit N . . .1E **45**
Rockfarm Dr. CH64: Lit N . . .1E **45**
Rockfarm Gro. CH64: Lit N . .1E **45**
ROCK FERRY 5B **22**
Rock Ferry By-Pass
CH42: Rock F 4C **22**
Rock Ferry Station (Rail) . .5B **22**
Rockfield Rd. L4: Walt 4H **7**
Rockland Rd. CH45: Wall . . .4D **4**
Rocklands, The CH43: Noct . .6B **12**
Rocklands Av. CH63: Beb . .2G **29**
Rocklands La.
CH63: Thorn H 3C **34**
Rock La. CH42: Rock F 6C **22**
(not continuous)
Rock La. W. CH42: Rock F . .6B **22**
Rocklee Gdns. CH64: Lit N . .1E **45**
Rockley St. L4: Kirkd 3G **7**
(not continuous)
Rocklis Grange CH64: Nest . .5C **38**
(off Tannery La.)
Rock Pk. CH42: Rock F 5C **22**
(not continuous)
Rock Pk. Rd. CH42: Rock F . .6D **22**
Rockpoint Av. CH45: New B . .4G **5**
Rock Retail Pk.
CH41: Birke 2A **22**
Rockville St. CH42: Rock F . .5B **22**
Rocky Bank Rd. CH42: Tran . .4H **21**
Rocky La. CH60: Hesw 3B **32**
Rocky La. Sth. CH60: Hesw . .3C **32**
Rococo Sq. CH45: New B . . .2G **5**
Roderick Rd. L4: Walt 1H **7**
Roderick St. L3: Liv 2G **15**
Rodney St. CH41: Birke . . .2H **21**
L1: Liv 5G **15**
Roe All. L1: Liv 4F **15**
(off Wood St.)
Roe St. L1: Liv 4F **15**
Roften Works Ind. Est.
CH66: Hoot 4F **41**
Rokeby Cl. L3: Liv 2G **15**
Rokeby St. L3: Liv 2G **15**
Roker Av. CH44: Wall 2E **13**
Roklis Bldg. CH44: Wall 1H **13**
(off Liscard Rd.)
Roklis Ct. CH49: Upton 3G **19**
(off Rake La.)
Roland Av. CH63: Hghr B . . .3D **28**
Rolleston Dr. CH45: Wall . . .4D **4**
CH63: Beb 5G **29**
Rollo St. L4: Kirkd 4F **7**
Roman Ct. CH64: Lit N 6D **38**
Roman Rd. CH43: Pren 1A **28**
CH47: Meols 4F **9**
CH63: Store 1A **28**
Romiley Rd. CH66: Ell P . . .1E **49**
Romley St. L4: Walt 2H **7**
Romney Cl. CH64: Lit N . . .6C **38**
Romney Ct. CH64: Lit N . . .6D **38**
Romney Way CH64: Lit N . . .6D **38**
Rona Av. CH65: Ell P 6A **50**
Ronaldsway CH49: Upton . .1F **19**
CH60: Hesw 5B **32**
Rone Cl. CH46: More 5D **10**
Rooks Way CH60: Hesw . . .3A **32**
Roper St. L8: Liv 2H **23**
Ropewalk, The CH64: Park . .4A **38**
Ropewalks Sq. L1: Liv 5G **15**
(off Wood St.)
Rosalind Av. CH63: Hghr B . .2E **29**
Rosalind Way L20: Kirkd . . .2F **7**
Rosclare Dr. CH45: Wall 5D **4**

Roscoe La. L1: Liv 5G **15**
Roscoe Pl. L1: Liv 5G **15**
Roscoe St. L1: Liv 5G **15**
Roscommon St. L5: Liv 1G **15**
Roscote, The CH60: Hesw . .4B **32**
Roscote Cl. CH60: Hesw . . .4B **32**
Roseacre CH48: W Kir 4C **16**
Roseate Ct. CH45: Wall 3C **4**
Rosebery Av. CH44: Wall . . .1G **13**
Rosebery Gro. CH42: Tran . .5F **21**
Rosebery St. L8: Liv 6H **15**
Rosebrae Ct. CH41: Birke . .6B **14**
CH60: Hesw 2C **32**
Rosebrae Wlk. CH41: Birke . .6C **14**
Rose Ct. CH41: Birke 1H **21**
Rosecroft CH62: Brom 5A **36**
Rosecroft Ct. CH7: Hoy 1C **16**
Rosedale Rd. CH42: Tran . . .4A **22**
Rosefield Av.
CH63: Hghr B 2E **29**
Rose Gdns. CH64: Lit N 1D **44**
Rose Hill L3: Liv 2F **15**
Roselands Ct.
CH42: Rock F 6A **22**
Roselee Ct. CH42: Rock F . .6C **22**
Rosemary Cl. CH43: Bid 5C **12**
Rosemead Av. CH61: Pens . .5B **26**
Rosemere Dr. CH1: Back . . .6A **48**
Rose Mt. CH43: Oxton 4F **21**
Rosemount Cl. CH43: Oxton . .4E **21**
Rose Mt. Dr. CH45: Wall 5E **5**
Rosemount Pk.
CH43: Oxton 3E **21**
Rose Pl. CH42: Tran 3H **21**
L3: Liv 2F **15**
(not continuous)
Rose St. L1: Liv 4F **15**
Rose Va. L5: Liv 1G **15**
(not continuous)
Rosewood Dr. CH46: More . . .5B **10**
Roslin Ct. CH43: Oxton 3F **21**
Roslin Rd. CH43: Oxton . . .3F **21**
CH61: Irby 3H **25**
Roslyn St. CH41: Tran 4B **22**
Rossall Ct. CH46: Leas 3F **11**
Rossall Gro. CH66: Lit Sut . .1D **48**
Rossall Rd. CH46: More 4F **11**
Ross Av. CH46: Leas 1A **12**
Rossbank Rd. CH65: Ell P . . .6G **43**
Rosscliffe Rd. CH65: Ell P . . .6G **43**
Rosscourt Vw.
CH42: Rock F 5D **22**
Ross Dr. CH65: Gt Sut 2C **48**
Rossendale Cl. CH43: Noct . .3B **20**
Rossfield Rd. CH65: Ell P . . .6G **43**
Rossiter Dr. CH43: Bid 1A **20**
Rosslyn Cres. CH46: More . .5E **11**
Rosslyn Dr. CH46: More . . .5E **11**
Rosslyn Pk. CH46: More . . .6E **11**
Rossmore Bus. Pk.
CH65: Ell P 6H **43**
Rossmore Bus. Village
CH65: Ell P 6H **43**
Rossmore Ct. CH66: Ell P . . .1E **49**
Rossmore Gdns.
CH66: Lit Sut 1D **48**
Rossmore Ind. Est.
CH65: Ell P 6G **43**
(not continuous)
Rossmore Rd. E.
CH65: Ell P 6F **43**
Rossmore Rd. W.
CH66: Ell P, Lit Sut 6D **42**
Rossmore Trad. Est.
CH65: Ell P 1G **49**
Rossmount Rd. CH65: Ell P . .1G **49**
Ross Rd. CH65: Ell P 1G **49**
Ross Twr. Ct. CH45: New B . .3G **5**
Rosswood Rd. CH65: Ell P . .1G **49**
Rostherne Av. CH44: Wall . . .2E **13**
CH66: Gt Sut 1G **49**
Rothbury Cl. CH46: More . . .5C **10**
Rother Dr. CH65: Ell P 6G **43**
Rother Dr. Bus. Pk.
CH65: Ell P 6G **43**
Rotherwood Cl. CH43: Noct . .2B **20**
Rotherwood Cl.
CH63: Hghr B 3D **28**
Rothesay Ct. CH63: Beb . . .5F **29**
Rothesay Dr. CH62: East . . .1G **41**

Rothesay Gdns. CH43: Pren . . .6D **20**
Rothsay Cl. L5: Liv 1H **15**
Rotunda St. L5: Liv 6F **7**
Roughley Ho. CH41: Birke . .6B **14**
(off Bridge St.)
Row, The CH47: Hoy 6D **8**
Rowan Ct. CH49: Grea 5B **18**
CH63: Hghr B 3D **28**
Rowan Gro. CH63: Hghr B . .5E **29**
Rowan Tree Cl. CH49: Grea . .4B **18**
Rowson Cl. CH45: New B 3F **5**
(off Pickering Rd.)
Rowson St. CH45: New B 2F **5**
Rowton Cl. CH43: Oxton . . .4D **20**
Roxburgh Av. CH42: Tran . . .5H **21**
Roxburgh Rd.
CH66: Lit Sut 1H **47**
Roxburgh St. L4: Kirkd 1G **7**
L20: Boot 1G **7**
Royal, The CH47: Hoy 1B **16**
Royal Ct. CH42: Rock F 6C **22**
(off Rock La. W.)
Royal Court Theatre 4F **15**
Royal Liverpool Golf Course
. . . . .2B **16**
ROYAL LIVERPOOL
UNIVERSITY HOSPITAL
. . . . .3H **15**
Royal Mail St. L3: Liv 4G **15**
Royal Quay L3: Liv 5E **15**
Royal Shop. Arc.
CH64: Nest 6C **38**
Royal Standard Way
CH42: Tran 4B **22**
Royal St. L4: Walt 4G **7**
Royden Av. CH44: Wall 6H **5**
Royden Rd. CH49: Upton . . .1E **19**
Royden Way L3: Liv 4G **23**
Royston Cl. CH66: Gt Sut . . .4F **49**
Rubbing Stone CH48: Caldy . .4B **24**
Ruby St. L8: Liv 4H **23**
(not continuous)
Rudd St. CH47: Hoy 6D **8**
Rudgrave M. CH44: Wall 6H **5**
Rudgrave Pl. CH44: Wall 6H **5**
Rudgrave Sq. CH44: Wall . . .6H **5**
Rudstone Cl. CH66: Lit Sut . .2B **48**
Rufford Rd. CH44: Wall 2G **13**
Rugby Rd. CH44: Wall 6D **4**
CH65: Ell P 4A **50**
Rugby Wlk. CH65: Ell P 4B **50**
Rullerton Rd. CH44: Wall . . .1E **13**
Rumford Pl. L3: Liv 3E **15**
Rumford St. L2: Liv 3E **15**
Rumney Pl. L4: Kirkd 3G **7**
(not continuous)
Rumney Rd. L4: Kirkd 3G **7**
Rumney Rd. W. L4: Kirkd . . .3F **7**
Rundle St. CH41: Birke 5E **13**
Runnell, The CH64: Nest . . .2B **38**
Rupert Dr. L6: Liv 1H **15**
Rushgreen Cl. CH43: Bid . . .6A **12**
Rushtons, The
CH66: Lit Sut 6C **42**
Ruskin Av. CH42: Rock F . . .6B **22**
CH44: Wall 2E **13**
Ruskin Cl. L20: Boot 1E **7**
Ruskin Dr. CH65: Ell P 4B **50**
Ruskin St. L4: Kirkd 2G **7**
Ruskin Way CH43: Noct . . .4B **20**
Rusland Av. CH61: Pens . . .5B **26**
Russell Rd. CH42: Rock F . . .4B **22**
(not continuous)
CH44: Wall 6C **4**
Russell St. CH41: Birke 6A **14**
L3: Liv 4G **15**
Ruthin Ct. CH65: Ell P 4B **50**
Rutland Cl. L5: Liv 6H **7**
Rutter St. L8: Liv 2G **23**
Rycroft Rd. CH44: Wall 5G **13**
CH47: Meols 5G **9**
Rydal Av. CH43: Noct 2A **20**
Rydal Bank CH44: Wall 1G **13**
CH63: Beb 2G **29**
Rydal Cl. CH61: Pens 5B **26**
CH64: Lit N 1D **44**
Rydal St. L5: Liv 5A **50**
Ryecroft Rd. CH60: Hesw . . .4E **33**
Ryland Pk. CH61: Thing 4C **26**
Rylands Hey CH49: Grea . . .3D **18**

S

Ryleys Gdns. L2: Liv 3E 15
(off Tempest Hey)
Rymer Gro. L4: Walt 2H 7

Saddlestone Gro. L8: Liv 2G 15
St Agnes Rd. L4: Kirkd 3F 7
St Aidan's Ct. CH43: Clau 1D 20
St Aidan's Ter. CH43: Clau 1D 20
St Albans Ct. L5: Liv 6E 7
St Albans Rd. CH43: Clau 6E 13
CH44: Wall 1F 13
L20: Boot 1E 7
St Alban's Sq. L20: Boot 1E 7
St Alexander Cl. L20: Kirkd 2F 7
St Ambrose Way L5: Liv 1G 15
(off Everton Brow)
St Andrews Ct. CH43: Noct 1B 20
CH65: Ell P 5C 50
St Andrews Gdns. L3: Liv 3G 15
St Andrews Rd. CH43: Oxton . . .1F 21
CH63: Beb 5G 29
CH65: Ell P 4B 50
St Andrew St. L3: Liv 4H 15
St Annes Cl. CH41: Birke 6H 13
St Annes Ct. L3: Liv 2G 15
(off St Anne St.)
St Annes Gro. CH41: Birke 5G 13
St Anne's Ho. L20: Boot 1F 7
(off University Rd.)
St Annes Pl. CH41: Birke 5G 13
St Annes Ter. CH41: Birke 5G 13
St Anne St. CH41: Birke 6H 13
(Livingstone Gdns.)
CH41: Birke 6H 13
(Robert St.)
CH41: Birke 5G 13
(St Anne's Pl.)
L3: Liv 1G 15
St Annes Way CH41: Birke 6H 13
St Anthony's Shop. Cen.
L5: Liv 6G 7
St Asaph Rd.
CH66: Gt Sut . . . .6E 49 & 6A 48
St Augustine St. L5: Liv 6F 7
St Austell Cl. CH46: More 4B 10
St Austells Rd. L4: Walt 1G 7
St Bartholomew Rd. L3: Liv . . .2F 15
St Bride's Rd. CH44: Wall 6H 5
St Bride St. L8: Liv 5H 15
St Bridget's La.
CH48: W Kir 6D 16
St Brigid's Cres. L5: Liv 6E 7
(off Silvester St.)
St Catherines Gdns.
CH42: Tran 3H 21
**ST CATHERINE'S HOSPITAL
(BIRKENHEAD)** **3H 21**
St Catherine's Rd. L20: Boot . .1E 7
St Columba's Cl. CH44: Wall . . .6H 5
St David Rd. CH43: Clau 1E 21
CH62: East 5E 37
St Davids Dr. CH66: Gt Sut . . .6A 48
St Davids La. CH43: Noct 2B 20
St Domingo Gro. L5: Liv 5H 7
St Domingo Rd. L5: Liv 4G 7
St Domingo Va. L5: Liv 5H 7
St Edmond's Rd. L20: Boot 1E 7
St Edmunds Ho. CH65: Ell P . .3C 50
St Edmund's Rd. CH63: Beb . . .4F 29
St Edwards Cl. CH41: Birke 5F 13
St Edwards M. CH41: Birke 5F 13
(off Old Bidston Rd.)
St Elmo Rd. CH44: Wall 6H 5
St Georges Av. CH42: Tran 5H 21
CH66: Gt Sut 6A 48
St George's Gro.
CH46: More 5D 10
St George's Hall **3F 15**
St George's Hill L5: Liv 6H 7
St George's Mt. CH45: New B . .3E 5
St George's Pk. CH45: New B . . .3F 5
St George's Pl. L1: Liv 3F 15
St George's Rd. CH45: Wall 5C 4
St George's Way
CH63: Thorn H 5A 34
L1: Liv 4F 15
(off St John's Cen.)

St Gerard Cl. L5: Liv 5F 7
St Helens Cl. CH43: Clau 1F 21
St Hilary Brow CH44: Wall 1D 12
St Hilary Dr. CH45: Wall 6D 4
St Hilda St. L4: Walt 3G 7
St Hugh's Cl. CH43: Clau 1F 21
St Hugh's Ho. L20: Boot 1E 7
St Ives Cl. CH43: Clau 6E 13
St Ives Rd. CH43: Clau 1E 21
St James Cl. CH43: Clau 3D 18
St James Ct. CH45: New B 3F 5
(off Victoria Rd.)
St James Pl. L8: Liv 1G 23
St James Rd. CH43: Birke 5D 12
CH45: New B 3F 5
L1: Liv 6G 15
St James St. L1: Liv 6F 15
St John's Cen. L1: Liv 4F 15
St John's Ct. CH47: Meols 5F 9
ST JOHN'S HOSPICE IN WIRRAL
. . . .**2E 35**
St Johns Ho. CH65: Ell P 2C 50
L20: Boot 1F 7
St John's La. L1: Liv 3F 15
St John's Pavement
CH41: Birke 1H 21
St John's Rd. CH45: Wall 6C 4
CH62: East 6E 37
L20: Boot 1D 6
St John's Sq. CH41: Birke 1H 21
L1: Liv 4F 15
(off St John's Cen.)
St John's Ter. L20: Boot 2D 6
(off St John's Rd.)
St John St. CH41: Birke 1H 21
St John's Way L1: Liv 4F 15
(off St John's Cen.)
St Josephs Cres. L3: Liv 2G 15
St Kilda Cl. CH65: Ell P 6A 50
St Kilda's Rd. CH46: More 6E 11
St Laurence Cl.
CH41: Birke 6H 13
St Laurence Dr.
CH41: Birke 6H 13
St Lawrence Cl. L8: Liv 3H 23
St Lucia Rd. CH44: Wall 6H 5
St Luke's Ct. L4: Walt 1H 7
St Lukes Pl. L1: Liv 5G 15
St Margaret's Rd.
CH47: Hoy 1C 16
St Marks Cl. CH43: Oxton 2F 21
St Marks Cres.
CH66: Gt Sut 6A 48
St Martins Dr. CH66: Gt Sut . . .5D 48
St Martin's Ho. L20: Boot 1E 7
St Martins M. L5: Liv 1G 15
St Mary's Av. CH44: Wall 1F 13
St Mary's Ct. CH45: Upton 3G 19
St Mary's Ga. CH41: Birke 1B 22
St Mary's La. L4: Walt 1H 7
St Mary's Pl. L4: Walt 1H 7
St Mary's St. CH44: Wall 1F 13
St Mary's Tower **1B 22**
St Michael's Gro.
CH46: More 5D 10
St Michaels Pk.
CH62: Port S 3H 29
St Nicholas Pl. L3: Liv 4D 14
(not continuous)
St Nicholas' Rd. CH45: Wall 6B 4
St Oswald's Av. CH43: Bid 4A 12
St Oswald's M. CH43: Bid 4A 12
St Paul's Av. CH44: Wall 3A 14
St Paul's Cl. CH42: Rock F 5A 22
St Pauls Gdns.
CH66: Lit Sut 6B 42
St Pauls Pl. L20: Boot 1F 7
St Paul's Rd. CH42: Rock F . . .5B 22
CH44: Wall 3H 13
St Paul's Sq. L3: Liv 3D 14
St Paul's Vs. CH42: Rock F 5B 22
St Peters Cl. CH60: Hesw 4B 32
St Peter's Ct. CH42: Rock F . . .6C 22
St Peter's Ho. L20: Boot 1F 7
St Peter's M. CH42: Rock F . . .6D 22
St Peter's Rd.
CH42: Rock F 6C 22
St Peter's Sq. L1: Liv 5F 15
(off Fleet St.)
St Peter's Way CH43: Noct 3A 20

St Richards Cl. L20: Kirkd 2F 7
St Seiriol Gro. CH43: Clau 1E 21
St Stephens Cl.
CH60: Hesw 5E 33
St Stephen's Ct. CH42: Tran . . .6F 21
St Stephen's Pl. L3: Liv 2F 15
St Stephen's Rd.
CH42: Tran 6D 21
St Thomas' Vw. CH65: Whit . . .3H 49
St Vincent Rd. CH43: Clau 1E 21
CH44: Wall 6H 5
St Vincent St. L3: Liv 3G 15
St Vincent Way L3: Liv 3G 15
(off Nelson St.)
St Werburgh's Sq.
CH41: Birke 1A 22
St Winifred Rd. CH45: New B . . .4F 5
Saker St. L4: Walt 4H 7
Salacre Cl. CH49: Upton 3G 19
Salacre Cres. CH49: Upton 3G 19
Salacre La. CH49: Upton 2G 19
Salacre Ter. CH49: Upton 2G 19
(off Salacre La.)
Salem Vw. CH43: Oxton 4F 21
Salisbury Av. CH48: W Kir 5C 16
Salisbury Cl. CH66: Gt Sut 6A 48
Salisbury Ct. CH42: Rock F . . .6A 22
Salisbury Dr. CH62: New F 2H 29
Salisbury Rd. CH45: New B 3E 5
L5: Liv 5H 7
Salisbury St. CH41: Birke 2H 21
L3: Liv 1H 15
Salop St. L4: Walt 3H 7
Saltburn Rd. CH45: Wall 6B 4
Saltergate Rd. L4: Walt 3H 23
Saltersgate CH66: Gt Sut 5F 49
Salthouse Quay L3: Liv 5E 15
Saltney St. L3: Liv 1D 14
Samaria Av. CH62: New F 2A 30
Sandalwood Dr. CH43: Noct . . .3B 20
Sandbanks CH47: Hoy 6C 8
Sandbeck St. L8: Liv 4H 23
Sandbourne CH46: More 5G 11
Sandbrook Cl. CH46: More 5E 11
Sandbrook La. CH46: More 5E 11
Sandcliffe Rd. CH45: Wall 3C 4
Sandfield Av. CH47: Meols 4F 9
Sandfield Cl. CH63: Hghr B . . .3D 28
Sandfield Pk. CH60: Hesw 3H 31
Sandfield Rd. CH45: New B 4F 5
CH49: Woodc 5H 19
CH63: Hghr B 3D 28
L20: Boot 1F 7
Sandfield Ter. CH45: New B 4F 5
Sandford St. CH41: Birke 6A 14
Sandham Gro. CH60: Hesw . . .3E 33
Sandhey Rd. CH47: Meols 5E 9
Sandheys CH64: Park 4A 38
Sandheys Cl. L4: Walt 4G 7
Sandheys Rd. CH45: New B 4F 5
Sandhills, The CH46: Leas 2E 11
Sandhills Bus. Est. L5: Kirkd . . .5E 7
Sandhills Bus. Pk. L5: Kirkd . . .4E 7
Sandhills La. L5: Kirkd 4D 6
Sandhills Station (Rail) **5E 7**
Sandhills Vw. CH45: Wall 6B 4
Sandino St. L8: Liv 1H 23
Sandiway CH47: Meols 4F 9
CH63: Brom 5A 36
Sandiways Rd. CH45: Wall 5C 4
Sandlea Pk. CH48: W Kir 5C 16
Sandon Cres. CH64: Lit N 2C 44
Sandon Ind. Est. L5: Kirkd 5D 6
Sandon Prom. CH44: Wall 1A 14
Sandon Rd. CH44: Wall 1A 14
Sandon St. L8: Liv 5H 15
Sandon Way L5: Kirkd 5D 6
Sandpiper Cl. CH49: Upton . . .1D 18
Sandpipers Ct. CH47: Hoy 6D 8
Sandridge Rd. CH45: New B 4F 5
CH61: Pens 4B 26
Sandringham Av.
CH47: Meols 5E 9
Sandringham Cl.
CH47: Meols 5E 9
CH62: New F 2G 29
Sandringham Dr.
CH45: New B 3E 5
Sandringham Gdns.
CH65: Ell P 5B 50

Sandringham M.
CH47: Meols 6E 9
Sandrock Cl. CH45: New B 4F 5
Sandrock Rd. CH45: New B 4F 5
Sandstone CH45: Wall 6G 5
Sandstone Dr. CH48: W Kir . . .5G 17
Sandstone Wlk.
CH60: Hesw 4C 32
Sandy La. CH45: Wall 5C 4
CH48: W Kir 6D 16
CH60: Hesw 2C 32
CH61: Irby 2G 25
CH64: Lit N 6E 39
Sandy La. Nth. CH61: Irby 2G 25
Sandymount Dr. CH45: Wall . . .4E 5
CH63: Beb 5F 29
Sandy Way CH43: Oxton 2E 21
Sankey St. L1: Liv 5G 15
Sark Av. CH65: Ell P 6H 49
SAUGHALL MASSIE **1C 18**
CH49: Upton 2E 19
Saughall Massie La.
CH49: Grea, Upton 4F 17
Saughall Massie Rd.
CH48: W Kir 4F 17
CH49: Grea, Upton 4F 17
Saughall Rd. CH46: More 6C 10
CH49: Upton 6C 10
Saxon Rd. CH46: More 4F 11
CH47: Meols 5E 9
Saxon Way CH66: Gt Sut 6A 48
Scafell Cl. CH62: East 2F 41
CH66: Ell P 6F 43
Scholars' Ct. CH64: Nest 5C 38
(off Cross St.)
School Av. CH46: Lit N 1D 44
School Cl. CH46: More 4F 11
Schoolfield Cl.
CH49: Woodc 5H 19
Schoolfield Rd.
CH49: Woodc 5H 19
School Hill CH60: Hesw 4B 32
School La. CH43: Bid 4A 12
CH44: Wall 6C 4
CH45: Wall 1C 12
CH47: Hoy 6D 8
(not continuous)
CH47: Meols 4F 9
CH61: Thurs 3F 25
CH62: New F 2H 29
CH63: Hghr B 3D 28
CH64: Lit N 1D 44
CH64: Nest 3F 39
CH64: Park 4A 38
CH66: Chil T 4H 41
L1: Liv 4F 15
School Rd. CH65: Ell P 2H 49
Schubert Cl. CH66: Gt Sut 3E 49
Scilly Cl. CH65: Ell P 6A 50
Scoresby Rd. CH46: Leas 2H 11
Scotia Av. CH62: New F 2A 30
Scotland Rd. L3: Liv 2F 15
L5: Liv 2F 15
Scott Cl. L4: Walt 4H 7
Scotton Av. CH66: Lit Sut 2B 48
Scotts Pl. CH41: Birke 6D 12
Scotts Quays CH41: Birke 4A 14
Scott St. CH45: Wall 6F 5
Scythes, The CH49: Grea 3C 18
Scythia Cl. CH62: New F 1A 30
Seabank Av. CH44: Wall 6G 5
Seabank Ct. CH48: W Kir 6C 16
Seabank Rd. CH44: Wall 6G 5
CH45: New B, Wall 3F 5
CH60: Hesw 5A 32
SEACOMBE **4H 13**
Seacombe Dr. CH66: Gt Sut . . .4E 49
Seacombe Prom.
CH44: Wall 1A 14
(not continuous)
Seacombe Vw. CH44: Wall 3A 14
Sea Ct. CH45: Wall 4D 4
Seafield Av. CH60: Hesw 5A 32
Seafield Dr. CH45: Wall 4E 5
Seafield Rd. CH62: New F 1H 29
Seaforth Dr. CH46: More 6E 11
Sealy Cl. CH63: Spit 2G 35
Sea Rd. CH45: Wall 3D 4
Seaton Rd. CH42: Tran 3G 21
CH45: Wall 5E 5
Sea Vw. CH64: Lit N 3C 44

Seaview CH47: Hoy 6D 8
Seaview Av. CH45: Wall 6E 5
CH61: Irby 3H 25
CH62: East 5F 37
Seaview La. CH61: Irby 3H 25
Seaview Rd. CH45: Wall 5E 5
Seawood Gro. CH46: More 6D 10
Second Av. CH43: Bid 1H 19
Seddon St. L1: Liv 5F 15
Sedbergh Rd. CH44: Wall 6D 4
Sedgefield Cl. CH46: More 5G 11
Sedgefield Rd. CH46: More . .5G 11
Seeley Av. CH41: Birke 6E 13
Seel St. L1: Liv 4F 15
Sefton Av. CH42: Rock F 6C 22
CH45: New B 4F 5
CH62: New F 1G 29
Sefton St. L8: Liv 1F 23
Seiont Ho. L8: Liv 2H 23
Selborne Cl. L8: Liv 6H 15
Selborne St. L8: Liv 6H 15
Selbourne Cl. CH49: Woodc . .4A 20
Selby St. CH45: Wall 6F 5
Selina Rd. L4: Walt 1G 7
Selkirk Av. CH62: East 1G 41
Selkirk Cl. CH66: Lit Sut 2H 47
Sellar St. L4: Kirkd 4G 7
Selston Cl. CH63: Spit 1G 35
Selwyn St. L4: Kirkd 2G 7
Serpentine Rd. CH44: Wall . . .6G 5
Sessions Rd. L4: Kirkd 3G 7
Seven Acres La.
CH61: Thing 3C 26
Sevenoaks Cl. L8: Liv 6G 7
Seven Row CH64: Lit N 2C 44
L5: Liv 5H 7
Severn St. CH41: Birke 4E 13
Severnvale CH65: Whit 4H 49
Seymour Ct. CH41: Tran 3A 22
Seymour Dr. CH66: Ell P 1E 49
Seymour Pl. E. CH45: New B . .3G 5
Seymour Pl. W. CH45: New B . .3F 5
Seymour St. CH42: Tran 3A 22
CH45: New B 3F 5
L3: Liv 3G 15
L20: Boot 1D 6
Seymour Ter. L3: Liv 3G 15
(off Seymour St.)
Shackleton Rd. CH46: Leas . . .1H 11
Shadwell St. L5: Liv 6D 6
Shaftesbury St. L8: Liv 1G 23
Shakespeare Av.
CH42: Rock F 6B 22
Shakespeare Rd.
CH44: Wall 3H 13
CH64: Nest 4C 38
Shalem Cl. CH63: Hghr B . . .3D 28
Shalford Gro. CH48: W Kir . . .5F 17
Shallmarsh Cl.
CH63: Hghr B 4D 28
Shallmarsh Rd.
CH63: Hghr B 4D 28
Shamrock Rd. CH41: Birke . .6D 12
Shannon Ho. CH46: Leas 1E 11
Shannon St. CH41: Birke 4D 12
Sharpeville Cl. L4: Kirkd 4F 7
Shavington Av. CH43: Oxton . .4D 20
Shawbury Av.
CH63: Hghr B 2D 28
Shaw Cl. CH66: Gt Sut 3F 49
Shaw Hill St. L1: Liv 3F 15
Shaw La. CH49: Grea 5C 18
Shaws All. L1: Liv 5F 15
Shaws Dr. CH47: Meols 5F 9
Shaw St. CH41: Birke 2H 21
CH47: Hoy 6D 8
L6: Liv 1H 15
Shearman Cl. CH61: Pens . . .5C 26
Shearman Rd. CH61: Pens . . .5C 26
Sheen Rd. CH45: New B 4G 5
Sheepfield Cl.
CH66: Lit Sut 6C 42
Sheldon Cl. CH63: Spit 2G 35
Sheldrake Gro. CH46: Lit N . .2C 44
Shelley Way CH48: W Kir 1A 24
Shelmore Dr. L8: Liv 3H 23
Shelton Rd. CH45: Wall 5E 5
Shenley Cl. CH63: Beb 3F 29
Shepherd Cl. CH49: Grea . . .3C 18

Shepherd St. L6: Liv 3H 15
Shepsides Cl. CH66: Gt Sut . .4C 48
Shepston Av. L4: Walt 2H 7
Shepton Rd. CH66: Gt Sut . .5E 49
Sherbourne Rd.
CH65: Ell P 4B 50
Sheriff Cl. L5: Liv 1G 15
Sheringham Cl.
CH49: Upton 6G 11
Sherlock La. CH44: Wall 3E 13
Sherry La. CH49: Woodc 5G 19
Sherwood Av. CH61: Irby . . .2G 25
Sherwood Dr. CH63: Hghr B . .2E 29
Sherwood Gro. CH47: Meols . .5H 9
Sherwood Rd. CH44: Wall . . .2G 13
CH47: Meols 5H 9
Sherwood St. L3: Liv 1D 14
Shetland Dr. CH62: Brom . . .3C 36
CH65: Ell P 6A 50
Shewell Cl. CH42: Tran 3H 21
Shiel Rd. CH45: New B 4F 5
Shipton Cl. CH43: Pren 6C 20
Shirley St. CH44: Wall 2A 14
Shones Cft. CH64: Ness 2E 45
Shore Bank CH62: New F 1A 30
Shore Dr. CH62: Port S 3A 30
Shorefields CH62: New F 1A 30
Shorefields Ho.
CH62: New F 2A 30
Shorefields Village L8: Liv . .4H 23
Shore La. CH48: Caldy 2A 24
Shore Rd. CH41: Birke 6B 14
CH48: Caldy 2A 24
Shore Road Pumping Station
. . . . .6B 14
Shortfield Rd. CH49: Upton . .3G 19
Shortfield Way CH49: Upton . .3G 19
Shotwick Helsby By-Pass
CH2: Lit Stan 6D 50
CH65: Ell P 6A 50
CH66: Back 6A 48
Shrewsbury Cl. CH43: Clau . .1D 20
Shrewsbury Dr.
CH49: Upton 1G 19
Shrewsbury Rd. CH43: Clau . .6D 12
CH44: Wall 6D 4
CH48: W Kir 6C 16
CH60: Hesw 2C 32
CH65: Ell P 2A 50
(off Norfolk Rd.)
Shropshire Rd.
CH2: Lit Stan 4D 50
Sidlaw Av. CH66: Lit Sut 1A 48
Sidney Av. CH45: New B 3E 5
Sidney Cl. CH64: Nest 4D 38
Sidney Ct. CH42: Tran 4A 22
Sidney Rd. CH42: Tran 3A 22
CH64: Nest 4D 38
L20: Boot 1F 7
Sidney St. CH41: Birke 6A 14
Sidney Ter. CH42: Tran 4A 22
Silkhouse Ct. L2: Liv 3E 15
(off Tithebarn St.)
Silkhouse La. L3: Liv 3E 15
(off George St.)
Silverbeech Rd. CH44: Wall . .2G 13
Silverbirch Gdns. CH44: Wall . .6C 4
Silverbirch Way CH66: Whit . .6A 48
Silverburn Av. CH46: More . . .4E 11
Silverdale Rd. CH43: Oxton . .3E 21
CH63: Hghr B 2F 29
Silverlea Av. CH45: Wall 6F 5
Silverne Dr. CH65: Whit 5G 49
Silvester St. L5: Liv 6E 7
Simon Ct. CH48: W Kir 5C 16
Simonsbridge CH48: Caldy . .3B 24
Simpson St. CH41: Birke 1H 21
L1: Liv 6F 15
Sim St. L3: Liv 2G 15
Singleton Av. CH42: Tran 4G 21
Singleton Rd. CH65: Gt Sut . .3F 49
Sir Howard St. L8: Liv 5H 15
Sir Howard Way L8: Liv 5H 15
(off Sir Howard St.)
Sir Thomas St. L1: Liv 3F 15
Sisters Way CH41: Birke 1H 21
Skelhorne St. L3: Liv 4G 15
Skiddaw Rd. CH62: Brom . . .1C 36
Skipton Dr. CH66: Lit Sut 3C 48

Skirving Pl. L5: Liv 5F 7
Skirving St. L5: Liv 5G 7
Skye Cl. CH65: Ell P 6A 50
Slackswood Cl. CH65: Ell P . .6H 43
Slater Pl. L1: Liv 5F 15
Slater St. L1: Liv 5F 15
Slatey Rd. CH43: Oxton 1F 21
Sleepers Hill L4: Walt 4H 7
Slessor Av. CH48: W Kir 4F 17
Slingsby Dr. CH49: Upton . . .3G 19
Smallacres CH65: Ell P 6F 43
Smallridge Cl. CH61: Pens . . .5A 26
Smallwood M. CH60: Hesw . .1A 32
Smeaton St. L4: Kirkd 2G 7
(not continuous)
Smilie Av. CH46: More 4C 10
Smith Av. CH41: Birke 5E 13
Smithfield St. L3: Liv 3E 15
Smith Pl. L5: Kirkd 5F 7
Smith St. L5: Kirkd 4G 7
Smithy Cl. CH64: Ness 3E 45
Smithy Ct. CH66: Lit Sut 1C 48
Smithy Hey CH48: W Kir 5E 17
Smithy Hill CH63: Thorn H . . .5A 34
Smithy La. CH63: Will 5C 40
CH66: Lit Sut 1C 48
Smugglers Way CH45: Wall . . .3C 4
Snab La. CH64: Ness 3D 44
Snabwood Cl. CH64: Lit N . . .2C 44
Snowberry Way CH66: Whit . .6A 48
Snowden Rd. CH46: More . . .5C 10
Snowdon Cl. CH66: Lit Sut . . .1A 48
Snowdon La. L5: Liv 6E 7
Snowdon Rd. CH42: Tran . . .5H 21
Snowdrop Av. CH41: Birke . . .5D 12
Snowdrop St. L5: Kirkd 4F 7
Soho Pl. L3: Liv 2G 15
Soho St. L3: Liv 2G 15
(not continuous)
Solly Av. CH42: Rock F 5A 22
Solway St. CH41: Birke 4E 13
Somerset Rd. CH45: Wall 6C 4
CH48: W Kir 4E 17
CH61: Pens 5A 26
Somerville Cl. CH63: Brom . .5H 35
CH64: Lit N 2C 44
Somerville Cres.
CH65: Ell P 3A 50
Sorrel Cl. CH43: Noct 2B 20
South Bank CH43: Oxton . . .4F 21
Southbourne Rd. CH45: Wall . .6B 4
Sth. Chester St. L8: Liv 1H 23
Southcroft Rd. CH45: Wall 6B 4
Southdale Rd.
CH42: Rock F 5A 22
South Dr. CH49: Upton 2G 19
CH60: Hesw 4C 32
CH61: Irby 4G 25
Southern Cres. L8: Liv 2G 23
Sth. Ferry Quay L3: Liv 1F 23
Southfield Rd.
CH66: Lit Sut 1C 48
South Hey Rd. CH61: Irby . . .4H 25
South Hill Gro. CH43: Oxton . .4F 21
South Hill Rd. CH43: Oxton . .3G 21
L8: Liv 4H 23
Sth. Hunter St. L1: Liv 5H 15
Sth. John St. L1: Liv 4E 15
South Pde. CH48: W Kir 5C 16
CH64: Park 5A 38
South Pk. Ct. CH44: Wall 2A 14
(off Demesne St.)
South Pk. Way L20: Boot 1F 7
Sth. Pier Rd. CH65: Ell P 2H 43
Southport Rd. L20: Boot 1G 7
South Quay L3: Liv 6E 15
Southridge Rd. CH61: Pens . .4C 26
South Rd. CH42: Tran 4G 21
CH48: W Kir 6C 16
CH65: Ell P 2D 50
(Bridges Rd.)
CH65: Ell P 4A 50
(Malvern Av.)
CH65: Hoot 2C 42
Sth. Sefton Bus. Cen.
L20: Boot 1D 6
South Vw. CH62: Brom 4B 30
L8: Liv 3F 23
(off Dentwood St.)
South Vs. CH45: New B 4F 5

Southwell Pl. L8: Liv 2G 23
Southwell St. L8: Liv 2G 23
Southwick Rd. CH42: Tran . . .4A 22
Sth. Wirral Retail Pk.
CH62: Brom 6B 30
Southwood Rd.
CH62: Brom 2D 36
Sovereign Way CH41: Birke . .4H 13
Spaceport 3B 14
Sparks La. CH61: Thing 3C 26
Sparling St. L1: Liv 6F 15
(not continuous)
Speedwell Cl. CH60: Hesw . . .3E 33
Speedwell Dr. CH60: Hesw . . .3E 33
Speedwell Rd. CH41: Birke . .6D 12
Spellow La. L4: Walt 3H 7
Spellow Pl. L3: Liv 3D 14
(off Union St.)
Spencer Av. CH46: More 4G 11
Spencer St. L6: Liv 1H 15
Spenser Av. CH42: Rock F . . .6B 22
Spenser Rd. CH64: Nest 4C 38
Spindle Cl. L6: Liv 1H 15
Spindrift Ct. CH48: W Kir 6C 16
Spinney, The CH48: W Kir . . .5G 17
CH49: Upton 1G 19
CH60: Hesw 6E 33
CH63: Spit 6H 29
CH64: Park 4B 38
Spinney Dr. CH66: Gt Sut . . .5D 48
SPITAL 6H 29
Spital Heyes CH63: Spit 6H 29
Spital Rd.
CH62: Brom, Spit 6G 29
CH63: Spit 6G 29
Spital Station (Rail) 6H 29
Sprainger St. L3: Liv 1D 14
Spring Av. CH66: Lit Sut 1C 48
Springcroft CH64: Park 4A 38
Springdale Cl. CH46: More . . .4G 11
Springfield L3: Liv 2G 15
(not continuous)
Springfield Av. CH48: W Kir . .4G 17
Springfield Cl.
CH49: Woodc 5A 20
Springfield Pl. CH41: Birke . .1H 13
Springfield Sq. L4: Walt 3H 7
Spring Gdns. CH66: Lit Sut . .1C 48
Springhill Av. CH62: Brom . . .5B 36
Spring St. CH42: Tran 4B 22
Spring Vale CH45: Wall 4C 4
Springwood Way
CH62: New F 1G 29
Spruce Cl. CH42: Tran 3H 21
Spunhill Av. CH66: Gt Sut . . .4C 48
Spurgeon Cl. L5: Liv 6H 7
Spurstow Cl. CH43: Oxton . . .4D 20
Squibb Dr. CH46: Leas 3G 11
Stable Cl. CH49: Grea 3D 18
Stackfield, The
CH48: W Kir 4H 17
Stadium Ct. CH62: Brom 1D 36
Stadium Rd. CH62: Brom 6C 30
Staffin Av. CH65: Ell P 6H 49
Stafford Gdns. CH65: Ell P . . .2H 49
Staffordshire Cl. L5: Liv 5G 7
Stafford St. L3: Liv 3G 15
Stakes, The CH46: Leas 2E 11
Stamford St. CH65: Ell P 4A 50
Stanbury Av. CH63: Beb 3G 29
Standingford Rd.
CH65: Ell P 6H 43
Standish St. L3: Liv 3F 15
Stanfield Av. L5: Liv 6H 7
Stanfield Dr. CH63: Beb 6F 29
Stanford Av. CH45: New B . . .4F 5
Stanhope Dr. CH62: Brom . . .2B 36
Stanhope St. L8: Liv 1F 23
(not continuous)
Stanlaw Abbey Bus. Cen.
CH65: Ell P 5B 50
Stanlaw Rd. CH65: Ell P 3A 50
Stanley Av. CH45: Wall 5E 5
CH63: Hghr B 1B 28
Stanley Cl. CH44: Wall 3A 14
L4: Kirkd 4F 7
Stanley Ct. CH42: Tran 4B 22
Stanley La. CH62: East 1H 41
Stanley Pk. 3H 7
Stanley Pct. L20: Boot 1E 7

Stanley Rd. CH41: Birke 4D 12
  CH47: Hoy 2A 16
  CH62: New F 1G 29
  CH65: Ell P 2G 43
  L5: Kirkd 2F 7
  L20: Boot, Kirkd 1E 7
  L20: Kirkd 2F 7
Stanley St. CH44: Wall 3A 14
  L1: Liv 3E 15
Stanley Ter. CH45: New B 4F 5
  L8: Liv 6H 15
  (off Up. Parliament St.)
Stanley Theatre **4H 15**
Stanmore Pk. CH49: Grea 4B 18
Stanney Cl. CH62: East 2G 41
  CH64: Nest 6C 38
Stanney La. CH2: Lit Stan 6C 50
  CH65: Ell P 3H 49
  (not continuous)
Stanney Mill Ind. Est.
  CH2: Lit Stan 4D 50
Stanney Mill La.
  CH2: Lit Stan 6D 50
Stanney Mill Rd.
  CH2: Lit Stan 4D 50
Stanney Oaks Leisure Cen. .**6A 50**
Stanney Ten Ind. Est.
  CH2: Lit Stan 5D 50
Stanney Wood Local Nature Reserve
  . . . .**6H 49**
Stanney Woods Av.
  CH65: Ell P 6A 50
Stanton Ct. CH64: Nest 5C 38
Stanton Rd. CH63: Beb 6E 29
Stanza Ct. L5: Liv 6G 7
Stapleford Ct. CH66: Ell P 5F 43
Staplehurst Dr.
  CH42: Rock F 6B 22
Stapleton Av. CH49: Grea 3D 18
Starbeck Dr. CH66: Lit Sut 2B 48
Stargazer, The **3C 12**
Star St. L8: Liv 1G 23
Starworth Dr. CH62: New F . . .2A 30
Statham Rd. CH43: Bid 5A 12
Station App. CH46: More 3E 11
  CH47: Meols 5G 9
Station Av. CH66: Lit Sut 6C 42
  CH64: Nest 6D 38
Station Ct. CH66: Lit Sut 6C 42
Station Grn. CH66: Lit Sut 6C 42
Station Rd. CH41: Birke 4D 12
  CH44: Wall 1E 13
  CH47: Hoy 1D 16
  CH60: Hesw 5B 32
  CH61: Barn 4F 27
  CH61: Thurs 6D 24
  CH63: Store 4F 27
  CH64: Burt 5E 45
  CH64: Nest 6C 38
  (not continuous)
  CH64: Park 5A 38
  CH65: Ell P 1A 50
  (not continuous)
  CH66: Lit Sut 1C 48
Stavordale Rd. CH46: More . . .4F 11
Steble St. L8: Liv 2H 23
Steel Av. CH45: Wall 5G 5
Steel Ct. L5: Liv 6E 7
Steeple, The CH48: Caldy 3B 24
Steeple Ct. CH64: Nest 6C 38
Steinberg Ct. L3: Liv 1E 15
Stephens Gdns.
  CH66: Lit Sut 1B 48
Stephens La. *L2: Liv* *3E 15*
  (off Tithebarn St.)
Stephens Ter. CH66: Lit Sut . . .1B 48
Stepney Gro. L4: Walt 2H 7
Sterling Way L5: Kirkd 5F 7
Stevenson Dr. CH63: Spit 6F 29
Stevens Rd. CH60: Hesw 4E 33
Stewart Ct. CH61: Pens 6A 26
Stillington Rd. L8: Liv 3H 23
Stiperstones Cl.
  CH66: Lit Sut 1A 48
Stirling Ct. CH65: Ell P 4B 50
Stirling St. CH44: Wall 3F 13
Stoak Lodge CH65: Ell P 3A 50
Stockbridge St. L5: Liv 6H 7
Stockdale Cl. L3: Liv 2E 15
Stoddart Rd. L4: Walt 1H 7

Stoke Cl. CH62: East 2G 41
Stoke Gdns. CH65: Ell P 3A 50
Stokesay CH43: Noct 1B 20
Stokesay Ct. CH65: Ell P 4C 50
Stoke St. CH41: Birke 5F 13
Stoke Wlk. CH65: Ell P 3A 50
Stonebank Dr. CH64: Lit N 1E 45
Stoneby Dr. CH45: Wall 4E 5
Stonegate Dr. L8: Liv 3H 23
Stonehey Dr. CH48: W Kir 6E 17
Stonehill Av. CH63: Beb 3G 29
Stonehouse Rd. CH44: Wall . . .6C 4
Stoneleigh Gro.
  CH42: Rock F 1F 29
Stoneridge Ct. CH43: Bid 5A 12
Stone St. L3: Liv 1D 14
Stoneway Ct. CH60: Hesw 2B 32
Stoney Hey Rd. CH45: New B . .4E 5
Stonham Cl. CH49: Upton 2E 19
Stopford St. L8: Liv 3H 23
Store St. L20: Kirkd 2F 7
STORETON **4A 28**
STORETON BRICKFIELDS . . .**4G 27**
Storeton Cl. CH43: Oxton 4F 21
Storeton La. CH61: Barn 6E 27
Storeton Rd. CH42: Tran 4F 21
  CH43: Oxton 4F 21
Stourcliffe Rd. CH44: Wall 1E 13
Stour Cl. CH65: Ell P 6H 43
Stourport Cl. CH49: Grea 3C 18
Stourton St. CH44: Wall 3G 13
Stowell St. L7: Liv 5H 15
Strada Way L3: Liv 2H 15
Straker Av. CH65: Ell P 1F 49
Strand, The L2: Liv 4E 15
Strand Rd. CH47: Hoy 6D 8
Strand St. L1: Liv 4E 15
Stratford Rd. CH64: Nest 1B 44
Strathallan Cl. CH65: Hesw . . .1A 32
Strathcona Rd. CH45: Wall 5F 5
Strathearn Rd. CH60: Hesw . . .5B 32
Strathlorne Cl. CH42: Tran 4B 22
Stratton Cl. CH45: Wall 5G 5
Strawberry Cross CH1: Back . .6B 48
Strawberry Dr. CH66: Whit 6B 48
Strawberry Grn. CH66: Whit . . .6B 48
Strawberry Pk. CH66: Whit 6B 48
Street Hey La. CH64: Will 3D 40
Stretton Av. CH44: Wall 1E 13
Stretton Cl. CH43: Oxton 4C 20
  CH62: East 2G 41
Stringhey Rd. CH44: Wall 6G 5
Stroma Av. CH65: Ell P 6H 49
Stroud Cl. CH49: Grea 4C 18
Stuart Av. CH46: More 5G 11
Stuart Cl. CH46: More 5G 11
Stuart Gro. L20: Kirkd 2F 7
Stuart Rd. CH42: Tran 4H 21
  L4: Walt 1G 7
Stuart Rd. Nth. L20: Boot 1G 7
Stubbs La. CH43: Noct 4C 20
Studholme St. L20: Kirkd 4E 7
Studley Rd. CH45: Wall 5C 4
Sudworth Rd. CH45: New B 4E 5
Suffield Rd. L4: Kirkd 3F 7
Suffolk Av. CH65: Ell P 2G 49
Suffolk St. L1: Liv 5F 15
Sugnall St. L7: Liv 5H 15
  (not continuous)
Sullivan Av. CH49: Upton 3F 19
Summerfield CH62: Brom 1B 36
Summerford Cl. CH42: Tran . . .4A 22
Summer Seat L3: Liv 1F 15
Summers Rd. L3: Liv 2F 23
Summertrees Av.
  CH49: Grea 3D 18
Summertrees Cl.
  CH49: Grea 3D 18
Summertrees Rd.
  CH66: Gt Sut 5E 49
Summerwood CH61: Irby 2H 25
Summit, The CH44: Wall 6G 5
Sumner Cl. L5: Liv 6E 7
Sumner Rd. CH43: Bid 5D 12
Sunbury Rd. CH44: Wall 2G 13
Suncroft Rd. CH60: Hesw 4E 33
Sunfield Cl. CH66: Gt Sut 4D 48
Sunfield Rd. CH46: More 3F 11
Sunlight Lodge
  CH62: Port S 3H 29

Sunlight Vision Mus. **3H 29**
Sunningdale CH46: More 5G 11
Sunningdale Dr.
  CH61: Thing 4C 26
  CH63: Brom 5H 35
Sunningdale Rd. CH45: Wall . .3D 4
Sunningdale Way
  CH64: Lit N 2C 44
Sunny Bank CH63: Hghr B 3D 28
Sunnybank CH49: Upton 1F 19
Sunnybank Av. CH43: Noct . . .3B 20
Sunnyside CH46: More 3D 10
  CH65: Ell P 1A 50
Sunset Cotts. CH64: Ness 3E 45
Surrey Av. CH49: Upton 2E 19
Surrey Dr. CH48: W Kir 1A 24
Surrey St. CH44: Wall 2E 13
  L1: Liv 5F 15
Susan Gro. CH46: More 5D 10
Sussex Cl. CH61: Pens 5A 26
Sussex Rd. CH48: W Kir 4E 17
Sutherland Dr. CH62: East 1E 41
Sutton Av. CH64: Nest 1C 44
Sutton Cl. CH62: East 2G 41
Sutton Community Sports Cen.
  . . . .**1E 49**
Sutton Hall Dr.
  CH66: Lit Sut 1A 48
Sutton Hall Gdns.
  CH66: Lit Sut 1A 48
Sutton Rd. CH45: New B 4F 5
Sutton Way
  CH65: Gt Sut, Whit 3D 48
  CH66: Gt Sut 3D 48
Swaledale Cl. CH62: East 6C 36
Swale Rd. CH65: Ell P 6G 43
Swan Cl. CH66: Gt Sut 5D 48
Swan Ct. CH43: Pren 5D 20
Swanston Av. L4: Walt 2H 7
Sweetfield Gdns.
  CH66: Lit Sut 6D 42
Sweetfield Rd.
  CH66: Lit Sut 6D 42
Sweeting St. L2: Liv 4E 15
Swift's Weint *CH64: Park* *4A 38*
  (off Coastguard La.)
Swindon Cl. CH49: Grea 3C 18
  L5: Kirkd 4F 7
Swindon St. L5: Kirkd 4F 7
Sybil Rd. L4: Walt 4H 7
Sycamore Av. CH49: Upton . . .6D 10
Sycamore Cl. CH49: Upton 6D 10
Sycamore Dr. CH66: Whit 6F 49
Sycamore Ri. CH49: Grea 5C 18
Sycamore Rd. CH42: Tran 3H 21
Sylvandale Gro.
  CH62: Brom 1B 36
Synergy Bus. Pk.
  CH2: Lit Stan 5D 50
Syren St. L20: Kirkd 3E 7
Sytchcroft CH64: Nest 5C 38

T

Tabley Cl. CH43: Oxton 5D 20
Tabley St. L1: Liv 5F 15
Tace Cl. L8: Liv 6H 15
Talbot Av. CH63: Brim 2A 34
  CH64: Lit N 1D 44
Talbot Cl. CH64: Lit N 1D 44
Talbot Ct. CH43: Oxton 3E 21
Talbot Gdns. CH64: Lit N 1D 44
Talbot Rd. CH43: Oxton 3E 21
  CH64: Gt Sut 4F 49
Taliesin St. L5: Liv 6F 7
Tamar Cl. L5: Liv 1H 15
Tamar Gro. CH46: More 5D 10
Tam O'Shanter Urban Farm
  . . . .**6C 12**
Tamworth St. L8: Liv 2G 23
Tanar Cl. CH63: Spit 6H 29
Tancred Rd. CH45: Wall 6E 5
  L4: Walt 4H 7
Tannery La. CH64: Nest 5C 38
Tansley Cl. CH48: W Kir 5G 17
Tanworth Gro. CH46: More 4B 10
Tapestry Gdns. CH41: Birke . . .4D 12
Tara Pk. Cvn. Site L3: Liv 2D 14

Tarbot Hey CH46: More 5C 10
Target Rd. CH60: Hesw 3F 31
Tariff St. L5: Liv 6F 7
Tarleton St. L1: Liv 4F 15
Tarnmere Cl. L4: Walt 1H 7
Tarn Rd. CH46: More 3D 10
Tarporley Cl. CH43: Oxton 4D 20
Tarporley Rd. CH66: Gt Sut . . .3E 49
Tarran Dr. CH46: More 3D 10
Tarran Rd. CH46: More 3D 10
Tarran Way E. CH46: More 3D 10
Tarran Way Nth.
  CH46: More 3D 10
Tarran Way Sth.
  CH46: More 3D 10
Tarran Way W. CH46: More 2D 10
Tarvin Cl. CH65: Ell P 3A 50
Tarvin Rd. CH62: East 1H 41
Tate Liverpool **5D 14**
Tate St. L4: Walt 3H 7
Tatlock St. L5: Liv 1E 15
Tattersall Pl. L20: Boot 1D 6
Tatton Rd. CH42: Tran 2H 21
Taunton Rd. CH45: Wall 5C 4
Tavener Cl. CH63: Brom 6A 36
Tavistock Rd. CH45: Wall 5C 4
Tavy Rd. L6: Liv 1H 15
Tawd St. L4: Kirkd 3G 7
Taylor St. CH41: Birke 6A 14
  L5: Liv 6F 7
Taylor St. Ind. Est. L5: Liv 6G 7
Teals Way CH60: Hesw 3H 31
Tebay Rd. CH62: East 3C 36
Teehey Cl. CH63: Hghr B 3D 28
Teehey Gdns. CH63: Hghr B . . .3D 28
Teehey La. CH63: Hghr B 3D 28
Tees Cl. L4: Kirkd 2G 7
Tees Ct. CH65: Ell P 6G 43
Teesdale Rd. CH63: Beb 5E 29
Tees Pl. L4: Kirkd 2G 7
Tees St. CH41: Birke 4D 12
  L4: Kirkd 2F 7
Teign Cl. L6: Liv 1H 15
Teilo St. L8: Liv 2H 23
Telary Cl. L5: Liv 6E 7
Telegraph La. CH45: Wall 6A 4
Telegraph Rd. CH48: Caldy 2D 24
  CH60: Hesw 2D 24
  CH61: Thurs 2D 24
Telford Cl. CH43: Oxton 3F 21
Telford Rd. CH65: Ell P 3C 50
Telford's Quay CH65: Ell P 2H 43
Tempest Hey L2: Liv 3E 15
Temple Ct. L2: Liv 4E 15
Temple La. L2: Liv 3E 15
Templemore Rd.
  CH43: Oxton 3E 21
Temple Rd. CH42: Tran 5G 21
Temple St. L2: Liv 3E 15
Tenby Dr. CH46: More 5F 11
Tenby St. L5: Liv 5H 7
Tennyson Av. CH42: Rock F . . .6B 22
Tennyson Rd. CH65: Whit 3G 49
Tenpin
  Ellesmere Port **6B 50**
Tenterden St. L5: Liv 1F 15
Terminus Rd. CH62: Brom 6B 30
Tern Way CH46: More 4B 10
Tetbury St. CH41: Birke 2G 21
Tetchill Cl. CH65: Gt Sut 5D 48
Tetlow St. L4: Walt 3H 7
Tetlow Way L4: Walt 3H 7
Teulon Cl. L4: Walt 3H 7
Tewkesbury Cl.
  CH66: Gt Sut 6A 48
Thackeray Cl. L8: Liv 1H 23
Thackeray Ct. *L8: Liv* *1H 23*
  (off Pomfret St.)
Thamesdale CH65: Whit 4G 49
Thames Gdns. CH65: Whit 4G 49
Thames Side CH65: Whit 4H 49
The . . . .
  Names prefixed with 'The'
  for example 'The Akbar' are
  indexed under the main
  name such as 'Akbar, The'
Thelwall Rd. CH66: Gt Sut 3E 49
Thermal Rd. CH62: Brom 5B 30
Thermopylae Pas.
  CH43: Noct 1B 20
THINGWALL **4D 26**

Thingwall Dr. CH61: Irby 3C 26
Thingwall Grange
  CH61: Thing 3D 26
Thingwall Recreation Cen. . . .3D 26
Thingwall Rd. CH61: Irby 3H 25
Thingwall Rd. E.
  CH61: Thing 3C 26
Third Av. CH43: Bid 1H 19
Thirlmere Av. CH43: Noct 1A 20
Thirlmere Dr. CH45: Wall 6F 5
Thirlmere Rd. CH64: Nest 1C 44
  CH65: Whit 5H 49
Thistledown Cl. L17: Aig 4H 23
Thistleton Av. CH41: Birke . . .5D 12
Thomas Cl. CH45: Whit 5H 49
Thomas Ct. CH43: Oxton 2G 21
Thomas Steers Way L1: Liv . . .4E 15
Thomas St. CH41: Birke 2A 22
Thomaston St. L5: Liv 5G 7
  (not continuous)
Thomas Winder Ct. L5: Kirkd . . .5F 7
  (off Sterling Way)
Thompson St. CH41: Tran 3A 22
Thorburn Cl. CH62: New F . . .1H 29
Thorburn St. CH62: New F . . .6D 22
Thorburn Cres.
  CH62: New F 1H 29
Thorburn Lodge
  CH62: New F 6D 22
Thorburn Rd. CH62: New F . . .1H 29
Thorncliffe Rd. CH44: Wall . . .2E 13
Thorncroft Dr. CH61: Barn . . .5D 26
Thorne Dr. CH66: Lit Sut 2B 48
Thorne La. CH44: Wall 6D 4
Thorness Cl. CH49: Grea 5C 18
Thorneycroft St. CH41: Birke . .5E 13
Thornfield Hey CH63: Spit 1G 35
Thornham Cl. CH49: Upton . . .6G 11
Thornleigh Av. CH62: East . . .2H 41
Thornleigh Dr. CH66: Ell P . . .1E 49
Thornley Rd. CH46: More 6C 10
Thornridge CH46: More 5G 11
Thorns Dr. CH49: Grea 5C 18
Thornton Av. CH63: Hghr B . . .1D 28
Thornton Comn. Rd.
  CH63: Raby M, Thorn H
  . . . . .4B 34
Thornton Cres. CH60: Hesw . .5D 32
Thornton Gro. CH63: Hghr B . .1D 28
THORNTON HOUGH 5A 34
Thornton M. CH66: Chil T 5B 42
Thornton Rd. CH45: Wall 5E 5
  CH63: Hghr B 1D 28
  CH65: Ell P 3B 50
Thornton St. CH41: Birke 5E 13
Thorntree Cl. L17: Aig 4H 23
Thornwythe Gro.
  CH66: Gt Sut 3E 49
Thorpe Bank CH42: Rock F . . .1F 29
Thorstone Dr. CH61: Irby 2G 25
Thorsway CH42: Rock F 5B 22
  CH48: Caldy 1B 24
THREE LANES END 2B 18
Thresher Av. CH49: Grea 3C 18
Thursby Rd. CH62: Brom 1C 36
THURSTASTON 4F 25
Thurstaston Common
  Local Nature Reserve . . .1E 25
Thurstaston Rd.
  CH60: Hesw 2A 32
  CH61: Irby, Thurs 4F 25
Thurston Billiard & Snooker Mus.
  . . . . .2G 15
Tichbourne Way L6: Liv 2H 15
Tide Way CH45: Wall 3C 4
Tillotson Cl. L8: Liv 2G 23
Tilstock Av. CH62: New F 1H 29
Tilstock Cres. CH43: Pren 6D 20
Tilston Rd. CH45: Wall 5E 5
Tinas Way CH49: Upton 2G 19
Tinsley St. L4: Walt 4H 7
Tintern Dr. CH46: More 5E 11
Titchfield St. L3: Liv 1E 15
  L5: Liv 1E 15
Tithebarn Cl. CH60: Hesw . . .4B 32
Tithebarn Dr. CH64: Park 3A 58
Tithebarn St. L2: Liv 3E 15
Tiverton Av. CH44: Wall 1E 13
Tobin Cl. L5: Liv 1E 15
Tobin St. CH44: Wall 1H 13

Toleman Av. CH63: Beb 4G 29
Tollemache Rd.
  CH41: Birke 6C 12
  CH43: Bid 6C 12
  CH43: Clau 6D 12
Tollemache St. CH45: New B . .3G 5
Tolpuddle Way L4: Kirkd 3F 7
Tom Mann Cl. L3: Liv 3F 15
Topaz Cl. L4: Walt 1G 7
Topgate Cl. CH60: Hesw 3D 32
Tordelow Cl. L6: Liv 1H 15
Toronto St. CH44: Wall 2A 14
Torr Dr. CH62: East 4E 37
Torridon Gro. CH66: Gt Sut . . .4F 49
Torrington Dr. CH61: Thing . . .3D 26
Torrington Gdns.
  CH61: Thing 2D 26
Torrington Rd. CH44: Wall . . .1E 13
Torwood CH43: Noct 6B 12
Total Fitness
  Prenton 6B 20
Tourist Info. Cen.
  Liverpool, Salthouse Quay
  . . . . .5E 15
  Liverpool, Williamson St.
  . . . . .4F 15
Tower Gdns. L3: Liv 4D 14
Tower Hill CH42: Tran 4H 21
Tower Prom. CH45: New B . . .2G 5
Tower Quays CH41: Birke 5A 14
Tower Rd. CH41: Birke 5A 14
  CH42: Tran 6F 21
  (Reservoir Rd.)
  CH42: Tran 4H 21
  (Tower Hill)
Tower Rd. Nth. CH60: Hesw . .1A 32
Tower Rd. Sth. CH60: Hesw . .2B 32
Towers, The CH47: Hoy 5A 22
Tower St. L3: Liv 2F 23
Tower Wharf CH41: Birke 5A 14
Townfield Cen. CH43: Oxton . .4C 20
Townfield Cl. CH43: Oxton . . .4C 20
Townfield Gdns.
  CH63: Hghr B 2F 29
Townfield La. CH43: Oxton . . .4C 20
  CH63: Beb 2F 29
  CH63: Beb, Hghr B 2F 29
Townfield Rd. CH48: W Kir . . .5D 16
Town Flds. CH45: Wall 5C 4
Townfield Way CH44: Wall . . .1F 13
Town La. CH63: Hghr B 3D 28
  CH64: Lit N 1D 44
Townley Ct. CH47: Hoy 6D 8
  (off Seaview)
Town Mdw. La. CH46: More . . .5B 10
Town Rd. CH42: Tran 4H 21
Townsend St. CH41: Birke . . .4C 12
  L5: Kirkd 5E 7
Townshend Av. CH61: Irby . . .4H 25
Town Vw. CH43: Oxton 2G 21
Town Vw. M. CH43: Oxton . . .2G 21
Towson St. L5: Liv 5H 7
  (Adam St.)
  L5: Liv 5H 7
  (Hartnup St.)
TOXTETH 1G 23
Toxteth Gro. L8: Liv 3H 23
Toxteth St. L8: Liv 2H 23
  (not continuous)
Tradewind Sq. L1: Liv 5G 15
  (off Kent St.)
TRAFALGAR 5G 29
Trafalgar Av. CH44: Wall 6H 5
Trafalgar Dr. CH63: Beb 5G 29
Trafalgar Rd. CH44: Wall 6G 5
Trafalgar Way L6: Liv 1H 15
TRANMERE 4A 22
Tranmere Recreation Cen. . .5G 21
Tranmere Rovers FC 5G 21
Traynor Ct. CH43: Oxton 2E 21
  (off Beresford Rd.)
Treborth St. L8: Liv 2H 23
Treetops Cl. CH41: Birke 3C 44
Treetops Dr. CH41: Birke 4B 12
Trefoil Cl. L8: Liv 1H 23
Treforris Rd. CH45: Wall 4D 4
Trentdale CH65: Whit 4H 49
Trentham Rd. CH44: Wall 2G 13
Trent St. CH41: Birke 4D 12
  L5: Kirkd 5E 7

Trent Way CH60: Hesw 5D 32
Trevelyan St. L9: Walt 1H 7
Trimley Cl. CH49: Upton 2E 19
Tring Cl. CH49: Upton 6G 11
Trinity Ct. CH47: Hoy 6D 8
Trinity Gdns. CH43: Oxton . . .2D 20
  CH47: Hoy 6D 8
Trinity La. CH41: Birke 6A 14
Trinity Pl. L20: Boot 1F 7
Trinity Rd. CH44: Wall 6F 5
  CH47: Hoy 6D 8
  CH65: Ell P 3B 50
  L20: Boot 1E 7
Trinity St. CH41: Birke 6G 13
Trinity Wlk. L3: Liv 2G 15
  (off Springfield)
Troon Cl. CH63: Brom 6A 36
Troutbeck Cl. CH49: Woodc . .5G 19
Trowbridge St. L3: Liv 4G 15
Trueman Cl. CH43: Bid 5A 12
Trueman St. L3: Liv 3F 15
Trumans La. CH66: Lit Sut . . .6C 42
Truro Cl. CH66: Gt Sut 6A 48
Tryfan Cl. CH66: Ell P 6F 43
Tudor Av. CH44: Wall 3A 14
  CH63: Beb 6G 29
Tudor Cl. CH66: Gt Sut 6A 48
  L7: Liv 4H 15
Tudor Grange CH49: Grea 4D 18
Tudor Rd. CH42: Tran 4A 22
Tudorville Rd. CH63: Beb 4F 29
Tudor Way CH60: Hesw 3D 32
Tulip Av. CH41: Birke 5D 12
Tunnage Sq. L1: Liv 5F 15
  (off Duke St.)
Tunnel Rd. CH41: Birke 2B 22
Tunstall Cl. CH49: Upton 2E 19
Tupman St. L8: Liv 2H 23
Turmar Av. CH61: Thing 3D 26
Turnberry Cl. CH46: More 4B 10
Turner St. CH41: Birke 2G 21
Turners Vw. CH64: Nest 3B 38
Turney Rd. CH44: Wall 1E 13
Turret Rd. CH45: Wall 5E 5
Turriff Dr. CH63: East 1E 41
Turrocks Cl. CH64: Lit N 2C 44
Turrocks Cft. CH64: Lit N 2C 44
Turton St. L5: Kirkd 5F 7
Tweed St. CH41: Birke 4E 13
Twickenham Dr. CH46: Leas . .2F 11
Two Acre Gro. CH66: Gt Sut . .6F 49
Twomey Cl. L5: Liv 1E 15
Tyburn Cl. CH63: Spit 1F 35
Tyburn Rd. CH63: Spit 1F 35
Tyne Cl. L4: Kirkd 3G 7
Tynemouth Cl. L5: Liv 6H 7
Tynesdale CH65: Whit 4H 49
Tyne St. CH41: Birke 4D 12
Tynron Gro. CH43: Noct 3B 20
Tynwald Rd. CH48: W Kir 5C 16
Tyrer St. CH41: Birke 4D 12
  L1: Liv 4F 15

U

U-boat Story 6C 14
Ullapool Cl. CH66: Lit Sut 1H 47
Ullswater Av. CH43: Noct 1B 20
Ullswater Rd. CH65: Ell P 5A 50
Ulverscroft CH43: Oxton 3D 20
Underley Ter. CH62: New F . . .2H 29
Underwater Street 4D 14
  (in Cunard Building, Water St.)
Underwood Dr.
  CH65: Ell P, Whit 5H 49
Unicorn Way CH41: Tran 2B 22
Union Cl. L2: Liv 4E 15
Union St. CH42: Tran 4B 22
  CH44: Wall 1H 13
  L3: Liv 3D 14
Union Ter. CH45: New B 2F 5
Unity Bldg. L3: Liv 2F 15
  (off Chapel St.)
Unity Theatre 5G 15
  (off Hope Pl.)
University of Liverpool
  Biosciences Building . . .4H 15
  Cambridge St. 5H 15
  Central Campus 4H 15

University of Liverpool
  North Campus 4H 15
  Peach St. 4H 15
University of Liverpool Library
  . . . . .5H 15
  (off Chatham St.)
University of Liverpool Sports Cen.
  . . . . .4H 15
University Rd. L20: Boot 1F 7
Upavon Av. CH49: Grea 4B 18
Upchurch Cl. L8: Liv 3H 23
Upland Rd. CH49: Upton 1F 19
Uplands, The CH43: Oxton . . .3C 20
Uplands Rd. CH62: Brom 2A 36
Up. Beau St. L5: Liv 1G 15
Up. Beckwith St.
  CH41: Birke 5F 13
UPPER BIDSTON VILLAGE . .4A 12
Up. Brassey St.
  CH41: Birke 5D 12
Up. Bute St. L5: Liv 1G 15
Up. Duke St. L1: Liv 5G 15
Up. Essex St. L8: Liv 2H 23
Up. Flaybrick Rd.
  CH41: Birke 6C 12
Up. Frederick St. L1: Liv 5F 15
  (not continuous)
Up. Hampton St. L8: Liv 6H 15
Up. Harrington St. L8: Liv 1G 23
Up. Hill St. L8: Liv 1G 23
  (not continuous)
Up. Hope Pl. L7: Liv 5H 15
Up. Huskisson St. L8: Liv 6H 15
Up. Mann St. L8: Liv 1G 23
  (not continuous)
Up. Mersey St. CH65: Ell P . . .2G 43
Upper Newington L1: Liv 4G 15
Up. Park St. L8: Liv 2H 23
Up. Parliament St. L8: Liv 6G 15
Up. Pitt St. L1: Liv 5F 15
  (not continuous)
Up. Pownall St. L1: Liv 5F 15
Up. Raby Rd. CH63: Raby 3E 39
  CH64: Nest 3E 39
Up. Rice La. CH44: Wall 6G 5
Up. Stanhope St. L8: Liv 6G 15
  (not continuous)
Up. Warwick St. L8: Liv 1H 23
Up. William St. L3: Liv 1D 14
Uppingham Rd. CH44: Wall . . .6D 4
UPTON 2G 19
Upton By-Pass CH49: Upton . .1E 19
Upton Cl. CH49: Upton 2F 19
Upton Ct. CH49: Upton 1F 19
Upton Pk. Dr. CH49: Upton . . .1G 19
Upton Rd. CH41: Birke 2A 20
  CH43: Bid, Noct 2A 20
  CH46: More 5E 11
  CH66: Gt Sut 3D 48
Upton Station (Rail) 2A 20
Ure Ct. CH65: Ell P 6G 43
Urmson Rd. CH45: Wall 6F 5
Ursula St. L20: Boot 2D 7
Utkinton Cl. CH43: Oxton 4D 20
UVECO Bus. Cen.
  CH41: Birke 4F 13

V

Vale Dr. CH45: New B 4G 5
Vale Gdns. CH65: Whit 3H 49
Valentia Rd. CH47: Hoy 1C 16
Valerian Rd. CH41: Birke 6D 12
Vale Rd. CH65: Whit 3H 49
Valiant Ho. CH41: Birke 1B 22
Valiant Way CH41: Tran 3B 22
Valkyrie Rd. CH45: Wall 6E 5
Valleybrook Gro.
  CH63: Spit 1H 35
Valley Dr. CH66: Gt Sut 2D 48
Valley Rd. CH41: Birke 3B 12
  CH62: Brom 3B 36
Valley Rd. Bus. Pk.
  CH41: Birke 4C 12
Valley Vw. CH66: Gt Sut 2D 48
Vanderbyl Av. CH62: Spit 1A 36
Vandries St. L3: Liv 1D 14
Vanguard St. L5: Liv 5H 7
Vanguard Way CH41: Tran . . .4B 22

Vardon St. CH41: Birke 5H 13
Varthen St. L5: Liv 5H 7
Vaughan Rd. CH45: New B 3G 5
Vaughan St. CH41: Birke 5D 12
VAUXHALL 1E 15
Vauxhall Bus. Cen. L3: Liv . . .2E 15
(off Eaton St.)
Vauxhall Motors FC 4C 42
Vauxhall Rd. L3: Liv 2E 15
L5: Liv 2E 15
Venables Cl. CH63: Spit 2H 35
Venables Dr. CH63: Spit 1G 35
Venice St. L5: Liv 5H 7
Venmore St. L5: Liv 5H 7
(not continuous)
Venture Ct. CH41: Birke 2A 22
Vere St. L8: Liv 2G 23
Vernon Av. CH44: Wall 3H 13
CH66: Hoot 3A 42
Vernon St. L2: Liv 3E 15
Verona St. L5: Liv 5H 7
Veronica Way CH66: Lit Sut . . .6D 42
Verwood Cl. CH61: Irby 2H 25
Vescock St. L5: Liv 1F 15
Vesuvius Pl. L5: Kirkd 5F 7
Vesuvius St. L5: Kirkd 5F 7
Vicarage Cl. CH42: Tran 6F 21
Vicarage Gro. CH44: Wall 6G 5
Vicarage La. CH64: Burt 5H 45
Viceroy St. L5: Liv 5H 7
Victoria Av. CH60: Hesw 5B 32
VICTORIA CENTRAL HOSPITAL
. . . . .2F 13
Victoria Ct. CH42: Rock F 6C 22
Victoria Dr. CH42: Rock F 6C 22
CH48: W Kir 5C 16
Victoria Flds. CH42: Tran 3G 21
Victoria Gallery & Mus. 4H 15
Victoria Gdns. CH43: Oxton . . .3F 21
Victoria Hall L2: Liv 3E 15
(off Tithebarn St.)
Victoria La. CH43: Oxton 3F 21
Victoria M. CH65: Ell P 2H 49
(off Victoria Rd.)
Victoria Mt. CH43: Oxton 3F 21
Victoria Pde. CH45: New B . . .2G 5
Victoria Pk. Rd.
CH42: Tran 5H 21
Victoria Pl. CH44: Wall 3B 14
Victoria Rd. CH42: Tran 3G 21
CH45: New B 3E 5
CH48: W Kir 6C 16
CH63: Hghr B 3D 28
CH64: Lit N 1D 44
CH65: Ell P 2H 49
Victoria St. CH62: Port S 4H 29
L1: Liv 4E 15
L2: Liv 4E 15
Victoria Vw. CH45: New B 3E 5
Vienna St. L5: Liv 5H 7
View 146 L5: Liv 6G 7
Village, The CH63: Beb 3G 29
CH64: Burt 6G 45
Village Cl. CH45: Wall 5C 4
Village Ct. CH43: Oxton 3E 21
CH61: Irby 3H 25
Village Grn. Ct. CH43: Bid 5A 12
Village M. CH45: Wall 5C 4
CH63: Hghr B 3D 28
Village Rd. CH43: Oxton 3E 21
CH48: W Kir 6D 16
CH60: Hesw 4B 32
CH63: Hghr B 3D 28
Village Sq. CH64: Will 5B 40
(off Buckley La.)
Village St. L6: Liv 1H 15
Village Way CH45: Wall 6C 4
Vincent Ct. L1: Liv 5F 15
Vincent Naughton Ct.
CH41: Birke 2A 22
Vincent St. CH41: Birke 1H 21
Vine Rd. CH66: Gt Sut 6F 49
Vine St. L7: Liv 5H 15
Vining St. L8: Liv 1H 23
Viola St. L20: Boot 2E 7
Violet Cft. CH63: Beb 5F 29
Violet Rd. CH41: Birke 6D 12
Virgil St. L5: Liv 1G 15
Virginia Rd. CH45: New B 2F 5
Virginia Ter. CH66: Chil T 5A 42

Vittoria Cl. CH41: Birke 6H 13
Vittoria Ct. CH41: Birke 6H 13
Vittoria St. CH41: Birke 6G 13
Vivian Av. CH44: Wall 3A 14
Vue Cinema
Birkenhead 1A 22
Ellesmere Port 5B 50
Vulcan Cl. CH41: Birke 5D 12
Vulcan St. CH41: Birke 5D 12
L3: Liv 1D 14
Vyner Cl. CH43: Noct 1C 20
Vyner Ct. CH43: Noct 1C 20
Vyner Pk. CH43: Noct 1C 20
Vyner Rd. CH45: Wall 6D 4
Vyner Rd. Nth. CH43: Bid 6B 12
Vyner Rd. Sth.
CH43: Bid, Noct 1B 20
Vyrnwy St. L5: Liv 5H 7

W

Wadham Pk. L20: Boot 1F 7
Wadham Rd. L20: Boot 2E 7
Wakefield Dr. CH46: Leas 1F 11
Wakefield Rd.
CH66: Gt Sut 6E 49
Wakefield St. L3: Liv 2G 15
Walby Cl. CH49: Woodc 5A 20
Walden Dr. CH1: Woodb 6F 47
Waldron Cl. L3: Liv 2E 15
Walford Cl. CH63: Spit 1F 35
Walker Art Gallery 3F 15
Walker Hgts. CH42: Tran 4H 21
(off Walker St.)
Walker M. CH42: Tran 4H 21
Walker Pl. CH42: Tran 4H 21
Walker's Cft. CH45: Wall 6D 4
Walkers La. CH66: Lit Sut 1C 48
Walker St. CH42: Tran 4H 21
CH47: Hoy 6D 8
CH62: Port S 3H 29
L6: Liv 2H 15
Wallacre Rd. CH44: Wall 1C 12
WALLASEY 6C 4
Wallasey Bri. Rd.
CH41: Birke 4D 12
Wallasey Grove Road Station (Rail)
. . . . .5C 4
Wallasey Rd. CH44: Wall 1D 12
CH45: Wall 1D 12
Wallasey Village CH44: Wall . .5C 4
CH45: Wall 5C 4
Wallasey Village Station (Rail)
. . . . .6C 4
Wallasey Waterfront
Retail & Leisure Pk.
CH45: New B 2E 5
Wallcroft CH64: Will 6C 40
Waller Cl. L4: Kirkd 4G 7
Wallingford Rd.
CH49: Upton 3F 19
Wallrake CH60: Hesw 4B 32
Wall St. L1: Liv 4E 15
Walmsley St. CH44: Wall 6G 5
L5: Liv 6E 7
Walnut Gro. CH66: Whit 6F 49
Walnut St. L7: Liv 4H 15
(off Mt. Pleasant)
Walsh Cl. L5: Liv 1E 15
Walsingham Ct.
CH44: Wall 2H 13
(off Liscard Rd.)
Walsingham Rd.
CH44: Wall 2H 13
Walter St. L5: Liv 6D 6
Walton Breck Rd. L4: Walt 4H 7
Walton La. L4: Walt 4H 7
Walton Rd. L4: Walt 4G 7
Walton St. CH41: Birke 1A 22
Walton Village L4: Walt 1H 7
(not continuous)
Wapping L1: Liv 5E 15
Warden St. L4: Walt 3G 7
Ward Gro. CH42: Rock F 1F 29
Ward St. L3: Liv 3G 15
Waring Av. CH42: Tran 5H 21
Warkworth Cl. CH65: Ell P 4C 50
Warren, The CH49: Upton 2H 19
Warren Ct. CH66: Gt Sut 4D 48

Warrender Dr. CH43: Bid 5D 12
Webster St. L3: Liv 3F 15
Warren Dr. CH43: Bid 1A 20
CH45: Wall, New B 3D 4
CH66: Ell P 6E 43
Warren Hey CH63: Spit 2G 35
Warren Hurst CH45: New B 3E 5
Warren La.
CH62: Brom, East 2D 36
(not continuous)
Warren Pk. CH45: Wall 4D 4
Warren Point CH45: Wall 3D 4
Warren Rd. CH47: Hoy 6C 8
Warren St. L3: Liv 4G 15
Warren Way CH60: Hesw 2H 31
Warrington Av. CH65: Whit . . .5H 49
Warrington St. CH41: Tran 3A 22
Warwick Cl. CH43: Oxton 2G 21
CH64: Nest 2C 44
Warwick Ct. CH65: Ell P 5C 50
L8: Liv 1H 23
(off Gwent St.)
Warwick Dr. CH45: Wall 5G 5
CH48: W Kir 1A 24
Warwick Rd. CH45: Upton 2E 19
Warwick St. L8: Liv 1G 23
Washbrook Av. CH43: Bid 5A 12
Wastdale Av. CH46: More 4C 10
Wastdale Dr. CH46: More 4C 10
Wastdale M. CH46: More 4C 10
Water Bus. Pk. CH65: Ell P . . .2H 43
Waterfall Dr. L4: Walt 1H 7
Waterfield Cl.
CH63: Hghr B 4D 28
Waterford Dr. CH64: Lit N 6E 39
Waterford Rd. CH43: Oxton . . .2D 20
Waterfront Bus. Area
L8: Liv 6G 15
Waterfront Bus. Area
Parliament St. Nth.
L1: Liv 6G 15
(off New Bird St.)
L1: Liv 6F 15
(off Simpson St.)
Waterfront Bus. Area
Parliament St. Sth.
L8: Liv 1G 23
(off Stanhope St.)
Waterloo Cl. CH65: Ell P 2A 50
Waterloo Ct. CH65: Beb 3G 29
Waterloo Dock L3: Liv 2D 14
Waterloo Pl. CH41: Birke 2A 22
Waterloo Quay L3: Liv 2D 14
Waterloo Rd. CH45: New B 2F 5
L3: Liv 1D 14
Waterpark Cl. CH43: Pren 6D 20
Waterpark Ho. CH42: Tran . . .5F 21
(off Storeton Rd.)
Waterpark Rd. CH42: Tran 6D 20
CH43: Pren 6D 20
Watersedge Apartments
CH45: New B 2G 5
(off Tower Prom.)
Waters Rd. CH65: Ell P 2H 43
Water St. CH41: Birke 1B 22
CH44: Wall 1H 13
CH62: Port S 4A 30
L2: Liv 4E 15
L3: Liv 4D 14
Water Twr. Rd. CH64: Nest . . .4C 38
Waterworks La.
CH66: Hoot 4G 41
Watkinson St. L1: Liv 6F 15
Watmough St. L5: Liv 1G 15
Watson Ct. CH41: Birke 6B 14
(off Argyle St.)
Watson St. CH41: Birke 6H 13
Waverley Gro. CH42: Tran 5G 21
Waverley Rd. CH47: Hoy 6E 9
Waverton Av. CH43: Oxton 5C 20
Wavertree Ct. CH66: Ell P 6F 49
Weald Dr. CH66: Lit Sut 1A 48
Weatherstones Bus. Cen.
CH64: Nest 5G 39
Weatherstones Cotts.
CH64: Nest 5H 39
Weaver Rd. CH65: Ell P 4A 50
Weaver St. L9: Walt 1H 7
Webster Av. CH44: Wall 6H 5
Websters Holt CH49: Upton . . .1F 19

Websters La. CH66: Gt Sut 5F 49
Webster St. L3: Liv 3F 15
Weldon St. L4: Walt 1H 7
Welford Av. CH43: Pren 5D 20
Welland Rd. CH63: Hghr B 4D 28
Wellbrae Cl. CH49: Upton 2D 18
Well Cl. CH64: Ness 3E 45
Weller St. L8: Liv 2H 23
Wellesbourne Cl.
CH64: Nest 1B 44
Wellesley Av. CH65: Ell P 2A 50
Wellesley Gro. CH63: Beb 3G 29
Wellesley Rd. CH44: Wall 1F 13
(not continuous)
Wellesley Wlk. CH65: Ell P . . .2A 50
(off Wellesley Av.)
Wellington Cl. CH63: Beb 3G 29
CH65: Ell P 2A 50
Wellington Ct. CH65: Ell P . . .2A 50
(off Arthur Av.)
Wellington Employment Pk. Sth.
L5: Kirkd 5E 7
Wellington Mans.
CH45: New B 2E 5
(off Atherton St.)
Wellington Rd. CH43: Oxton . . .2E 21
CH45: New B 2E 5
CH63: Beb 3G 29
CH65: Ell P 3H 49
(not continuous)
L8: Liv 3H 23
Wellington Rd. Nth.
CH65: Ell P 2A 50
Wellington St. L3: Liv 2F 15
Wellington Ter. CH41: Birke . . .2H 21
L8: Liv 2H 23
Well La. CH42: Rock F, Tran . . .4H 21
CH49: Grea 4C 18
CH60: Hesw 5C 32
CH63: Hghr B 3D 28
CH64: Ness 2D 44
Wells Cl. CH66: Gt Sut 6A 48
Wellswood Rd. CH66: Ell P . . .6E 43
Wellwood Cl. CH65: Ell P 6H 43
Welshampton Cl.
CH66: Gt Sut 5D 48
Welsh Rd. CH1: Woodb 6F 47
CH66: Led, Lit Sut, Chil T
. . . . .6F 47
Welton Av. CH49: Upton 2F 19
Welton Rd. CH62: Brom 1B 36
Wendover Cl. CH43: Noct 3B 20
Wenlock Gdns.
CH66: Gt Sut 5F 49
Wenlock La. CH66: Gt Sut 5F 49
Wensleydale Av. CH62: East . .6C 36
Wentworth Av. CH45: New B . . .4F 5
Wentworth Cl. CH43: Noct 3B 20
Wentworth Dr. CH63: Brom . . .6A 36
L5: Liv 1H 15
Wernbrook Cl. CH43: Noct 3B 20
Wervin Cl. CH43: Oxton 5C 20
Wervin Rd. CH43: Oxton 5C 20
Wesley Av. CH44: Wall 6G 5
Wesley Cl. CH64: Park 5B 38
Wesley Gro. CH44: Wall 2A 14
W. Alfred Ct. CH43: Oxton . . .2G 21
(off Alfred Rd.)
Westbank Av. CH45: New B 4G 5
Westbank Rd. CH42: Tran 4G 21
Westbourne Av.
CH48: W Kir 5D 16
Westbourne Gro.
CH48: W Kir 5D 16
Westbourne Rd.
CH41: Birke 2G 21
CH43: Oxton 2G 21
CH44: Wall 1D 12
CH48: W Kir 5C 16
Westbrook Rd. CH46: More . . .6C 10
W. Brow Gdns. CH43: Bid 5A 12
Westbury St. CH41: Tran 3A 22
West Cheshire Sailing Club . . .4B 4
West Cl. CH43: Noct 2H 19
Westcott Way CH43: Noct 3B 20
Westdale Rd. CH42: Rock F . . .5A 22
W. Derby St. L7: Liv 3H 15
West Dr. CH49: Upton 2G 19
CH60: Hesw 4C 32
CH64: Nest 1B 44

Westenra Av. CH65: Ell P 1F **49**
Western Approaches Mus.
(Underground Wartime Mus.)
. . . .**3E 15**
Western Av. CH62: Brom 6B **30**
Westfield Rd. CH44: Wall 4H **13**
W. Float Ind. Est.
CH41: Birke 3F **13**
Westgate Rd. CH62: Port S . .5H **29**
West Gro. CH60: Hesw 3B **32**
Westhouse Cl. CH63: Brom . . .6A **36**
WEST KIRBY **5C 16**
West Kirby Concourse (Leisure Cen.)
. . . .**4C 16**
W. Kirby Rd. CH46: More 1C **18**
West Kirby Station (Rail) . .**5C 16**
West Knowe CH43: Oxton . . .3D **20**
Westlands Cl. CH64: Nest 4D **38**
W. Lodge Dr. CH48: W Kir . . .4C **16**
Westminster Bri.
CH65: Ell P 2A **50**
Westminster Chambers
L1: Liv 3F **15**
(off Crosshall St.)
Westminster Cl. L4: Kirkd . . .3G **7**
Westminster Ct.
CH43: Oxton 2D **20**
Westminster Dr.
CH62: Brom 4B **36**
Westminster Gro.
CH65: Ell P 1A **50**
Westminster Ind. Pk.
CH65: Ell P 1F **49**
Westminster Retail Pk.
CH65: Ell P 1B **50**
Westminster Rd.
CH44: Wall 1F **13**
CH65: Ell P 1A **50**
L4: Kirkd 2F **7**
Westmoreland Rd.
CH45: New B 4G **5**
Westmorland Dr. L3: Liv 2E **15**
Westmorland Pl. L5: Liv 6F **7**
West Pk. Dr. CH66: Gt Sut . . .6A **48**
West Pk. Gdns. CH43: Bid . . .5A **12**
Westport Bus. Pk. L20: Kirkd . .4E **7**
West Rd. CH43: Noct 2B **20**
CH65: Ell P 4A **50**
CH65: Ell P, Hoot 2C **42**
Westry Cl. CH46: More 5B **10**
West St. CH45: Wall 6F **5**
West Twr. L3: Liv 3D **14**
(off Brook St.)
Westview CH43: Noct 3B **20**
Westward Ho CH48: Caldy . . .3B **24**
Westward Vw. L17: Aig 4H **23**
Westway CH43: Noct 3B **20**
CH46: More 4E **11**
CH49: Grea 3D **18**
CH60: Hesw 5B **32**
Westway Sq. CH46: More 4E **11**
Westwood Ct. CH43: Oxton . . .2D **20**
CH64: Nest 3C **38**
Westwood Gro. CH44: Wall . . .1E **13**
Westwood Rd. CH43: Bid 1A **20**
Wetherby Av. CH45: Wall 6C **4**
Wetherby Way
CH66: Lit Sut 1B **48**
Wethersfield Lodge
CH43: Noct 3C **20**
Wethersfield Rd.
CH43: Noct 4C **20**
Wetstone La. CH48: W Kir . . .6E **17**
Wexford Cl. CH43: Oxton 3C **20**
Wexford Rd. CH43: Oxton . . .3D **20**
Weybourne Cl. CH49: Upton . .6G **11**
Weymoor Cl. CH63: Spit 1F **35**
Whaley La. CH61: Irby 3B **26**
Whalley Rd. CH42: Tran 2H **21**
Whalley St. L8: Liv 3H **23**
Wharfedale Av. CH42: Tran . . .5F **21**
Wharfedale Dr. CH62: East . . .6D **36**
Wharfedale Rd. CH45: Wall . . .5D **4**
Wharfe La. CH65: Ell P 6G **43**
Wharf St. CH62: Port S 4A **30**
Wharton Cl. CH49: Upton 1D **18**

Wheatfield Cl. CH46: More . . .6F **11**
CH66: Gt Sut 4C **48**
Wheatland Bus. Pk.
CH44: Wall 3H **13**
Wheatland La. CH44: Wall . . .3H **13**
Wheatland Rd. CH60: Hesw . .4E **33**
Wheldrake Cl.
CH66: Lit Sut 2B **48**
Whetstone Ct. CH41: Birke . . .2H **21**
(off Whetstone La.)
Whetstone Hey
CH66: Gt Sut 2D **48**
Whetstone La. CH41: Birke . .2H **21**
Whinmoor Cl. CH43: Noct . . .1B **20**
WHITBY **3G 49**
Whitby Av. CH45: Wall 6C **4**
WHITBYHEATH **5G 49**
Whitby Rd. CH1: Back 6B **48**
CH65: Ell P, Whit 3H **49**
(not continuous)
Whitebeam Av.
CH66: Gt Sut 6F **49**
Whitebeam Wlk.
CH49: Grea 5B **18**
Whitechapel L1: Liv 4F **15**
Whitecroft Rd.
CH66: Gt Sut 5E **49**
Whitefield Av. L4: Kirkd 3G **7**
Whitefield Cl.
CH49: Woodc 4H **19**
Whitegates Cl. CH64: Will . . .4A **40**
Whitegates Cres.
CH64: More 5A **40**
Whitehall Cl. L4: Kirkd 2G **7**
Whitehaven Rd. L5: Liv 5H **7**
Whiteheath Way
CH46: Leas 2F **11**
Whitehouse La.
CH60: Hesw 2E **33**
CH63: Brim 2E **33**
Whitelands Mdw.
CH49: Upton 2E **19**
White Lodge Cl.
CH62: Brom 6B **36**
Whitemere Ct. CH65: Ell P . . .2G **43**
Whiteside Cl. CH49: Upton . . .3G **19**
L5: Liv 6F **7**
Whitewell Dr. CH49: Upton . . .1F **19**
Whitfield Ct. CH42: Tran 3H **21**
Whitfield La. CH60: Hesw . . .1C **32**
Whitford Rd. CH42: Tran 3H **21**
Whitford Rd. CH42: Tran 3G **21**
Whitley Dr. CH44: Wall 6H **5**
Whitley St. L3: Liv 1D **14**
Whittle Cl. L5: Kirkd 5G **7**
Whittle St. L5: Kirkd 5G **7**
Wickham Cl. CH44: Wall 3H **13**
Wicklow Cl. CH66: Lit Sut . . .1A **48**
Widgeons Covert
CH63: Thorn H 6H **33**
Wiend, The CH42: Rock F . . .6H **21**
Wight Cl. CH65: Ell P 6A **50**
Wilbraham Pl. L5: Liv 6F **7**
Wilbraham St. CH41: Birke . . .1A **22**
L5: Liv 6F **7**
Wilburn St. L4: Walt 2H **7**
Wilcock Cl. L5: Liv 6F **7**
Wildbrook Dr. CH41: Birke . . .4B **12**
Wilde St. L3: Liv 3G **15**
Wilfred Owen Dr.
CH41: Birke 6C **12**
Wilkes Av. CH46: Leas 2H **11**
Wilkinson St.
CH41: Birke 2G **21**
CH65: Ell P 1H **49**
Wilkinson St. M.
CH65: Ell P 1A **50**
(off Wilkinson St. Nth.)
Wilkinson St. Nth.
CH65: Ell P 1A **50**
Wilkin St. L4: Kirkd 4G **7**
Willan St. CH43: Oxton 3F **21**
WILLASTON **5B 40**
Willaston Grn. M.
CH64: Will 5B **40**
Willaston Rd. CH46: More . . .4D **10**
CH63: Raby, Thorn H 4D **34**
William Brown St. L3: Liv . . .3F **15**
(not continuous)

William Ct. CH64: Nest 3D **38**
William Henry St. L3: Liv 2G **15**
L20: Boot 1D **6**
William Jessop Way
L3: Liv 3D **14**
William Johnson Gdns.
CH65: Ell P 1H **49**
William Moult St. L5: Liv 6F **7**
Williamson Art Gallery & Mus.
. . . .**2F 21**
Williamson Sq. L1: Liv 4F **15**
Williamson St. L1: Liv 4F **15**
William St. CH41: Birke 1A **22**
CH44: Wall 3A **14**
Willington Av. CH62: East . . .2G **41**
Willmer Rd. CH42: Tran 2G **21**
Willoughby Rd. CH44: Wall . .1D **12**
Willow Bank CH44: Wall 3F **13**
Willowbank Rd. CH42: Tran . .4H **21**
CH62: New F 3H **29**
Willowbrow Rd.
CH63: Raby 1G **39**
Willow Cl. CH44: Wall 3F **13**
Willow Ct. CH63: Hghr B 3D **28**
Willowcroft Rd. CH44: Wall . .3G **13**
Willowdale Way
CH66: Gt Sut, Whit 6F **49**
Willow Gro. CH46: More 6D **10**
CH66: Whit 6G **49**
Willow La. CH63: Raby 2H **39**
Willow Lea CH43: Oxton 3E **21**
Willow Moss Cl.
CH46: More 3G **11**
Willow Pk. CH49: Grea 3C **18**
Willows, The CH45: Wall 4C **4**
Wilmslow Cl. CH66: Gt Sut . . .2E **49**
Wilmslow Dr. CH66: Gt Sut . . .2E **49**
Wilne Rd. CH45: Wall 5E **5**
Wilson Av. CH44: Wall 1A **14**
Wilson Rd. CH44: Wall 1A **14**
Wilsons La. CH65: Whit 4G **49**
Wilstan Av. CH63: Hghr B . . .4D **28**
Wilstone Cl. L6: Liv 1H **15**
Wilton Grange CH48: W Kir . .3C **16**
Wilton Rd. CH42: Rock F 6C **22**
Wilton St. CH44: Wall 1F **13**
L3: Liv 2G **15**
(off Soho St.)
Wimbledon St. CH45: Wall . . .6F **5**
Wimborne Av. CH61: Thing . . .4C **26**
Wimborne Way CH61: Irby . . .2H **25**
Wimbrick Cl. CH46: More 5F **11**
Wimbrick Ct. CH46: More 5F **11**
Wimbrick Hey CH46: More . . .5F **11**
Winchester Av. CH65: Ell P . .3B **50**
Winchester Dr. CH44: Wall . . .1E **13**
Windermere Cl.
CH64: Lit N 6D **38**
Windermere Ct.
CH41: Birke 2G **21**
(off Penrith St.)
Windermere Rd.
CH43: Noct 2A **20**
CH65: Ell P 5A **50**
Windfield Gdns.
CH66: Lit Sut 6D **42**
Windle Ct. CH64: Nest 3C **38**
WINDLE HILL **5G 39**
Windmill Gdns. CH43: Bid . . .5A **12**
Windsor Cl. CH49: Grea 4D **18**
CH62: New F 2G **29**
Windsor Ct. L8: Liv 1H **23**
(off Northumberland St.)
Windsor Dr. CH65: Whit 4G **49**
Windsor M. CH62: New F 2G **29**
Windsor St. CH41: Birke 2G **21**
CH45: New B 2F **5**
L8: Liv 6H **15**
Windways CH66: Lit Sut 6D **42**
Windy Bank CH62: Port S . . .3H **29**
(not continuous)
Winford St. CH44: Wall 2H **13**
Winfrith Cl. CH63: Spit 1F **35**
Winfrith Dr. CH63: Spit 1F **35**
Wingate Cl. CH43: Noct 3C **20**
Wingate Rd. CH62: East 6C **36**
Winkle St. L8: Liv 2H **23**
Winnington Rd. CH47: Hoy . . .2C **16**
Winsford Gro. CH66: Gt Sut . .4C **48**
Winslow St. L4: Walt 2H **7**

Winstanley Ho.
CH62: New F 2H **29**
(off Winstanley Rd.)
Winstanley Rd.
CH62: New F 2H **29**
CH64: Lit N 2C **44**
Winston Dr. CH43: Noct 2A **20**
Winston Gro. CH46: More 5E **11**
Winterhey La. CH44: Wall 3F **13**
Winter St. L6: Liv 2A **16**
Winthrop Pk. CH43: Oxton . . .2C **20**
Winton Cl. CH45: New B 3E **5**
Wirral Beach Cvn. Pk.
CH47: Meols 3H **9**
Wirral Bus. Cen.
CH41: Birke 3G **13**
Wirral Cl. CH63: Beb 6F **29**
Wirral Country Pk. **5D 24**
Wirral Country Pk. Vis. Cen.
. . . .**6D 24**
Wirral Cres. CH64: Lit N 2D **44**
Wirral Gdns. CH63: Beb 6F **29**
Wirral Intl. Bus. Pk.
CH62: Brom 2D **36**
Wirral Leisure Pk.
CH62: Brom 6C **30**
Wirral Little Theatre **1G 21**
Wirral Mt. CH45: Wall 6D **4**
CH48: W Kir 5F **17**
Wirral Mus. **1B 22**
Wirral Sailing Cen. **5B 16**
Wirral Tennis & Sports Cen.
. . . .**3B 12**
Wirral Transport Mus. **6A 14**
Wirral Vs. CH45: Wall 5C **4**
Wirral Way CH43: Noct 2A **20**
Withburn Cl. CH49: Upton . . .1E **19**
Withensfield CH45: Wall 5F **5**
Withens La. CH44: Wall 5F **5**
CH45: Wall 5F **5**
Wither Av. CH63: Hghr B 1D **28**
Withington Rd. CH44: Wall . . .2G **13**
Witley Av. CH46: More 4E **11**
Witley Cl. CH46: More 4E **11**
Witney Cl. CH49: Grea 4C **18**
Witsun Dr. L4: Kirkd 4G **7**
Wittenham Cl. CH49: Upton . .3F **19**
Wittering La. CH60: Hesw . . .3H **31**
Witterings, The CH64: Nest . .4C **38**
Woburn Pl. CH42: Rock F 5C **22**
Woburn Rd. CH45: Wall 5F **5**
Wolferton Cl. CH49: Upton . . .6H **11**
Wolfe St. L8: Liv 2G **23**
Wolfrick Dr. CH63: Spit 2H **35**
Wolsey St. L20: Kirkd 2E **7**
Wolstenholme Sq. L1: Liv . . .5F **15**
WOLVERHAM **3B 50**
Wolverham Rd. CH65: Ell P . .4A **50**
Woodacre Gro. CH66: Ell P . . .5F **43**
Woodacre Rd. CH66: Ell P . . .5E **43**
Woodbank Pk. CH43: Oxton . .3D **20**
Woodbank Rd. CH65: Whit . . .5H **49**
Woodberry Cl. CH43: Noct . . .3B **20**
Woodbine St. L5: Kirkd 4F **7**
Woodburn Blvd.
CH63: Hghr B 1E **29**
Woodburn Dr. CH60: Hesw . . .5B **32**
WOODCHURCH **5H 19**
Woodchurch Ct. CH42: Tran . .4G **21**
Woodchurch La. CH42: Tran . .5F **21**
CH49: Woodc 1E **27**
CH49: Woodc 1E **19**
Woodchurch Leisure Cen. . . .**4A 20**
Woodchurch Rd.
CH41: Birke 4G **21**
CH42: Tran 6H **19**
CH43: Pren 6H **19**
CH49: Woodc 6H **19**
Wood Cl. CH41: Birke 6H **13**
CH66: Hoot 4A **42**
Woodcote Av. CH65: Whit . . .5H **49**
Woodcote Bank
CH42: Rock F 2G **29**
Woodcotes, The
CH62: Brom 5B **36**
Woodcot La. CH60: Hesw . . .2A **32**
Woodcroft Dr. CH61: Hesw . . .1B **32**
Woodcroft La.
CH63: Hghr B 1F **29**
Woodend CH61: Pens 4B **26**

Woodend La. CH64: Burt 3A **46**
Woodend Rd. CH65: Ell P 1F **49**
Woodfall Cl. CH64: Lit N 1E **45**
Woodfall Gro. CH64: Lit N 1E **45**
Woodfall La. CH64: Lit N 1D **44**
Woodfield Av.
  CH63: Hghr B 2E **29**
Woodfield Rd. CH61: Pens 5A **26**
  CH63: Beb 6G **29**
  CH65: Ell P 2A **50**
Woodfield Rd. Nth.
  CH65: Ell P 2A **50**
Woodford Rd. CH62: New F . . .1H **29**
Wood Grn. CH43: Bid 5A **12**
Woodham Gro. CH64: Lit N . . .2D **44**
Woodhead Rd.
  CH62: Port S 3A **30**
Woodhead Row
  CH62: Port S 4A **30**
Woodhead St. CH62: New F . . .2H **29**
Wood Heath Way
  CH62: East 4E **37**
WOODHEY **2E 29**
Woodhey Ct. CH63: Hghr B . . .1F **29**
Woodhey Gro.
  CH63: Hghr B 2F **29**
Woodhey Rd. CH63: Hghr B . . .2F **29**
Woodhouse Cl. L4: Walt 4G **7**
Woodin Rd. CH42: Rock F 1G **29**
Woodkind Hey CH63: Spit 1G **35**
Woodland Av. CH47: Meols 4F **9**
Woodland Dr. CH45: New B . . .4G **5**
  CH49: Woodc 4G **19**
Woodland Gro.
  CH42: Rock F 1F **29**
Woodland Rd.
  CH42: Rock F 1F **29**
  CH48: W Kir 5G **17**
  CH49: Woodc 4G **19**
  CH65: Whit 5G **49**
Woodlands, The
  CH41: Birke 2H **21**
  CH49: Upton 1F **19**

Woodlands Cl. CH64: Park 5B **38**
Woodlands Dr. CH61: Barn 5E **27**
Woodlands La. CH48: W Kir . . .6F **17**
Woodlands Rd. CH61: Irby 4H **25**
  CH64: Park 5B **38**
Woodland Vw. CH66: Chil T . . .5B **42**
Woodland Wlk.
  CH62: Brom 2A **36**
Wood La. CH45: Wall 5C **4**
  CH49: Grea 2D **18**
  CH64: Burt 5G **45**
  CH64: Park 3A **38**
  CH64: Will 4C **40**
Woodlea Cl. CH62: Brom 6B **36**
Woodpecker Cl.
  CH49: Upton 2D **18**
Woodruff St. L8: Liv 3H **23**
Woodside CH65: Whit 5A **50**
Woodside Av. CH46: More 6D **10**
Woodside Bus. Pk.
  CH41: Birke 6B **14**
Woodside Ferry App.
  CH41: Birke 6B **14**
Woodside Rd. CH61: Irby 3A **26**
Woodside Walkway
  CH41: Birke 6B **14**
Woodsome Cl. CH65: Whit 6H **49**
Woodsome Dr. CH65: Whit 6H **49**
Woodsorrel Rd.
  CH41: Birke 6D **12**
Woodstock Rd. CH44: Wall 2E **13**
Woodstock St. L5: Liv 6F **7**
Wood St. CH41: Birke 6H **13**
  CH47: Hoy 6D **8**
  CH62: Port S 4H **29**
  L1: Liv 4F **15**
Woodvale Cl. CH43: Bid 1A **12**
Woodvale Ct. *CH49: Woodc . . .6G 19*
  (off Childwall Grn.)
Woodvale Rd.
  CH66: Lit Sut 1D **48**
Woodview Av. CH44: Wall 3A **14**
Woodville Rd. CH42: Tran 3G **21**

Woodward Rd.
  CH42: Rock F 1G **29**
Woodway CH49: Grea 3D **18**
Woodway Ct. CH62: Brom 1C **36**
Woodyear Rd. CH62: Brom 4C **36**
Wooler Cl. CH46: More 5C **10**
Woollam Dr. CH66: Lit Sut 6D **42**
Woolton Ct. CH66: Ell P 5F **43**
Worcester Ct. L20: Boot 1F **7**
Worcester Rd. CH43: Bid 5B **12**
Worcester St. CH65: Ell P 1A **50**
Worcester Wlk. CH65: Ell P . . .1A **50**
Wordsworth Av.
  CH42: Rock F 6B **22**
Wordsworth Wlk.
  CH48: W Kir 1A **24**
Wordsworth Way
  CH66: Gt Sut 6E **49**
World Mus. Liverpool **3F 15**
Wrenbury Cl. CH43: Oxton 5D **20**
Wright St. CH44: Wall 1H **13**
  L5: Liv 6F **7**
Wroxham Cl. CH49: Upton 2G **19**
Wroxham Ct. *CH49: Upton 2G 19*
  (off Wroxham Cl.)
Wroxham Dr. CH49: Upton 3G **19**
Wroxham Way CH49: Upton . . .2G **19**
Wrynose Rd. CH62: Brom 3C **36**
Wulstan St. L4: Kirkd 4F **7**
Wycherley Rd. CH42: Tran 4H **21**
Wychwood CH49: Upton 2F **19**
Wycliffe Rd. CH65: Gt Sut 4F **49**
Wycliffe St. CH42: Rock F . . .5B **22**
Wye Cl. CH42: Rock F 4B **22**
Wyedale CH65: Whit 4H **49**
Wye St. L5: Liv 5H **7**
Wykeham St. L4: Kirkd 4F **7**
Wykeham Way L4: Kirkd 4F **7**
Wyncroft Cl. CH65: Whit 4H **49**
Wyncroft St. L8: Liv 3H **23**
Wyndham Cres.
  CH66: Gt Sut 5E **49**
Wyndham Rd. CH45: Wall 6B **4**

Wyndham St. L4: Walt 1H **7**
Wynstay Rd. CH47: Meols 5E **9**
Wyre Rd. L5: Liv 4H **7**
Wyvern Rd. CH46: More 5E **11**

X

X Building L3: Liv 3E **15**

Y

Yardley Dr. CH63: Spit 2G **35**
Yates St. L8: Liv 2G **23**
Yelverton Rd. CH42: Tran 4A **22**
Yeoman Cotts. CH47: Hoy 1E **17**
Yeoman Way CH66: Gt Sut . . .6E **49**
Yewdale Dr. CH66: Whit 6F **49**
Yewdale Pk. CH43: Oxton 3F **21**
Yewtree Cl. CH64: Lit N 6D **38**
Yew Tree Ct. CH60: Hesw 3C **32**
Yew Tree La. CH48: W Kir 5D **16**
Yew Tree Rd. CH46: More 3F **11**
  CH63: Hghr B 5E **29**
Yew Way CH46: More 4F **11**
York Av. CH44: Wall 2H **13**
  CH48: W Kir 6D **16**
York Rd. CH44: Wall 3H **13**
  CH65: Ell P 2A **50**
York St. CH62: Brom 4B **30**
  L1: Liv 5F **15**
  L9: Walt 1H **7**
York Ter. L5: Liv 5G **7**

Z

Zante Cl. L5: Liv 5G **7**
Zetland Rd. CH45: Wall 4D **4**
Zetland St. CH41: Birke 2H **21**
Zig Zag Rd. CH45: Wall 5F **5**

SAFETY CAMERA INFORMATION

Safety camera locations are publicised by the Safer Roads Partnership which operates them in order to encourage drivers to comply with speed limits at these sites. It is the driver's absolute responsibility to be aware of and to adhere to speed limits at all times.

By showing this safety camera information it is the intention of Geographers' A-Z Map Company Ltd., to encourage safe driving and greater awareness of speed limits and vehicle speed. Data accurate at time of printing.

Printed and bound in the United Kingdom by Gemini Press Ltd., Shoreham-by-Sea, West Sussex
Printed on materials from a sustainable source